ALWAYS RUNNING

La Vida Loca:
Gang Days in L.A.

by
LUIS J. RODRIGUEZ

CURBSTONE PRESS

Cover design by Stone Graphics
Printed in the U.S. by BookCrafters

Curbstone Press is a 501(c)(3) nonprofit literary arts organization whose operations are supported in part by private donations and by grants from the ADCO Foundation, the Bissell Foundation, the Connecticut Commission on the Arts, the Lila Wallace-Reader's Digest Literary Publishers Marketing Development Program, administered by the Council of Literary Magazines and Presses, the Andrew W. Mellon Foundation, the National Endowment for the Arts, and the Plumsock Fund.

Some of the material in this book has appeared as poetry and prose in *Poems Across The Pavement* (1989, Tía Chucha Press, Chicago), *The Concrete River* (1991, Curbstone Press, Connecticut), and in the following publications (often in versions different than contained here): *Puerto del Sol, Cambio, TriQuarterly, The Chicago Review, 201: Homenaje A La Ciudad De Los Angeles* (anthology by the LA Latino Writers Association), *Left Curve, Milestones, Obras, ChismeArte, El Grito*, and *When I Was A Child* (anthology published by the Children's Literature Association). Parts of the preface and epilogue originally appeared in *The Los Angeles Times, Centro De Estudios Puertorriqueños Bulletin*, and *The National Catholic Reporter*. The author wishes to thank the Illinois Arts Council for their support with an Artists Fellowship Award.

The epigram in Chapter Eight comes from "Tin Tan Tan," a story in *Woman Hollering Creek*, copyright © 1991 Sandra Cisneros. Published in the United States by Vintage Books, a division of Random House, Inc. Originally published in hard cover by Random House, Inc., New York in 1991. Reprinted by permission of Susan Bergholz Literary Services, New York.

Library of Congress Cataloging-in-Publication Data

Rodriguez, Luis J., 1954-
　　　Always running: la vida loca, gang days in L.A. / by Luis J.
　　Rodriguez. — 1st ed.
　　　　p. cm.
　　ISBN 1-880684-06-3: $19.95
　　　　1. Rodriguez, Luis J., 1954- . 2. Gangs—California—Los
　　Angeles—Biography. 3. Mexican American youth—California—Los
　　Angeles—Biography. I. Title.
　　HV6439.U7L77　1993
　　364.1'092—dc20
　　[B]　　　　　　　　　　　　　　　　　　　　　　　　92-39002

distributed in the U.S. by
INBOOK
Box 120261, East Haven, CT 06512

published by
CURBSTONE PRESS
321 Jackson Street, Willimantic, CT 06226

This work is dedicated to:

Antonio Gutierrez
Carlos Mancillas
Eddie Lozano
Linda Treviño
John "Spook" Fabela
Marlene "Negra" Domínguez
Don "Sonny" López
Miguel Robles
Elías Avila
Richard "Porky" Sierra
Lenard "Gallo" Ocaña
Fernando "Caballo" Arredondo
Martín Alvarado
Fidel "Puppet" Hernández
Marcelino "Daddio" Cabrera
David "Puppet" Alcon
Freddie Mendoza
David "Loco" Domínguez
Ricky Herrera
René Molinar
Al "Pache" Alvarez
Leonard "Lalo" Villaseñor
Ruben "Sharkie" Martínez
Daniel "Indio" Cabrera
and
Rodolfo "Sonny" Gómez

My life is a poem to their memory.

—Luis J. Rodríguez

ALWAYS RUNNING

There is no absolute peril except for him who abandons himself; there is no complete death except for him who acquires a taste for dying.
— *Jacques Rivière*

PREFACE

"We have the right to lie, but not about the heart of the matter."
— Antonin Artaud

Late winter Chicago, early 1991: The once-white snow which fell in December had turned into a dark scum, mixed with ice-melting salt, car oil and decay. Icicles hung from rooftops and windowsills like the whiskers of old men.

For months, the bone-chilling "hawk" swooped down and forced everyone in the family to squeeze into a one-and-a-half bedroom apartment in a gray-stone, three-flat building in the Humboldt Park neighborhood.

Inside tensions built up like fever as we crammed around the TV set or kitchen table, the crowding made more intolerable because of heaps of paper, opened file drawers and shelves packed with books that garnered every section of empty space (a sort of writer's torture chamber). The family included my third wife Trini; our child, Rubén Joaquín, born in 1988; and my 15-year-old son Ramiro (a 13-year-old daughter, Andrea, lived with her mother in East Los Angeles).

We hardly ventured outside. Few things were worth heaving on the layers of clothing and the coats, boots and gloves required to step out the door.

Ramiro had been placed on punishment, but not for an act of disobedience or the usual outburst of teenage anxiety. Ramiro had been on a rapidly declining roller coaster ride into the world of street-gang America, not unexpected for this neighborhood, once designated as one of the 10 poorest in the country and also known as one of the most gang-infested.

Humboldt Park is a predominantly Puerto Rican community with growing numbers of Mexican immigrants and uprooted blacks and sprinklings of Ukrainians and Poles from previous generations. But along with the greater West Town area it was considered a "changing neighborhood," dotted here and there with rehabs, signs of gentrification and for many of us, imminent displacement.

Weeks before, Ramiro had received a 10 day suspension from Roberto Clemente High School, a beleaguered school with a good number of caring personnel, but one which, unfortunately, was an epicenter of gang activity. The suspension came after a school fight which involved a war between "Insanes" and "Maniacs," two factions of the "Folks" ("Folks" are those gangs allied with the Spanish Cobras and Gangster Disciples; the "People" are gangs tied to the Latin Kings and Vice Lords, symbolic of the complicated structures most inner-city gangs had come to establish). There was also an "S.O.S." — a "smash-on-sight" — contract issued on Ramiro. As a result I took him out of Clemente and enrolled him in another school. He lasted less than two weeks before school officials there kicked him out. By then I also had to pick him up from local jails following other fighting incidents — and once from a hospital where I watched a doctor put 11 stitches above his eye.

Following me, Ramiro was a second-generation gang member. My involvement was in the late 1960s and early 1970s in Los Angeles, the so-called gang capital of the country. My teen years were ones of drugs, shootings and beatings, and arrests. I was around when South Central Los Angeles gave birth to the Crips and Bloods. By the time I turned 18 years old, 25 of my friends had been killed by rival gangs, police, drugs, car crashes and suicides.

If I had barely survived all this — to emerge eventually as a journalist, publisher, critic, and poet — it appeared unlikely my own son would make it. I had to cut his blood line to the street early, before it became too late. I had to begin the long, intense struggle to save his life from the gathering storm of street violence sweeping the country — some 20 years after I sneaked out of my 'hood in the dark of night, hid out in an L.A. housing project, and removed myself from the death-fires of *La Vida Loca*.

La Vida Loca or The Crazy Life is what we called the barrio gang experience. This lifestyle originated with the Mexican

Pachuco gangs of the 1930s and 1940s, and was later recreated with the *Cholos*. It became the main model and influence for outlaw bikers of the 1950s and 1960s, the L.A. punk/rock scene in the 1970s and 1980s, and the Crips and Bloods of the 1980s and early 1990s. As Leon Bing commented in her 1991 book *Do or Die* (HarperCollins): "It was the *cholo* homeboy who first walked the walk and talked the talk. It was the Mexican American *pachuco* who initiated the emblematic tattoos, the signing with hands, the writing of legends on walls."

One evening that winter, after Ramiro had come in late following weeks of trouble at school, I gave him an ultimatum. Yelling burst back and forth between the walls of our Humboldt Park flat. Two-year-old Rubén, confused and afraid, hugged my leg as the shouting erupted. In moments, Ramiro ran out of the house, entering the cold Chicago night without a jacket. I went after him, although by my mid-thirties I had gained enough weight to slow me down considerably. Still I sprinted down the gangway which led to a debris-strewn alley, filled with furniture parts and overturned trash cans. I saw Ramiro's fleeing figure, his breath rising above him in quickly-dissipating clouds.

I followed him toward Augusta Boulevard, the main drag of the neighborhood. People yelled out of windows and doorways: "*¿Qué pasa, hombre?*" Others offered information on Ramiro's direction. A father or mother chasing some child down the street is not an unfamiliar sight around here.

A city like Chicago has so many places in which to hide. The gray and brown brick buildings seem to suck people in. Ramiro would make a turn and then vanish, only to pop up again. Appearing and disappearing. He flew over brick walls, scurried down another alley then veered into a building that swallowed him up and spit him out the other side.

I kept after Ramiro until, unexpectedly, I found him hiding in some bushes. He stepped out, unaware I was to the side of him.

"Ramiro...come home," I gently implored, knowing if I pounced on him there would be little hope he'd come back. He sped off again.

"Leave me alone!" he yelled.

As I watched his escape, it was like looking back into a distant time, back to my own youth, when I ran and ran, when I jumped over peeling fences, fleeing *vatos locos,* the police or my own shadow in some drug-induced hysteria.

I saw Ramiro run off and then saw my body entering the mouth of darkness, my breath cutting the frigid flesh of night; it was my voice cracking open the winter sky.

Ramiro was born just prior to my 21st birthday. I had been working in a steel mill in Los Angeles. His mother Camila, not yet 19, was an East Los Angeles woman who grew up in one of East L.A.'s roughest barrios: *La Gerahty Loma.* Yet Camila and her five sisters, with the help of their mother, managed to stave off attempts to pull them into the street life there — even having battles on their front porch with the *locas* who tried to recruit them.

The media likens Los Angeles to a "Beirut by the Beach." For 1991, police cited these statistics: 100,000 gang members, 800 gangs, nearly 600 young people killed. Parts of the city, particularly the public housing projects, have been called "ungovernable." These stats have been used to create a hysteria against black and Latino youth. Police in L.A. have practically instituted martial law in the inner city. Michael Davis in his book *City of Quartz* (Verso Press, 1991) says that by 1990 the various law enforcement "operations" to destroy gangs (using helicopters, infra-red lights and made-over armored vehicles — not far behind what was used in "Desert Storm") detained or arrested 50,000 youth, in South Central alone.

"The Crazy Life" in my youth, although devastating, was only the beginning stages of what I believe is now a consistent and growing genocidal level of destruction predicated on the premise there are marginalized youth with no jobs or future, and therefore expendable.

Camila's brothers weren't spared. One of them became active in *Gerahty Loma*, a witness to a number of killings himself, and later a heroin addict and a convict. Another brother got jumped and stabbed seven times — but survived. And an older half-brother was killed while trying to exact some revenge one night near the Mexican border.

Later, her nephews from an older sister got involved in the barrio and one of them, known as Shorty, was murdered outside his home at the age of 17 (but not before he fathered a baby).

When Ramiro was two years old, and his sister only 10 months, Camila and I broke up. About seven years later, I moved to Chicago. After being left behind, Ramiro failed miserably in school, although he had been tested as a gifted child. He ran away from home a number of times. Once when he was about 10 years old he hopped a train from L.A. to Chicago, but police pulled him out of a boxcar before he passed the city limits. When he turned 13 years old, he came to stay with me. Because of what Camila and I had been through, we tried everything we could to keep him out of the "life," even after we divorced and lived a couple of thousands of miles apart. But often there was too much against us.

In East L.A. and in schools like Chicago's Clemente were some of the nation's highest drop-out rates. Youth unemployment hovered around 75 percent in the most neglected areas. And what of those who did everything right, got all the good grades and followed the "rules?" Camila, for example, had been an A student at Garfield High School (site of the 1988 movie "Stand and Deliver") and was active in school affairs. But after we married, she applied for work and was told she didn't know enough to get a basic 9 to 5 office job. She even had to go back to some classes to make up for the lack of schooling she received despite being one of the best students at Garfield! The fact the L.A. schools now give "warranties" only underscores the point.

7

With little productive to do, drug selling becomes a lucrative means of survival. A 10-year-old in Humboldt Park can make $80-$100 a day as a lookout for local dealers. The drug trade is business. It's capitalism: Cutthroat, profit-motivated and expedient. Also, the values which drive gangs are linked to the control of markets, in a way similar to what has created borders between nations. In communities with limited resources like Humboldt Park and East L.A., sophisticated survival structures evolved, including gangs, out of the bone and sinew tossed up by this environment.

After Ramiro ran away, he failed to return home for another two weeks. I was so angry at him for leaving, I bought locks to keep him out. I kept a vigil at home to catch him should he sneak in to eat. But then I remembered what I had been through. I recalled how many institutions and people had failed my son — and now he was expected to rise above all this! Soon I spent every night he was gone driving around the streets, talking to the "boys" in their street-corner domains, making daily calls to the police. I placed handwritten notes in the basement which said it was okay for him to come back. I left food for him to get to. Suddenly every teenage Latino male looked like Ramiro.

With the help of some of his friends, I finally found Ramiro in a rundown barrio hovel and convinced him to come home. He agreed to obtain help in getting through some deep emotional and psychological problems — stemming in large part from an unstable childhood, including abuse he sustained as a kid from his stepfathers, one who was an alcoholic and another who regularly beat him. And I could not remove myself from being struck by the hammerhead of responsibility. A key factor was my relative lack of involvement in Ramiro's life as I became increasingly active in politics and writing.

Although the best way to deal with one's own children is to help construct the conditions that will ensure the free and healthy development of all, it's also true you can't be for all children if you can't be for your own.

By mid-1991, Ramiro had undergone a few months in a psychiatric hospital and various counseling and family sessions that also involved bringing his mother in from L.A. We implemented an educational and employment plan, worked out with school officials, teachers and social workers (everyone who had dealings with him had to be involved, to get them on "our side" so to speak). I also learned a parent cannot just turn over a child to a school, a court, or hospital without stepping in at various times to insure his or her best interests are being met. My aim was to help Ramiro get through his teen-age years with a sense of empowerment and esteem, with what I call complete literacy: The ability to participate competently and confidently in any level of society one chooses.

There is an aspect of suicide in young people whose options have been cut off. They stand on street corners, flashing hand signs, inviting the bullets. It's either *la torcida* or death: A warrior's path, when even self-preservation is not at stake. And if they murder, the victims are usually the ones who look like them, the ones closest to who they are — the mirror reflections. They murder and they're killing themselves, over and over.

At the same time, individual efforts must be linked with social ones. I tried to get Ramiro to understand the systematic nature of what was happening in the street which in effect made choices for him before he was born. The thing is, no matter what one does individually, in this setting, the dangers keep lurking around every corner.

A couple of examples helped Ramiro see the point. Not long ago, a few of his friends were picked up by police, who drove them around in a squad car. The police took them to a rival gang neighborhood. There they forced Ramiro's friends to spray paint over the graffiti with their own insignias — as rival gang members watched — and then left them there to find their way home. It's an old police practice.

A second incident involved the shooting death of a Dragon, a Puerto Rican teenager named Efrain, who Ramiro knew. Soon after, we happened to drive through a Latin Kings' territory. The words "Efrain Rots" had been emblazoned on a wall. That night, Ramiro sat alone, intensely quiet, in the backyard, thinking about this for a long time.

Things between us, for now, are being dealt with day by day. Although Ramiro has gained a much more viable perspective on his place in the world, there are choices he has to make "not just once, but every time they come up."

Meanwhile I've pursued writing this book — after a 10-year lapse. The writing first began when I was 15, but the urgency of the present predicament demands it finally see the light of day. This work is an argument for the reorganization of American society — not where a few benefit at the expense of the many, but where everyone has access to decent health care, clothing, food and housing, based on need, not whether they can afford them. It's an indictment against the use of deadly force which has been the principal means this society uses against those it cannot accommodate (as I write this, Rodney King's beating by the LAPD continues to play itself out throughout the country. And the *Los Angeles Daily News* in late October 1991 reported that the L.A. County Sheriff's Department had shot 57 people since the first of the year — about 80 percent were people of color, and a few were disabled or mentally ill; all of them were unarmed or shot in the back).

Criminality in this country is a class issue. Many of those warehoused in overcrowded prisons can be properly called "criminals of want," those who've been deprived of the basic necessities of life and therefore forced into so-called criminal acts to survive. Many of them just don't have the means to buy their "justice." They are members of a social stratum which includes welfare mothers, housing project residents, immigrant families, the homeless and unemployed. This book is part of their story.

Although the work begins with my family's trek from Mexico when I was a child and touches on our early years in Watts, it primarily covers the period from ages 12 until 18 when I became active in *Las Lomas* barrio.

This work is not fiction, yet there are people I don't want hurt by having their names and stories made public. I've changed names and synthesized events and circumstances in keeping with the integrity of a literary, dramatic work, as an artist does in striving for that rare instance when, as a critic once said, "something of beauty collides with something of truth."

The more we know, the more we owe. This is a responsibility I take seriously. My hope in producing this work is that perhaps there's a thread to be found, a pattern or connection, a seed of apprehension herein, which can be of some use, no matter how slight, in helping to end the rising casualty count for the Ramiros of this world, as more and more communities come under the death grip of what we called "The Crazy Life."

July 1992

CHAPTER ONE

"Cry, child, for those without tears have a grief
which never ends." — Mexican saying

This memory begins with flight. A 1950s bondo-spackled Dodge
surged through a driving rain, veering around the potholes and
upturned tracks of the abandoned Red Line trains on Alameda.
Mama was in the front seat. My father was at the wheel. My
brother *Rano* and I sat on one end of the back seat; my sisters
Pata and *Cuca* on the other. There was a space between the boys
and girls to keep us apart.

"*Amá, mira a Rano,*" a voice said for the tenth time from the
back of the car. "He's hitting me again."

We fought all the time. My brother, especially, had it in
for *La Pata* — thinking of Frankenstein, he called her
"Anastein." Her real name was Ana, but most of the time we
went by the animal names Dad gave us at birth. I am *Grillo*,
which means cricket. *Rano* stands for "rana," the frog. *La Pata* is
the duck and *Cuca* is short for *cucaracha*: cockroach.

The car seats came apart in strands. I looked out at the
passing cars which seemed like ghosts with headlights rushing
past the streaks of water on the glass. I was nine years old. As
the rain fell, my mother cursed in Spanish intermixed with
pleas to saints and "*la Santísima Madre de Dios.*" She argued
with my father. Dad didn't curse or raise his voice. He just
stated the way things were.

"I'll never go back to Mexico," he said. "I'd rather starve
here. You want to stay with me, it has to be in Los Angeles.
Otherwise, go."

This incited my mother to greater fits.

We were on the way to the Union train station in downtown
L.A. We had our few belongings stuffed into the trunk and
underneath our feet. I gently held on to one of the comic books
Mama bought to keep us entertained. I had on my Sunday best

clothes with chewed gum stuck in a coat pocket. It could have been Easter, but it was a weeping November. I don't remember for sure why we were leaving. I just knew it was a special day. There was no fear or concern on my part. We were always moving. I looked at the newness of the comic book and felt some exhilaration of its feel in my hand. Mama had never bought us comic books before. It had to be a special day.

For months we had been pushed from one house to another, just Mama and us children. Mom and Dad had split up prior to this. We stayed at the homes of women my mom called *comadres,* with streams of children of their own. Some nights we slept in a car or in the living rooms of people we didn't know. There were no shelters for homeless families. My mother tried to get us settled somewhere but all indications pointed to our going back to the land of her birth, to her red earth, her Mexico.

The family consisted of my father Alfonso, my mom María Estela, my older brother, José René, and my younger sisters, Ana Virginia and Gloria Estela. I recall my father with his wavy hair and clean-shaven face, his correct, upright and stubborn demeanor, in contrast to my mother who was heavy-set with Native features and thick straight hair, often laughing heartily, her eyes narrowed to slits, and sometimes crying from a deep tomb-like place with a sound like swallowing mud.

As we got closer to the Union station, Los Angeles loomed low and large, a city of odd construction, a good place to get lost in. I, however, would learn to hide in imaginative worlds — in books; in TV shows, where I picked up much of my English; in solitary play with mangled army men and crumpled toy trucks. I was so withdrawn it must have looked scary.

ᛉ ᛉ ᛉ

This is what I know: When I was two years old, our family left Ciudad Juárez, Chihuahua, for Los Angeles. My father was an educated man, unusual for our border town, a hunger city filled to the hills with cardboard hovels of former peasants, Indians and dusk-faced children. In those days, an educated man had to be careful about certain things — questioning authority, for example. Although the principal of a local high school, my father failed to succumb to the local chieftains who were linked to the national party which ruled Mexico, as one famous Latin American writer would later say, with a "perfect dictatorship."

When Dad first became principal, there were no funds due to the massive bureaucratic maze he had to get through to get them. The woman he lived with then was an artist who helped raise money for the school by staging exhibitions. My father used his own money to pay for supplies and at one point had the iron fence around the school torn down and sold for scrap.

One year, Dad received an offer for a six-month study program for foreign teachers in Bloomington, Indiana. He liked it so much, he renewed it three times. By then, my father had married his secretary, my mother, after the artist left him. They had their first child, José René.

By the time my father returned, his enemies had mapped out a means to remove him — being a high school principal is a powerful position in a place like Ciudad Juarez. My father faced a pile of criminal charges, including the alleged stealing of school funds. Police arrived at the small room in the *vecindad* where Mama and Dad lived and escorted him to the city jail.

For months my father fought the charges. While he was locked up, they fed him scraps of food in a rusted steel can. They denied him visitors — Mama had to climb a section of prison wall and pick up 2-year-old José René so he could see his father. Finally, after a lengthy trial, my father was found innocent — but he no longer had his position as principal.

Dad became determined to escape to the United States. My mother, on the other hand, never wanted to leave Mexico; she did it to be with Dad.

Mama was one of two daughters in a family run by a heavy-drinking, wife-beating railroad worker and musician. My mother was the only one in her family to complete high school. Her brothers, Kiko and Rodolfo, were pistol-packing womanizers who often crossed the border to find work and came back with stories of love and brawls on the other side.

Their grandmother was a Tarahumara Indian who once walked down from the mountainous area in the state of Chihuahua where her people lived in seclusion for centuries. The Spanish never conquered them. But their grandmother never returned to her people. She eventually gave birth to my grandmother, Ana Acosta.

Ana's first husband was a railroad worker during the Mexican Revolution; he lost his life when a tunnel exploded during a raid. They brought his remains in a box. Ana was left alone with one son, while pregnant with a daughter. Lucita, the daughter, eventually died of convulsions at the age of four, and Manolo, the son, was later blinded after a bout with a deadly form of chicken pox which struck and killed many children in the area.

Later Ana married my grandfather, Mónico Jiménez, who like her first husband worked the railroads. At one point, Mónico quit the rails to play trumpet and sing for bands in various night clubs. Once he ended up in Los Angeles, but with another woman. In fact, Mónico had many other women. My grandmother often had to cross over to the railroad yards, crowded with prostitutes and where Mónico spent many nights singing, to bring him home.

When my parents married, Mama was 27; Dad almost 40. She had never known any other man. He already had four or five children from three or four other women. She was an emotionally-charged, border woman, full of fire, full of pain, full of giving love. He was a stoic, unfeeling, unmoved intellectual who did as he pleased as much as she did all she could to please him. This dichotomous couple, this sun and moon, this *curandera* and biologist, dreamer and realist, fire woman and water man, molded me; these two sides created a life-long conflict in my breast.

By the time Dad had to leave Ciudad Juarez, my mother had borne three of his children, including myself, all in El Paso, on the American side (Gloria was born later in East L.A.'s General Hospital). This was done to help ease the transition from alien status to legal residency. There are stories of women who wait up to the ninth month and run across the border to have their babies, sometimes squatting and dropping them on the pavement as they hug the closest lamppost.

We ended up in Watts, a community primarily of black people except for *La Colonia*, often called The Quarter — the Mexican section and the oldest part of Watts.

Except for the housing projects, Watts was a ghetto where country and city mixed. The homes were mostly single-family units, made of wood or stucco. Open windows and doors served as air conditioners, a slight relief from the summer desert air. Chicken coops graced many a back yard along with broken auto parts. Roosters crowed the morning to birth and an occasional goat peered from weather-worn picket fences along with the millions of dogs which seemed to populate the neighborhood.

Watts fed into one of the largest industrial concentrations in the country, pulling from an almost endless sea of cheap labor; they came from Texas, Louisiana, Mississippi, Oklahoma, Arkansas...from Chihuahua, Sonora, Sinaloa and Nayarit. If you moved there it was because the real estate concerns pushed you in this direction. For decades, L.A. was notorious for restrictive covenants — where some areas were off limits to "undesirables."

Despite the competition for jobs and housing, we found common ground there, among the rolling mills, bucket shops and foundries. All day long we heard the pounding of forges and the air-whistles that signaled the shift changes in the factories which practically lay in our backyards.

We moved to Watts at the behest of my oldest sister, really a half-sister, who was already married with two children of her own. Her family eventually joined us a few months later. Her name was Seni, a name my father invented (although rumor has it, it was an inversion of the name Inés, an old girlfriend of his). The name, however, has stayed in the family. Seni's first daughter was named Ana Seni and in later years, one of Ana Seni's daughters became Seni Bea.

When Seni was a child, my father often left her for long intervals with my grandmother Catita, whom she called Mama Piri. One family legend tells of a 9-year-old Seni answering the door during a pouring rain. A man, with soaked hat and coat, stood at the doorway. Seni yelled out: "Mama Piri, Mama Piri — there's a strange man at the door."

"Don't worry, *m'ija*," Catita said. "He's only your father."

Seni lived in several rentals in Watts until she found a two-story on 111th Street near a block of factories. The place later got razed to build Locke High School. I stayed there a couple of summers, sleeping in a cobweb-infested attic with exposed 2-by-4 studs. Rats and cockroaches roamed freely in that house: huge rats, huge cockroaches. Seni would place a chair at the bottom of the attic steps and she convinced me it could ward off the creatures. I believed it until one night I noticed the chair was gone. I ran down to tell Seni. But she yelled back in Spanish: "Go back to bed...that chair couldn't keep nothing away, and only a fool would believe it could."

I was devastated.

Seni was my father's daughter from one of his earlier relationships; her mother died giving birth to her. My father was handsome and athletic as a young man. He was the pole-vaulting champion at one of the schools he attended. But his looks apparently got him into a lot of trouble. His father Cristóbal, then a general in the Mexican army, once disowned him when Dad fell for a woman and neglected his studies in medical school. Dad quit school to be with the woman who would later become Seni's mother.

I also had two older half-brothers, Alberto and Mario, who lived in Mexico. Another half-sister, Lisa, died as an infant after she accidently ate some *chicharrones* my father was forced to sell on cobblestone streets in Mexico City after his father cut him off. My mother kept a sepia-colored black-and-white death photo of Lisa in a white lace baptism dress, looking like a doll, looking asleep, so peaceful, as she lay in a tiny wood coffin.

Our first exposure in America stays with me like a foul odor. It seemed a strange world, most of it spiteful to us, spitting and stepping on us, coughing us up, us immigrants, as if we were phlegm stuck in the collective throat of this country. My father was mostly out of work. When he did have a job it was in construction, in factories such as Sinclair Paints or Standard Brands Dog Food, or pushing door-bells selling insurance, Bibles or pots and pans. My mother found work cleaning homes or in the garment industry. She knew the corner markets were ripping her off but she could only speak with her hands and in a choppy English.

Once my mother gathered up the children and we walked to Will Rogers Park. There were people everywhere. Mama looked around for a place we could rest. She spotted an empty spot on a park bench. But as soon as she sat down an American woman, with three kids of her own, came by.

"Hey, get out of there — that's our seat."

My mother understood but didn't know how to answer back in English. So she tried in Spanish.

"Look spic, you can't sit there!" the American woman yelled. "You don't belong here! Understand? This is not your country!"

Mama quietly got our things and walked away, but I knew frustration and anger bristled within her because she was unable to talk, and when she did, no one would listen.

We never stopped crossing borders. The *Río Grande* (or *Río Bravo*, which is what the Mexicans call it, giving the name a power "Río Grande" just doesn't have) was only the first of countless barriers set in our path.

We kept jumping hurdles, kept breaking from the constraints, kept evading the border guards of every new trek. It was a metaphor to fill our lives — that river, that first crossing, the mother of all crossings. The L.A. River, for example, became a new barrier, keeping the Mexicans in their neighborhoods over on the vast east side of the city for years, except for forays downtown. Schools provided other restrictions:

Don't speak Spanish, don't be Mexican — you don't belong. Railroad tracks divided us from communities where white people lived, such as South Gate and Lynwood across from Watts. We were invisible people in a city which thrived on glitter, big screens and big names, but this glamour contained none of our names, none of our faces.

The refrain "this is not your country" echoed for a lifetime.

Although we moved around the Watts area, the house on 105th Street near McKinley Avenue held my earliest memories, my earliest fears and questions. It was a small matchbox of a place. Next to it stood a tiny garage with holes through the walls and an unpainted barn-like quality. The weather battered it into a leaning shed. The back yard was a jungle. Vegetation appeared to grow down from the sky. There were banana trees, huge "sperm" weeds (named that because they stunk like semen when you cut them), foxtails and yellowed grass. An avocado tree grew in the middle of the yard and its roots covered every bit of ground, tearing up cement walks while its branches scraped the bedroom windows. A sway of clothes on some lines filled the little bit of grassy area just behind the house.

My brother and I played often in our jungle, even pretending to be Tarzan (Rano mastered the Tarzan yell from the movies). The problem, however, was I usually ended up being the monkey who got thrown off the trees. In fact, I remember my brother as the most dangerous person alive. He seemed to be wracked with a scream which never let out. His face was dark with meanness, what my mother called *maldad*. He also took delight in seeing me writhe in pain, cry or cower, vulnerable to his own inflated sense of power. This hunger for cruelty included his ability to take my mom's most wicked whippings — without crying or wincing. He'd just sit there and stare at a wall, forcing Mama to resort to other implements of pain — but Rano would not show any emotion.

Yet in the streets, neighborhood kids often chased Rano from play or jumped him. Many times he came home mangled, his face swollen. Once somebody threw a rock at him which cut a gash across his forehead, leaving a scar Rano has to this day.

Another time a neighbor's kid smashed a metal bucket over Rano's head, slicing the skin over his skull and creating a horrifying scene with blood everywhere. My mother in her broken English could remedy few of the injustices, but she tried. When this one happened, she ran next door to confront that kid's mother.

The woman had been sitting on her porch and saw everything.

"¿Qué pasó aquí?" Mama asked.

"I don't know what you want," the woman said. "All I know is your boy picked up that bucket and hit himself over the head — that's all I know."

In school, they placed Rano in classes with retarded children because he didn't speak much English. They even held him back a year in the second grade.

For all this, Rano took his rage out on me. I recall hiding from him when he came around looking for a playmate. My mother actually forced me out of closets with a belt in her hand and made me play with him.

One day we were playing on the rooftop of our house.

"Grillo, come over here," he said from the roof's edge. "Man, look at this on the ground."

I should have known better, but I leaned over to see. Rano then pushed me and I struck the ground on my back with a loud thump and lost my breath, laying deathly still in suffocating agony, until I slowly gained it back.

Another time he made me the Indian to his cowboy, tossed a rope around my neck and pulled me around the yard. He stopped barely before it choked the life out of me. I had rope burns around my neck for a week.

His abuse even prompted neighborhood kids to get in on it. One older boy used to see how Rano tore into me. One day he peered over the fence separating his yard from ours.

21

"Hey, little dude...yeah you. Come over here a minute," he said. "I got something to show you."

This time I approached with caution. Little good that did me: I stepped into a loop of rope on the ground. He pulled on it and dragged me through the weeds and foxtails, up the splintery fence, and tied it down on his side. I hung upside down, kicking and yelling for what seemed like hours until somebody came and cut me down.

The house on 105th Street stayed cold. We couldn't always pay the gas or light bills. When we couldn't, we used candles. We cleaned up the dishes and the table where we ate without any light, whispering because that's what people do in the dark.

We took baths in cold water, and I remember wanting to run out of the bathroom as my mother murmured a shiver of words to comfort me:

"*Así es, así será,*" she explained as she dunked me into the frigid bath.

One night, my parents decided to take us to a restaurant since we had no heat to cook anything with. We drove around for awhile. On Avalon Boulevard we found one of those all-night, ham-eggs-&-coffee places. As we pulled up, I curled up in the seat.

"No, I don't want to go in," I yelled.

"And why not?" my mother demanded. "*Por el amor de Dios,* aren't you hungry?"

I pointed a finger to a sign on the door. It read: "Come In. Cold Inside."

Christmases came with barely a whimper. Once my parents bought a fake aluminum tree, placed some presents beneath it, and woke us up early to open them up. Most of the wrappings, though, had been haphazardly put together because Rano had sneaked into the living room in the middle of the night and torn them open to take a peek. The presents came from a church group which gave out gifts for the poor. It was our first Christmas. That day, I broke the plastic submarine, toy gun and metal car I received. I don't know why. I suppose in my mind it didn't seem right to have things that were in working order, unspent.

My mother worked on and off, primarily as a *costurera* or cleaning homes or taking care of other people's children. We sometimes went with her to the houses she cleaned. They were nice, American, white-people homes. I remember one had a swimming pool and a fireplace and a thing called rugs. As Mama swept and scrubbed and vacuumed, we played in the corner, my sisters and I, afraid to touch anything. The odor of these houses was different, full of fragrances, sweet and nauseating. On 105th Street the smells were of fried lard, of beans and car fumes, of factory smoke and home-made brew out of backyard stills. There were chicken smells and goat smells in grassless yards filled with engine parts and wire and wood planks, cracked and sprinkled with rusty nails. These were the familiar aromas: the funky earth, animal and mechanical smells which were absent from the homes my mother cleaned.

Mama always seemed to be sick. For one thing, she was overweight and suffered from a form of diabetes. She had thyroid problems, bad nerves and high blood pressure. She was still young then in Watts, in her thirties, but she had all these ailments. She didn't even have teeth; they rotted away many years before. This made her look much older until later when she finally obtained false ones. Despite this she worked all the time, chased after my brother with a belt or a board, and held up the family when almost everything else came apart.

⊹ ⊹ ⊹

Heavy blue veins streak across my mother's legs, some of them bunched up into dark lumps at her ankles. Mama periodically bleeds them to relieve the pain. She carefully cuts the engorged veins with a razor and drains them into a porcelain-like metal pail called a *tina*. I'm small and all I remember are dreams of blood, me drowning in a red sea, blood on sheets, on the walls, splashing against the white pail in streams out of my mother's ankle. But they aren't dreams. It is Mama bleeding — into day, into night. Bleeding a birth of memory: my mother, my blood, by the side of the bed, me on the covers, and her slicing into a black vein and filling the pail into some dark, forbidden red nightmare which never stops coming, never stops pouring, this memory of Mama and blood and Watts.

✝ ✝ ✝

One day, my mother asked Rano and me to go to the grocery store. We decided to go across the railroad tracks into South Gate. In those days, South Gate was an Anglo neighborhood, filled with the families of workers from the auto plant and other nearby industry. Like Lynwood or Huntington Park, it was forbidden territory for the people of Watts.

My brother insisted we go. I don't know what possessed him, but then I never did. It was useless to argue; he'd force me anyway. He was nine then, I was six. So without ceremony, we started over the tracks, climbing over discarded market carts and tore-up sofas, across Alameda Street, into South Gate: all-white, all-American.

We entered the first small corner grocery store we found. Everything was cool at first. We bought some bread, milk, soup cans and candy. We each walked out with a bag filled with food. We barely got a few feet, though, when five teenagers on bikes approached. We tried not to pay attention and proceeded to our side of the tracks. But the youths pulled up in front of us. While two of them stood nearby on their bikes, three of them jumped off theirs and walked over to us.

"What do we got here?" one of the boys said. "Spics to order — maybe with some beans?"

He pushed me to the ground; the groceries splattered onto the asphalt. I felt melted gum and chips of broken beer bottle on my lips and cheek. Then somebody picked me up and held me while the others seized my brother, tossed his groceries out, and pounded on him. They punched him in the face, in the stomach, then his face again, cutting his lip, causing him to vomit.

I remember the shrill, maddening laughter of one of the kids on a bike, this laughing like a raven's wail, a harsh wind's shriek, a laugh that I would hear in countless beatings thereafter. I watched the others take turns on my brother, this terror of a brother, and he doubled over, had blood and spew on his shirt, and tears down his face. I wanted to do something, but they held me and I just looked on, as every strike against Rano opened me up inside.

They finally let my brother go and he slid to the ground, like a rotten banana squeezed out of its peeling. They threw us back over the tracks. In the sunset I could see the Watts Towers, shimmers of 70,000 pieces of broken bottles, sea shells, ceramic and metal on spiraling points puncturing the heavens, which reflected back the rays of a falling sun. My brother and I then picked ourselves up, saw the teenagers take off, still laughing, still talking about those stupid greasers who dared to cross over to South Gate.

Up until then my brother had never shown any emotion to me other than disdain. He had never asked me anything, unless it was a demand, an expectation, an obligation to be his throwaway boy-doll. But for this once he looked at me, tears welled in his eyes, blood streamed from several cuts — lips and cheeks swollen.

"Swear — you got to swear — you'll never tell anybody how I cried," he said.

I suppose I did promise. It was his one last thing to hang onto, his rep as someone who could take a belt whipping, who could take a beating in the neighborhood and still go back risking more — it was this pathetic plea from the pavement I remember. I must have promised.

It was a warm September day when my mother pulled me out of bed, handed me a pair of pants and a shirt, a piece of burnt toast and dragged me by the arm toward 109th Street School. We approached a huge, dusty brick building with the school's name carved in ancient English lettering across the entrance. Mama hauled me up a row of steps and through two large doors.

First day of school.

I was six years old, never having gone to kindergarten because Mama needed me then to take care of La Pata and Cuca so she could work. When La Pata became old enough to enter kindergarten, it became time for me to go. Mama filled out some papers. A school monitor directed us to a classroom where Mama dropped me off and left to join some parents who gathered in the main hall.

The first day of school said a lot about my scholastic life to come. I was taken to a teacher who didn't know what to do with me. She complained about not having any room, about kids who didn't even speak the language. And how was she supposed to teach anything under these conditions! Although I didn't speak English, I understood a large part of what she was saying. I knew I wasn't wanted. She put me in an old creaky chair near the door. As soon as I could, I sneaked out to find my mother.

I found Rano's class with the retarded children instead and decided to stay there for a while. Actually it was fun; they treated me like I was everyone's little brother. But the teacher finally told a student to take me to the main hall.

After some more paperwork, I was taken to another class. This time the teacher appeared nicer, but distracted. She got the word about my language problem.

"Okay, why don't you sit here in the back of the class," she said. "Play with some blocks until we figure out how to get you more involved."

It took her most of that year to figure this out. I just stayed in the back of the class, building blocks. It got so every morning I would put my lunch and coat away, and walk to my corner where I stayed the whole day long. It forced me to be more withdrawn. It got so bad, I didn't even tell anybody when I had to go the bathroom. I did it in my pants. Soon I stunk back there in the corner and the rest of the kids screamed out a chorus of "P.U.!" resulting in my being sent to the office or back home.

In those days there was no way to integrate the non-English speaking children. So they just made it a crime to speak anything but English. If a Spanish word sneaked out in the playground, kids were often sent to the office to get swatted or to get detention. Teachers complained that maybe the children were saying bad things about them. An assumption of guilt was enough to get one punished.

A day came when I finally built up the courage to tell the teacher I had to go to the bathroom. I didn't quite say all the words, but she got the message and promptly excused me so I didn't do it while I was trying to explain. I ran to the bathroom and peed and felt good about not having that wetness trickle down my pants leg. But suddenly several bells went on and off. I hesitantly stepped out of the bathroom and saw throngs of children leave their classes. I had no idea what was happening. I went to my classroom and it stood empty. I looked into other classrooms and found nothing. Nobody. I didn't know what to do. I really thought everyone had gone home. I didn't bother to look at the playground where the whole school had been assembled for the fire drill. I just went home. It got to be a regular thing there for a while, me coming home early until I learned the ins and outs of school life.

Not speaking well makes for such embarrassing moments. I hardly asked questions. I just didn't want to be misunderstood. Many Spanish-speaking kids mangled things up; they would say things like "where the beer and cantaloupe roam" instead of "where the deer and antelope roam."

That's the way it was with me. I mixed up all the words. Screwed up all the songs.

Eventually I did make friends. My brother often brought home a one-armed Mexican kid named Jaime. Sometimes we all hung out together. Jaime lost his arm when he was a toddler. Somehow he managed to get the arm stuck in the wringer of one of those old washing machines which pulled the clothes through two rollers. It tore his arm off at the socket. But later he made up for it with soccer feet and even won a couple of fights with his one good arm.

And then there was Earl. I didn't really know him until one day when we lined up following recess, he pulled the *trenzas* of a Mexican girl in our class named Gabriela. We all liked Gabriela. But she was also quiet, like me. So Earl pulled on her braids, the girl wailed, turned around and saw me standing there. Just then the teacher ran out of the classroom. Gabriela pointed in my direction. The one who never says anything. Because of this, I suffered through an hour's detention, fuming in my seat the whole time.

Later that evening, Earl came to my sister's house where we were visiting. Seni answered the door and looked askance at him.

"What do you want?"

"I want to know if the boy upstairs can play?"

"I don't know, I don't think so."

"Tell him I got some marbles. If it's okay, I'd like him to play with me."

"I don't know, I don't think so."

I looked down from the attic window and saw the tall, thin boy in striped shirt and blue jeans. Under an arm was a coffee can. Inside the can, marbles rattled whenever Earl moved.

But going through Seni was becoming a chore. Earl looked past her to a large, round woman in a print dress: My mom. She looked at the boy and then yelled up the stairs in Spanish.

"Go and play, Grillo," she said. "You stay in the attic all the time. Go and play. Be like other boys. ¡Ya!"

Earl waited patiently as the Rodríguez household quaked and quavered trying to get me downstairs and into the yard. Finally, I came down. Earl smiled broadly and offered me the can of marbles.

"This is for taking the rap today, man."

I looked hard at him, still a little peeved, then reached out for the can and held the best marble collection I had ever seen. I made a friend.

Desert winds swept past the TV antennas and peeling fences, welcome breezes on sweltering dry summer days when people came out to sit on their porches, or beneath a tree in dirt yards, or to fix cars in the street.

But on those days the perils came out too — you could see it in the faces of street warriors, in the play of children, too innocent to know what lurked about, but often the first to fall during a gang war or family scuffle.

103rd Street was particularly hard. It was the main drag in Watts, where most of the businesses were located, and it was usually crowded with people, including dudes who took whatever small change one might have in their pocket.

On days like that Rano, Jaime, Earl and I ventured out to the "third," as 103rd Street was called, or by the factories and railroad tracks playing dirt war with other kids. Other times we played on the rooftop and told stories.

"Did you ever hear the one about the half-man?" Earl asked.

"The what?" Jaime replied. "What's a half-man?"

"Well, he's a dude who got cut in half at the railroad tracks over there by Dogtown."

"Yeah, go on."

"So now he haunts the streets, half of him one place, the other half in another place — and he eats kids."

"Man, that's sick," Rano said. "But I got one for you. It's about *el pie*."

"What the hell is that?"

"*Pie* means foot in Spanish...and that's all it is! One big foot, walking around."

Gusts of winds swirled around the avocado tree branches as the moonlight cast uncanny shadows near where we related our tales.

"And you heard about *La Llorona*, right?" Rano continued.

"Oh, yeah, sure..."

"She's an old Mexican lady —"

"You mean Mrs. Alvarez?"

We laughed.

"Nah, this lady once got all her children and cut them up into tiny pieces."

"And..."

"And then she went all over the neighborhood, sprinkling bits of their bodies everywhere."

"And then..."

"So then God saw what she did and cursed her to walk the world, looking for her children — weeping — for all eternity. That's why she's called *La Llorona*, the weeping woman. And you know what, she picks up other kids to make up for the ones she's killed."

The leaves rustled, giving out an eerie sound. All of us jumped up, including Rano. Before anyone could say good night, we stumbled over one another, trying to get out of there, climbed off the roof, and ran through bedsheets and dresses hanging on a line, dashing like mad as we made our way home.

We changed houses often because of evictions. My dad constantly tried to get better work; he tried so many things. Although he was trained as a teacher, graduated with a degree in biology and had published Spanish textbooks in Mexico, in Los Angeles everyone failed to recognize his credentials. In Los Angeles, he was often no more than a laborer.

One day a miracle happened. My dad obtained a substitute teaching job in the San Fernando Valley, at Taft High School in Woodland Hills, teaching Spanish to well-off white children.

My dad must have thought we had struck oil or something. He bought a house in Reseda. In those days, this made us the only Mexican family around. It was a big house. It had three bedrooms, which meant the boys could have their own room, the girls theirs and my parents could be alone. It had two baths, a large, grassy yard and an upstanding, stucco garage.

I went to a school on Shirley Avenue which actually had books. I remember being chased back home a lot by the Anglo kids. But we were so glad to be in Reseda, so glad to be away from South Central Los Angeles.

Even my brother enjoyed success in this new environment. He became the best fighter in the school, all that he went through in Watts finally amounting to something. The big white kids tried to pick on him, and he fought back, hammered their faces with quick hands, in street style, after which nobody wanted to mess with him. Soon the bullies stopped chasing me home when they found out I was José's brother.

My dad went nuts in Reseda. He bought new furniture, a new TV, and he had the gall to throw away the old black & white box we had in Watts. He bought a new car. He was like a starving man in a candy store, partaking of everything, touching whatever he couldn't eat. He sat on a mountain of debt. But his attitude was "who cares?" We were Americans now. We were on our way to having a little bit of that dream. He was even doing it as a teacher, what he was trained for. Oh what a time it was for my father!

My mother, I could tell, was uncomfortable with the whole set-up. She shied away from the neighbors. The other mothers around here were good-looking, fit and well-built. My pudgy mom looked dark, Indian and foreign, no matter what money could buy. Except she got her false teeth. It seemed Mama was just there to pick up the pieces when my father's house of cards fell. She knew it would.

When it happened, it happened fast, decisively. It turned out Taft High School hired my father to teach Spanish on a temporary basis. Apparently the white kids couldn't understand him because of his accent. He wrote letters to the school board proposing new methods of teaching Spanish to American children so he could keep working. They turned them down, and Taft High School let him go.

We weren't in Reseda very long, less than a school year. Then the furniture store trucks pulled into the driveway to take back the new sofas, the washing machine, the refrigerator — even the TV. A "For Sale" sign jabbed into the front lawn. The new car had been repossessed. We pulled out of Reseda in an old beat-up Dodge. Sad faces on our neighbors were our farewell. I supposed they realized we weren't so bad for being Mexican. We were going back to an old friend — *pobreza*.

We moved in with Seni, her husband, and their two daughters. They were then occupying an apartment just outside East Los Angeles. Seni's girls were about the same age as me, my brother and sisters, although we were their uncles and aunts. They also had nicknames. Ana Seni was called *Pimpos*, which doesn't mean anything I know of. But Rano called her "Beanhead" and that took. Aidé was called *La Banana* because as a baby she had shades of blonde hair. They later had another daughter named Beca, also *güerita*.

Like most Latinos, we had a mixture of blood. My half-brother Alberto looked Caribbean. His mother came from Veracruz on the Caribbean side of Mexico which has the touch of Africa. The rest of us had different shades of Spanish white to Indian brown.

Uprooted again, we stuffed our things in a garage. The adults occupied the only two bedrooms. The children slept on makeshift bedding in the living room. My grandmother Catita also stayed with us. There were eleven of us crushed into that place. I remember the constant fighting. My dad was dumped on for not finding work. Seni accused her husband of having affairs with other women. Mama often stood outside alone, crying, or in the garage next to all our things piled on top of each other.

Rano and I sought refuge in the street.

One night, we came home late after having stocked up on licorice and bubble gum. We walked past police cars and an ambulance. Colored lights whirled across the tense faces of neighbors who stood on patches of grass and driveway. I pushed through low voices and entered the house: Blood was splattered on a far wall.

Moments before, Seni had been brushing Pimpos' hair when, who knows why, she pulled at the long sections. The girl's screams brought in my sister's husband. An argument ensued. Vicious words. Accusations.

Seni then plucked a fingernail file from the bathroom sink. She flashed it in front of my brother-in-law's face. He grabbed for her hand. The nail file plunged into his arm. Mom and Dad rushed in, ramming my sister against the wall; nail file crashed steely bright onto the linoleum floor.

Soon after the incident, the landlord evicted us all. This was when my mother and father broke up. And so we began that car ride to the train station, on the way back to Mexico, leaving L.A., perhaps never to come back.

☦ ☦ ☦

We pull into a parking lot at the Union station. It's like a point of no return. My father is still making his stand. Mama looks exhausted. We continue to sit in our seats, quiet now as Dad maneuvers into an empty space. Then we work our way out of the car, straightening our coats, gathering up boxes and taped-over paper bags: our "luggage." Up to this juncture, it's been like being in a storm — so much instability, of dreams achieved and then shattered, of a silence within the walls of my body, of being turned on, beaten, belittled and pushed aside; forgotten and unimportant. I have no position on the issue before us. To stay in L.A. To go. What does it matter? I've been a red hot ball, bouncing around from here to there. Anyone can bounce me. Mama. Dad. Rano. Schools. Streets. I'm a ball. Whatever.

We are inside the vast cavern of the station. Pews of swirled wood are filled with people. We sit with our bags near us, and string tied from the bags to our wrists so nobody can take them without taking us too. My father turns to us, says a faint goodby, then begins to walk away. No hugs. He doesn't even look at us.
  "Poncho."
  The name echoes through the waiting area.
  "Poncho."
  He turns. Stares at my mother. The wet of tears covers her face. Mama then says she can't go. She will stay with him. In

L.A. I don't think she's happy about this. But what can a single mother of four children do in Mexico? A woman, sick all the time, with factory work for skills in a land where work is mainly with the soil. What good is it except to starve.

"*Está bien*," Dad says as he nears my mother. "We will make it, *mujer*. I know it. But we have to be patient. We have to believe."

Mama turns to us and announces we are not leaving. I'm just a ball. Bouncing outside. Bouncing inside. Whatever.

CHAPTER TWO

"If you ain't from no barrio, then you ain't born."
— a 10-year-old boy from South San Gabriel

One evening dusk came early in South San Gabriel, with wind and cold spinning to earth. People who had been sitting on porches or on metal chairs near fold-up tables topped with cards and beer bottles collected their things to go inside. Others put on sweaters or jackets. A storm gathered beyond the trees.

Tino and I strolled past the stucco and wood-frame homes of the neighborhood consisting mostly of Mexicans with a sprinkling of poor white families (usually from Oklahoma, Arkansas and Texas). *Ranchera* music did battle with Country & Western songs as we continued toward the local elementary school, an oil-and-grime stained basketball under my arm.

We stopped in front of a chain-link fence which surrounded the school. An old brick building cast elongated shadows over a basketball court of concrete on the other side of the fence. Leaves and paper swirled in tiny tornadoes.

"Let's go over," Tino proposed.

I looked up and across the fence. A sign above us read: NO ONE ALLOWED AFTER 4:30 PM, BY ORDER OF THE LOS ANGELES COUNTY SHERIFF'S DEPARTMENT. Tino turned toward me, shrugged his shoulders and gave me a who-cares look.

"Help me up, man, then throw the ball over."

I cupped my hands and lifted Tino up while the boy scaled the fence, jumped over and landed on sneakered feet.

"Come on, Luis, let's go," Tino shouted from the other side.

I threw over the basketball, walked back a ways, then ran and jumped on the fence, only to fall back. Although we were both 10 years old, I cut a shorter shadow.

"Forget you, man," Tino said. "I'm going to play without you."

"Wait!" I yelled, while walking further back. I crouched low to the ground, then took off, jumped up and placed torn sneakers in the steel mesh. I made it over with a big thud.

Wiping the grass and dirt from my pants, I casually walked up to the ball on the ground, picked it up, and continued past Tino toward the courts.

"Hey Tino, what are you waiting for?"

The gusts proved no obstacle for a half-court game of B-ball, even as dark clouds smothered the sky.

Boy voices interspersed with ball cracking on asphalt. Tino's lanky figure seemed to float across the court, as if he had wings under his thin arms. Just then, a black-and-white squad car cruised down the street. A searchlight sprayed across the school yard. The vehicle slowed to a halt. The light shone toward the courts and caught Tino in mid-flight of a lay-up.

The dribbling and laughter stopped.

"All right, this is the sheriff's," a voice commanded. Two deputies stood by the fence, batons and flashlights in hand.

"Let's get out of here," Tino responded.

"What do you mean?" I countered. "Why don't we just stay here?"

"You nuts! We trespassing, man," Tino replied. "When they get a hold of us, they going to beat the crap out of us."

"Are you sure?"

"I know, believe me, I know."

"So where do we go?"

By then one of the deputies shouted back: "You boys get over here by the fence — now!"

But Tino dropped the ball and ran. I heard the deputies yell for Tino to stop. One of them began climbing the fence. I decided to take off too.

It never stopped, this running. We were constant prey, and the hunters soon became big blurs: the police, the gangs, the junkies, the dudes on Garvey Boulevard who took our money, all smudged into one. Sometimes they were teachers who jumped on us Mexicans as if we were born with a hideous stain. We were always afraid. Always running.

Tino and I raced toward the dark boxes called classrooms. The rooms lay there, hauntingly still without the voices of children, the commands of irate teachers or the clapping sounds of books as they were closed. The rooms were empty, forbidden places at night. We scurried around the structures toward a courtyard filled with benches next to the cafeteria building.

Tino hopped on a bench, then pulled himself over a high fence. He walked a foot or two on top of it, stopped, and proceeded to climb over to the cafeteria's rooftop. I looked over my shoulder. The deputies weren't far behind, their guns drawn. I grabbed hold of the fence on the side of the cafeteria. I looked up and saw Tino's perspiring face over the roof's edge, his arm extended down toward me.

I tried to climb up, my feet dangling. But then a firm hand seized a foot and pulled at it.

"They got me!" I yelled.

Tino looked below. A deputy spied the boy and called out: "Get down here...you *greaser!*"

Tino straightened up and disappeared. I heard a flood of footsteps on the roof — then a crash. Soon an awful calm covered us.

"Tino!" I cried out.

A deputy restrained me as the other one climbed onto the roof. He stopped at a skylight, jagged edges on one of its sides. Shining a flashlight inside the building, the officer spotted Tino's misshapen body on the floor, sprinkled over with shards of glass.

☩ ☩ ☩

After the aborted trip to Mexico, a poverty agency helped our family find a rented place within our means: a square, one-bedroom clapboard house on La Presa Street in an unincorporated part of the county called South San Gabriel.

The living room served as sleeping quarters for my mom, sisters and dad. My brother and I had the only bedroom to ourselves, along with piles of stuffed boxes. On hot nights, Rano and I slept outside under the openness of the desert sky. It was similar to Watts, but at least it was a home of our own again.

Incorporated towns like Monterey Park, Rosemead and Montebello surrounded South San Gabriel. The area was located in the San Gabriel Valley, which for years consisted of incipient industry, farmland and migrant camps until Los Angeles stretched out fingers of suburban sprawl to the furthest reaches of the valley.

There used to be a corn field not far away from our house on La Presa Street. I remember playing there with my friends. Once, though, a farmer came at us with a loaded shotgun while we swerved and pivoted out of his range through the stalks of corn.

By the early 1970s, this area was torn up and office buildings, hotels and a couple of high rises replaced the rows of stalks which once swayed free in the wind, which once held our imaginations afire with war play, clod-throwing contests, and majestic worlds of conquest. By then, with the farmlands and many of the Mexicans of Klingerman Street removed, the City of Rosemead annexed this part of South San Gabriel and it ceased being unwanted county territory.

Unincorporated county territory was generally where the poorest people lived, the old barrios, which for the most part didn't belong to any city because nobody wanted them.

Most of Watts and a large section of East Los Angeles were unincorporated county territory. Sometimes they had no sewage system or paved roads. They included hills, ravines and hollows. The Los Angeles County Sheriff's Department — known as the most brutal of the local law enforcement agencies — policed these areas.

In the mid-60s, South San Gabriel included both flat areas and what we called the Hills, or *Las Lomas*. The Hills were made up of tiny houses patched together by weathered wood, chicken wire and creaking porches that buckled and swayed like a boat on an open sea. Cadavers of rusted cars filled up yellowed yards. Torn sofas, broken lamps and threadless tires were strewn about in vacant lots. The roads turned and twisted every which way; they were dusty, curbless streets that might have served as goat trails at one time. Coming down one of the dirt roads, you could encounter chickens, wild dogs or pigs. Some back yards held the wood-and-wire sheds of fighting cocks, or the copper pipings of a backyard still.

The Hills were unseen. Unvisited. Cars flew past north of here on the San Bernardino Freeway into Los Angeles, but most of the drivers never imagined such a place existed, a place you could have found in the Ozarks or the hills of Tijuana.

☦ ☦ ☦

Bruja, Bruja.

Whispers of morning, whispers of night, children without faces tormenting with a word, descending like a torrent of leaves, like the blaze of dawn. A never-ending litany.

Bruja, Bruja.

The conspiracy of voices greets the old woman who lives in an almost toppled, unpainted house next door; her back yard dense with overgrown weeds.

They say she is a witch. The children hide in bushes or behind fences and taunt her as she lumbers outside to put out trash or water her grassless yard.

"¡Bruja, Bruja!"

They sling dirt clods at her feet, tease her to tears, dare her to strike away at this cancer of childhood that makes her last days alone in this clapboard cottage feel like the hell fires she herself condemns the voices to.

The old woman grabs a trash-can lid or a broom and pursues the children who scamper out of the way, laughing and jeering as she creaks in her bones.

One Halloween, the woman offers the neighborhood children cookies — but the talk is she made them with cyanide. Nobody eats the cookies, but soon all the cats in the neighborhood vanish, and nobody knows why.

One morning, uniformed men bust into the old woman's house. Sheriff's deputies pull her from out of the debris-strewn guts of the wood-shingle dwelling; the woman never cleaned it. They take the woman away, never to come back.

It turns out she had been babysitting three small children when, for an unknown reason, the kids' parents never came back for them. The woman ran out of food. One day, trash collectors find three children in a playpen next to the morning garbage.

Angry voices close in on the woman's house after her removal. A few kids throw rocks at the windows, the glass falling like raindrops skewing down a marble wall. Somebody pours gasoline on the splintered porch. Somebody tosses a twirled newspaper lit at the top. Next door, the glow washes across faces as we observe the house crackle and tumble in a craze of flames.

The Mexicans who came to live in the San Gabriel Valley worked the fields, the railroads or in the encroaching industry which soon dotted the valley. Their barrios had names like *El Jardín* (the garden), *Monte Flores* (mountain flowers), *Canta Ranas* (singing frogs — named for the watery inhabitants of a local swamp), *Bolen* (a Spanish corruption of Baldwin Park), or *La Puente* (the bridge).

Las Lomas was an old barrio whose main rivals were to the west, in East Los Angeles, or the north in another barrio called *Sangra*.

Sangra was a corruption of San Gabriel, an incorporated city built around one of the Spanish Missions founded by Father Junípero Serra in the 1700s. A major Indian village, Yang Na, was once situated here. Later when the railroads linked many of the missions, they brought in Mexican laborers who became the first barrio residents.

It didn't take long for middle-income Anglos, primarily fleeing L.A.'s inner-city as it filled up with people of color, to move in and around these barrios and create the first suburbs. New tracts of homes suddenly appeared on previously empty space or by displacing the barrios. In later years, large numbers of Asians from Japan, Korea and Taiwan also moved into the area. Sections of Monterey Park and even San Gabriel became known as Little Japans or Chinatowns. It wasn't hard to find an unpaved road cluttered with shacks on one block while a row of stucco townhouses graced another.

The barrios which weren't incorporated, including Las Lomas, became self-contained and forbidden, incubators of rebellion which the local media, generally controlled by suburban whites, labeled havens of crime.

For years, nobody ventured into Las Lomas unless they had to be there. Buses refused to provide residents there any service. Sheriff's deputies entered it with full firepower and ample backup, hardly ever alone.

One of the county's most devastating increases in gang activity centered on Las Lomas.

✝ ✝ ✝

We didn't call ourselves gangs. We called ourselves clubs or *clicas*. In the back lot of the local elementary school, about a year after Tino's death, five of us gathered in the grass and created a club — "Thee Impersonations," the "Thee" being an old English usage that other clubs would adopt because it made everything sound classier, nobler, *badder*. It was something to belong to — something that was ours. We weren't in boy scouts, in sports teams or camping groups. Thee Impersonations is how we wove something out of the threads of nothing.

"We all taking a pledge," Miguel Robles said. "A pledge to be for each other. To stand up for the *clica*. Thee Impersonations will never let you down. Don't ever let Thee Impersonations down."

Miguel was 11 years old like the rest of us. Dark, curly-haired and good-looking, he was also sharp in running, baseball and schoolwork — and a leader. Miguel was not prone to loudness or needless talking, but we knew he was the best among us. We made him president of our club.

Thee Impersonations was born of necessity. It started one day at the school during lunch break. A few of us guys were standing around talking to some girls — girls we were beginning to see as women. They had makeup and short skirts. They had teased hair and menstruations. They grew breasts. They were no longer Yolanda, Guadalupe or María — they were Yoli, Lupe and Mari.

Some of the boys were still in grass-stained jeans with knee patches and had only begun getting uncontrollable hard-ons. The girls flowered over the summer, and it looked near impossible for some of us to catch up.

Older dudes from junior high school, or even some who didn't go to school, would come to the school and give us chilled looks as they scoped out the young women.

That day, a caravan of low-scraping cars slow-dragged in front of the school. A crew of mean-looking *vatos* piled out, armed with chains, bats, metal pipes and zip guns.

"Thee Mystics rule," one of them yelled from the other side of the school fence.

Thee Mystics were a tough up-and-coming group. They fired their rigged .22s at the school and broke a couple of windows with stones. They rammed through the gate and front entrances. Several not-so-swift dudes who stood in their way got beat. Even teachers ran for cover. Terror filled everyone's eyes.

I froze as the head-stomping came dangerously my way. But I was also intrigued. I wanted this power. I wanted to be able to bring a whole school to its knees and even make teachers squirm. All my school life until then had been poised against me: telling me what to be, what to say, how to say it. I was a broken boy, shy and fearful. I wanted what Thee Mystics had; I wanted the power to hurt somebody.

Police sirens broke the spell. Dudes scattered in all directions. But Thee Mystics had done their damage. They had left their mark on the school — and on me.

Miguel and the rest of us started Thee Impersonations because we needed protection. There were other clubs popping up all over, many challenging anybody who wasn't into anything. All of a sudden every dude had to claim a clique.

Some of these clubs included Thee Ravens, The Superiors, Latin Legions, Thee Imitations, Los Santos and Chug-a-lug (a curious mix of Anglo and Mexican dudes). These were the "Southside" clubs (for South San Gabriel). The biggest on the Southside then were Thee Illusions and their allies: Thee Mystics.

Over in San Gabriel, other cliques were formed such as Thee Regents, The Chancellors, Little Gents, The Intruders and Little Jesters.

Most of the clubs began quite innocently. Maybe they were a team of guys for friendly football. Sometimes they were set up for trips to the beach or the mountains. But some became more organized. They obtained jackets, with their own colors, and identification cards. Later a few of the cliques became car clubs, who invested what little they had in bouncing lowriders, street-wise "shorts," splashed with colors, which cruised the main drags of local barrios or the main cruising spot we called *the boulevard*: Whittier Boulevard in East Los Angeles.

Then also some of the clubs metamorphosed into something more unpredictable, more encompassing. Something more deadly.

Junior high school became the turning point.

After grammar school, I ended up going to Richard Garvey Intermediate School. My father had gotten a job as a "laboratory technician" at a Los Angeles community college. So we moved into a larger, two-bedroom place in territory which stood between the two major barrios: *Las Lomas* and *Sangra*. This meant I had to go to Garvey.

In the mid-1960s, the students at Garvey had some of the worst academic scores in the state. There were no pencils or papers. Books were discards from other suburban schools where the well-off students turned up. The kids who lived in the Hills found their way into Garvey. And for half of them, the school was the end of the line: It had more than a 50-percent dropout rate among Mexicans before they even got to high school.

There were only a couple of Impersonations who made it there. Miguel Robles and the others ended up in another school. Garvey was Illusions and Mystics territory. I was on my own.

Again the first thing I noticed were some of the girls. The ones from the Hills weren't just blossoming women, though; they were already hardened, sophisticated. Some of them called themselves *cholas*. They had long, teased hair, often peroxided black or red. They had heavy makeup, skirts which hugged their behinds, and they were all the time fighting, including with guys. The cholas laughed a lot and knew how to open up to every situation. They talked back, talked loud and talked tough. And they knew how to dance.

A few East L.A. people who moved into the Hills brought the East L.A. style with them. There were federally-subsidized housing projects not far from here called Maravilla. It was so-named in the 1920s when Los Angeles city officials rebuilt the downtown area and got rid of the Mexicans in the inner core by offering land on the far outreaches of town for a dollar. When the Mexicans got wind of this they exclaimed "¡*Qué Maravilla!*" — what a marvel! — and the name took.

My first love at 12 years old was a girl from Maravilla named Elena, a chola, who came to Garvey all *prendida*. She didn't just know how to kiss, but how to take my hand through sections of her body and teach a pre-teen something of his own budding sexuality.

At Garvey, the dudes began to sport cholo attire: the baggy starched pants and suspenders over white T-shirts, the flannel shirts clipped only from the top button, the bandannas and small brim hats. It was hip. It was different. And it was what the cholas liked.

This is what I remember of junior high: Cholas who walked up the stairs in their tight skirts, revealing everything, and looked down at us, smiling at their power. Bloody Kotexes on the hallway floor. Gang graffiti on every available space of wall. Fires which flared from restroom trash bins. Fights every day, including after school on the alley off Jackson Avenue. Dudes who sold and took drugs, mostly downers and *yesca*, but sometimes heroin which a couple of dudes shot up in the boys' room while their "homeys" kept a lookout.

Yet most of the Mexican girls weren't cholas; their families still had strong reins on many of them. Mexicans were mostly traditional and Catholic. Fathers, mothers or older brothers would drop off these girls and come get them after school so no perceived harm would come their way.

One of them was Socorro, from Mexico, who was straight and proper, and tried to stop me from being a cholo. I asked her to become my girlfriend when word got around she liked me and Elena had left me for Ratón, a down dude from the Hills.

"They're trash," Socorro would often say in Spanish about the *cholillos*. "If you keep hanging out with them, you can say goodby to me forever."

I liked her, but we didn't last too long as a couple. I didn't want to be straight and proper. My next girlfriend was Marina, a girl from Lomas who had one of the highest, peroxided teases on her head with blonde streaks that accentuated her dark face.

It was at Marina's urging that I obtained my first tattoo. A dude named Angel charged $5 for an hour's work beneath the school's bleachers. They were crude, unadorned, hand-etchings. Angel used sewing needles, sterilized by placing them over a match flame. He then tied a tight wound of sewing thread on the end. Enough of the needle's point stuck out to penetrate below the skin. Angel dipped the needle into a bottle of black India ink, allowing the thread to soak it up. Then he punctured the skin with quick up and down motions, filling the tiny holes with ink from the thread.

I got the tattoo on my upper right arm. It was an outline of a cross beneath the words "*Mi Vida Loca.*"

We drove teachers nuts at Garvey. A number of them were sent home with nervous breakdowns. We went through three teachers and five substitutes in my home room my first year at the school.

One of my teachers was a Cuban refugee named Mr. Enríquez. We made him wish he never left the island. He could hardly speak English. And when he spoke Spanish, it was a sure sign we were in trouble.

Every morning Mr. Enríquez entered the class and got bombarded with spit balls and jelly beans. Sometimes he'd turn around to write something on the chalk board and everyone would drop their books all at once.

Often you could find Mr. Enríquez with his head on his desk, cursing into folded arms.

Then there was the science teacher, Mrs. Krieger. She must have been 80 years old or more. It took her half the class period to walk up the stairs and down the hall to her classroom. By that time most of the class was gone. Once, as she creaked around to write something on the chalkboard, we threw her rain-stained, beat-up encyclopedias, which were as ancient as she was, out the windows. Then we threw out the desks and chairs. Before long, most of Mrs. Krieger's classroom was scattered across the front lawn — and she didn't realize it until a school official ran puffing up the stairs to investigate what the hell was going on.

The school's teachers were made up of misfits, those that other schools didn't want or who for some reason couldn't cut it. The gym teacher looked like a refugee from the Marines who shouted commands even in normal conversation, was always dressed in shorts and never failed to have a stainless steel whistle hanging from his bull-neck. The shop teacher was Mr. Stone, who acted exactly as if he were carved out of a thick piece of gray granite. He dealt with us harshly, always on his guard. But one day we broke through his defenses.

The shop class was inside an old bungalow at the back of the school. The front door had "Las Lomas" spray-painted on the outside followed by the words *Con Safos*, the cholo term that signified nobody should mess with this — if they valued their life. Mr. Stone was inside showing our class how to cut a piece of wood on a rotary saw.

Then Elías, one of the *vatitos,* started a racket from the back of the room. Mr. Stone turned around to discipline him. But he forgot to turn off the saw. It sliced away at the board...then his finger. Man, what a mess! Mr. Stone turned a sickening pale color as soon as he realized what had happened.

"God damn it!" he yelled, "God damn it!" as his face wrinkled with every throb of pain.

An ambulance came and rushed Mr. Stone away. School officials shoved everyone else into another classroom until they could hold meetings to determine who to blame. But Elías and I sneaked out and returned to the wood shop bungalow. The door was still open. We foraged through the piles of sawdust and wood pieces and found Mr. Stone's finger. It looked purplish with dried blood and bone chips on one end. Elías carefully placed it inside an empty cigar box.

For weeks we kept the finger in Elías' locker. He'd bring it out to scare some of the girls and to show it off to incoming students until it shriveled away, like a dried sliver of old fruit.

✟ ✟ ✟

"You can't be in a fire and not get burned."

This was my father's response when he heard of the trouble I was getting into at school. He was a philosopher. He didn't get angry or hit me. That he left to my mother. He had these lines, these cuts of wisdom, phrases and syllables, which swept through me, sometimes even making sense. I had to deal with him at that level, with my brains. I had to justify in words, with ideas, all my actions — no matter how insane. Most of the time I couldn't.

Mama was heat. Mama was turned-around leather belts and wailing choruses of Mary-Mother-of-Jesus. She was the penetrating emotion that came at you through·her eyes, the mother-guilt, the one who birthed me, who suffered through the contractions and diaper changes and all my small hurts and fears. For her, dealing with school trouble or risking my life was nothing for discourse, nothing to debate. She went through all this hell and more to have me — I'd better do what she said!

Mama hated the cholos. They reminded her of the rowdies on the border, I suppose our relatives, who fought all the time, talked that *caló* slang, drank mescal, smoked marijuana and left scores of women with babies bursting out of their bodies.

They were her uncles. Her father's friends. Her brothers. To see me become like them made her sick, made her cringe and cry and curse. Mama reminded us how she'd seen so much alcoholism, so much weed-madness, and she prohibited anything with alcohol in the house, even beer. I later learned this rage came from how Mama's father treated her siblings and her mother, how in drunken rages he'd hit her mom and drag her through the house by the hair.

The school informed my parents I had been wreaking havoc with a number of other young boys. I was to be part of a special class of troublemakers. We would be isolated from the rest of the school population and forced to pick up trash and clean graffiti during the rest of the school year.

"Mrs. Rodríguez, your son is too smart for this," the vice-principal told Mama. "We think he's got a lot of potential. But his behavior is atrocious. There's no excuse. We're sad to inform you of our decision."

They also told her the next time I cut class or even made a feint toward trouble, I'd be expelled. After the phone call, my mom lay on her bed, shaking her head while sobbing in-between bursts of how God had cursed her for some sin, how I was the devil incarnate, a plague, testing her in this brief tenure on earth.

My dad's solution was to keep me home after school. Grounded. Yeah, sure. I was 13 years old already. Already tattooed. Already sexually involved. Already into drugs. In the middle of the night I snuck out through the window and worked my way to the Hills.

At 16 years old, Rano turned out much better than me, much better than anyone could have envisioned during the time he was a foul-faced boy in Watts.

When we moved to South San Gabriel, a Mrs. Snelling took a liking to Rano. The teacher helped him skip grades to make up for the times he was pushed back in those classes with the retarded children.

Mrs. Snelling saw talent in Rano, a spark of actor during the school's thespian activities. She even had him play the lead in a class play. He also showed some facility with music. And he was good in sports.

He picked up the bass guitar and played for a number of garage bands. He was getting trophies in track-and-field events, in gymnastic meets and later in karate tournaments.

So when I was at Garvey, he was in high school being the good kid, the Mexican exception, the barrio success story — my supposed model. Soon he stopped being Rano or even José. One day he became Joe.

My brother and I were moving away from each other. Our tastes, our friends, our interests, were miles apart. Yet there were a few outstanding incidents I fondly remember in relationship to my brother, incidents which despite their displays of closeness failed to breach the distance which would later lie between us.

When I was nine, for example, my brother was my protector. He took on all the big dudes, the bullies on corners, the ones who believed themselves better than us. Being a good fighter transformed him overnight. He was somebody who some feared, some looked up to. Then he developed skills for racing and high-jumping. This led to running track and he did well, dusting all the competition.

I didn't own any talents. I was lousy in sports. I couldn't catch baseballs or footballs. And I constantly tripped when I ran or jumped. When kids picked players for basketball games, I was the last one they chose. The one time I inadvertently hit a home run during a game at school — I didn't mean to do it — I ended up crying while running around the bases because I didn't know how else to react to the cheers, the excitement, directed at something I did. It just couldn't be me.

But Rano had enemies too. There were two Mexican kids who were jealous of him. They were his age, three years older than me. One was named Eddie Gómez, the other Ricky Corral. One time they cornered me outside the school.

"You José's brother," Eddie said.

I didn't say anything.

"Wha's the matter? Can't talk?"

"Oh, he can talk all right," Ricky chimed in. "He acting the *pendejo* because his brother thinks he so bad. Well, he ain't shit. He can't even run."

"Yea, José's just a *lambiche*, a kiss ass," Eddie responded. "They give him those ribbons and stuff because he cheats."

"That's not true," I finally answered. "My brother can beat anybody."

"Oh, you saying he can beat me," Eddie countered.

"Sure sounds like he said that," Ricky added.

"I'm only saying that when he wins those ribbons, *está derecho*," I said.

"It sounds to me like you saying he better than me," Eddie said.

"Is that what you saying, man?" Ricky demanded. "Com' on — is that what you saying?"

I turned around, and beneath my breath, mumbled something about how I didn't have time to argue with them. I shouldn't have done that.

"What'd you say?" Eddie said.

"I think he called you a punk," Ricky agitated.

"You call me a punk, man?" Eddie turned me around. I denied it.

"I heard him, dude. He say you are a punk-ass *puto*," Ricky continued to exhort.

The fist came at me so fast, I don't even recall how Eddie looked when he threw it. I found myself on the ground. Others in the school had gathered around by then. When a few saw it was me, they knew it was going to be a slaughter.

I rose to my feet — my cheek had turned swollen and blue. I tried to hit Eddie, but he backed up real smooth and hit me again. Ricky egged him on, I could hear the excitement in his voice.

I lay on the ground, defeated. Teachers came and chased the boys out. But before Eddie and Ricky left they yelled back: "José ain't nothing, man. You ain't nothing."

Anger flowed through me, but also humiliation. It hurt so deep I didn't even feel the fracture in my jaw, the displacement which would later give me a disjointed, lopsided and protruding chin. It became my mark.

Later when I told Rano what happened, he looked at me and shook his head.

"You didn't have to defend me to those dudes," he said. "They're assholes. They ain't worth it."

I looked at him and told him something I never, ever told him again.

"I did it because I love you."

☦ ☦ ☦

Along the spine of the night, through the shrubbery, on the coarse roads, past the peeling shacks, past the walls filled with the stylized writing that proclaimed our existence, past La India's shed where boys discovered the secret of thighs, in the din of whispers, past Berta's garden of herbs and midnight incantations, past the Japo's liquor store, past the empty lots scattered around the barrio we called "the fields," overlooking Nina's house, pretty Nina, who lavished our dreams, there you'd find the newest and strongest clique. There you'd find the Animal Tribe.

We lingered in the dust: Clavo, Wilo, Chicharrón and I. We walked through these streets in pairs with a rhythm, slow, like a *bolero*. I had on a T-shirt, cut off at the shoulders, with "The Animal Tribe" in old English lettering on the back written in shoe polish and a long pair of county-jail pants, called "counties," over a couple of black Tijuana sandals.

Clavo, Wilo, Chicharrón and I. We picked up cigarettes at *la marqueta*. We strutted, like soldiers, and stopped for a while to look into the small, store-front church where Spanish-speaking holy rollers squirmed and shouted in their seats.

Clavo, Wilo, Chicharrón and I. We were *los cuatro del barrio*, the younger dudes, 13 and 14, who got swept up in the fast, tumultuous changes between the cliques and clubs in the area. The Animal Tribe was taking over everything: It did it through war, through a reputation, through the strong leadership of two key families: the López brothers and the Domínguezes.

The five López brothers got hooked up with the two Domínguez brothers and their four sisters. Lydia Domínguez ended up marrying Joaquín López, the Tribe's president, and this continued to pull the various groups into one, huge clique.

Thee Illusions and Mystics were gone. The other clubs also disappeared as The Animal Tribe consolidated them in as well. Even Thee Impersonations vanished; Miguel Robles joined the Tribe and later became one of its generals.

The Tribe, although based in the Hills, pulled in dudes from all over South San Gabriel, even from areas east of the Hills like Muscatel Street, Bartlett Street and Earle Avenue which had long-running feuds with Las Lomas.

Joaquín López was the leader, *el mero chingón*, as we'd say. Clavo, Wilo, Chicharrón and I were the peewees, the youngest set, who stood outside the Tribe meetings held in the fields or in the baseball diamond of Garvey Park, looking in until we could collect more experience and participate wholly with the others. Sometimes we were allowed to witness "the line." This is where new initiates were forced to run through two rows of Tribe members, absorbing a storm of fists and kicks. Inevitably, somebody used brass knuckles and some dude would end up with cracked ribs.

We tried being "the Southside Boys" for a short time while we were in Garvey school, getting brown-and-gold jackets and crashing parties and dances. But we got into trouble with dudes from Sangra who objected to us embroidering the term "South Sangra" on the jackets.

"There's only one Sangra," Chava from the Sangra Diablos told us one night at a *quinceñera*. He had a small brim hat and leaned on a silver-inlaid, porcelain-tipped mahogany cane. He looked Asian, like Fuji in the movies.

Next to him were Tutti, Negro and Worm, with scars and tattoos on their arms and faces, and extra-baggy pants and muscled torsos. Then they chased us down a number of streets and alleys. It was the death of the Southside Boys.

Miguel got us banging with The Tribe. It was during a dance at Garvey Park. The gym was opened one weekend for the local teenagers. Lowrider cars filled the front parking lot and side streets. Girls from barrios all over converged on the bungalow-type gym. That night I noticed there weren't the usual knots here and there of different club members with their own unique jackets and colors. Only a few still carried proud their old club insignias, including the few of us in the Southside Boys.

"*¿Qué hubo, ése?*" Miguel greeted as he walked up to me. It had been about two years since we were partners in Thee Impersonations. But this time he had on a black jacket with gold lettering on the back that read: The Animal Tribe.

I introduced him to the remaining Southside Boys. Miguel was kind, courteous, and invited us into the dance for free: This was a Tribe party; we were his guests.

Inside, the place was almost pitch black and reeked of cigarette and marijuana smoke. Although no alcoholic beverages were allowed, I could see outlines of dudes and their girlfriends drinking from bottles of cheap wine they had sneaked in.

A local band played some mean sounds, one of a number of street bands which were popping up all over the valley and east side of the county.

"I heard about what happened to you guys at Lola's *quinceñera*," Miguel said. "The old *veteranos* from Sangra, you see, are forcing all the cliques over there to claim their barrio.

There's no more Regents or Chancellors or Little Gents. They in Sangra or they dead."

"So why they messing with us?" Wilo asked. "We ain't in their barrio."

"You ain't in Lomas either, man," Miguel said. "That's the problem. You guys live in between the two largest 'hoods. You got to figure out which one to claim or you're going to get fucked by both of them."

"What do you say we do, Miguel?" Chicharrón asked.

"There's the Tribe, man. It's the one that's taking over all the south side cliques."

"I don't know, I mean, we still don't live in the Hills," I replied. "We could still get jumped."

"I'm telling you there's no choice," Miguel continued. "You wanta live, you wanta breathe air, you got to be in the Tribe man. *De verotas, ése.*"

That night, we took off our "Southside Boys" jackets and met with Joaquín, his brothers Ernie and Gregorio, and a few other dudes and *rucas* from the Tribe. They were in the darkest part of the park, beyond the gym dance area. Some of them had containers with pills they called *colies* or *blancas* (*colies* was short for *coloradas*, which meant "reds" or downers; *blancas* stood for "whites," uppers).

Miguel talked to Joaquín and Ernie separately for a while about us coming in. Gregorio and the others stayed with us. I looked over to one side where I thought I heard a girl's muffled voice. There seemed to be a figure on top of somebody, going up and down on a body laid out on the ground, moaning with every motion.

Gregorio eyed me. Just staring. Finally he spoke: "She's being initiated into the Tribe."

Then he laughed.

CHAPTER THREE

"You *cholos* have great stories about climbing fences."
— a barrio boxing coach

The Hills blistered below a haze of sun and smog. Mothers with wet strands of hair across their foreheads flung wash up to dry on weathered lines. Sweat-drenched men lay on their backs in the gravel of alleys, beneath broken-down cars propped up on cinder blocks. *Charrangas* and *corridos* splashed out of open windows.

Suddenly from over a hill, an ice cream truck raced by with packs of children running beside it. A hurried version of "Old McDonald Had A Farm" chimed through a speaker bolted on the truck's roof. The truck stopped long enough for somebody to toss out dozens of sidewalk sundaes, tootie-fruities and half-and-half bars to the children who gathered around, thrusting up small, dirt-caked hands that blossomed open as their shrieks blended with laughter.

Then the truck's transmission gears growled as it continued up the slope, whipped around a corner and passed a few of us *vatos* assembled on a field off Toll Drive. We looked over toward the echoes of the burdensome chimes, the slip and boom of the clutch and rasp of gears as the ice cream truck entered the dead-end streets and curves of Las Lomas.

"*Orale, ése, ¿qué está pasando?*" a dude named Little Man asked while passing a bottle of Tokay wine to Clavo.

"It's Toots and the *gaba*, you know, Axel," Clavo replied. "They just stole an ice cream truck on Portrero Grande Drive."

"*¡Qué cábula!*" Little Man said. "They sure is crazy."

We continued to talk and drink until the day melted into night.

Little Man and one of the López brothers, Fernie, all Tribe, were there in the field with me and my *camaradas* Clavo, Chicharrón, and Wilo. The four of us were so often together that the list of our names became a litany. We spray-painted our *placas* on the walls, followed by *AT* for Animal Tribe or *SSG* for South San Gabriel.

Everyone called me Chin because of my protruding jawbone. I had it tattooed on my ankle.

We sat around a small roasting pit Chicharrón made from branches and newspaper. Around us were ruins, remains of a home which had been condemned and later ravaged by fire. We assembled inside the old cement foundation with its scattered sections of brick and concrete walls splattered with markings and soot with rusted re-enforcing bars protruding from stone blocks.

We furnished the lot with beat-up couches and discarded sofas. Somebody hung plastic from a remaining cinder-block wall to a low branch so homeboys could sleep there — and miss most of any rain — when there was nowhere else to go. It was really a vacant lot but we called all such lots "the fields."

Even as we talked, there was Noodles, a wino and old *tecato,* crashed out on the sofa.

"Get up Noodles, time for some *refín*," Chicharrón exclaimed as he placed stolen hot dogs and buns on the fire. Wilo threw a dirt clod at the sofa and Noodles mumbled some incoherent words.

"*Orale,* leave the *vato* alone, *ése,*" Little Man said.

But Noodles got up, spittle dripping from his mouth.

"Hey *ése,* Noodles is awake, and man is he pissed," Wilo said.

"How can you tell?" Chicharrón asked.

"When he moves fast and you can't understand what he's saying, then he's pissed," Wilo answered. "When he moves slow and you still can't understand what he's saying, he's all right."

Noodles staggered toward us, his arms flailing, as if boxing — huffing, puffing and dropping mucus from his nose.

"Get the hell out of here, *pinche,*" Wilo said as he stood up and pushed the wino aside.

"You thinks youse are tuss dues...you ain't so tuss," Noodles said, throwing sloppy left hooks and uppercuts into the air.

Wilo placed his hand over Noodles' head, whose wiry body looked like a strand from a dirty mop. Wilo was also thin and slippery. The rest of us laughed and laughed at the two *flaquillos* goofing around.

"Ah leave the *vato* alone, homeboy," Clavo suggested. "Let's break out another bottle."

As we cooked, shared wine and told stories of *jainas* and the little conquests, of fights for honor, homeys and the 'hood, a gray Mercury sedan with its headlights turned off crept up the road. Wilo was the closest up the slope to the street. He looked over at the Mercury, then frowned.

"Anybody recognize the *ranfla?*" Wilo inquired.

"*Chale,*" Chicharrón responded. "It looks too funky to be gang-bangers."

"Unless that's what they want it to look like."

Wilo moved up the slope from the field, followed by Clavo, Chicharrón and Little Man. Fernie stayed back with Noodles and me. Wilo and Clavo were the first ones to hit the street as the Mercury delayed a turn around a curve.

Clavo moved to one side of the Mercury, its occupants covered in darkness. He stretched out his arms and yelled out: "Here stand The Animal Tribe — ¡y *qué!*"

The Mercury stopped. A shadow stepped out of a bashed-in side door, a sawed-off shotgun in his hands. Another shadow pushed an automatic rifle out the side window.

"Sangra Diablos! ¡*Qué rifa!*" the dude with the shotgun yelled out. Then a blast snapped at the night air.

Wilo and Chicharrón fell back down the slope. Automatic gunfire followed them as they rolled in the dirt. The bullets skimmed off tree branches, knocked over trash cans and ricocheted off walls. Wilo ended up face-down; Chicharrón landed on his butt. Noodles knelt behind the sofa, whimpering. The cracking sounds stopped. The Mercury sped off, its tires throwing up dirt and pebbles behind it.

I could see the car speeding down another hill. I ran up the slope, slipping and sliding toward the road. On the street, Little Man kneeled over Clavo, who lay sprawled on the ground and trembling. Half of Clavo's face was shot full of pellets, countless black, steaming round holes; his eye dripping into the dirt.

Wilo and the others climbed up and rushed up to Little Man. Fernie began jumping up and down like he had been jolted with lightning, letting out *gritos*. I kept looking at Clavo's face, thinking something stupid like how he was such a dummy, always taking chances, all the time being "the dude." Then I squatted on the ground, closed my eyelid and let a tear stream down the side of my face.

Windows flung upwards. Doors were pushed aside. People bolted out of their homes. Mothers cursed in Spanish from behind weather-beaten picket fences.

As Clavo was taken to the hospital, Fernie talked about getting all the Tribe together, about meeting later that night, about guns and warfare and "*ya estuvo*" — that's it. A war, fought for generations between Lomas and Sangra, flared up again.

Later, as I walked down the hills on the way back home, sirens tore across the sky and a sheriff's helicopter hovered nearby, beaming a spotlight across shacks and brush, over every hole and crevice of the neighborhood.

I mounted a fence which wound around a dirt embankment, hoping to get out of the helicopter's sights. I looked over the other side and there overturned at the bottom of the gully, to be ravaged by scavengers for parts, to be another barrio monument, lay an ice cream truck.

✝ ✝ ✝

A few years after our family moved to the L.A. area, other family members followed: cousins, aunts, uncles, grandmothers. Members of my mother's family in particular stayed with us for various periods and some later found work and their own places to live. I remember my cousins Lilo, Rafas, Bune, Miguelito, Alfonso and La Maye — later Gloria, Ninfa and her Anglo husband (both of whom later died in an auto accident while on a highway in Arizona).

Then Tío Kiko, his wife Agustina and their four children decided to stay and relocate to an apartment on Muscatel Street. There was also Tía Nieves and her ugly daughters, including Marta who managed to make the worst tortillas anyone's ever tasted.

And there was Tía Chucha, the one everyone called crazy. Oh sure, she once ran out naked to catch a postman with a letter that didn't belong to us. I mean she had this annoying habit of boarding city buses and singing at the top of her voice — one bus driver even refused to go on until she got off. But crazy? To me, she was the wisp of the wind's freedom, a music-maker, who often wrote song lyrics, told stories and recited dirty jokes. She would come unexpected — and often uninvited — and burst into our home with a guitar across her back and a bag full of presents, including homemade colognes and perfumes that smelled something like rotting fish at the tuna cannery.

I secretly admired Tía Chucha, the most creative influence in my childhood, while others talked holier-than-thou about her irreverence, her eccentricities, as if the craziness didn't threaten to thunder out of any of us at one time or another.

But the first one of the family I remember coming to visit us in South San Gabriel was my cousin Pancho. I was about 10 years old, Rano was 13, when Pancho entered our lives.

In his late teens, Pancho was muscular, darkly handsome with fine features and tightly-woven hair. Pancho traveled throughout the country: working in Texas, staying in a Tucson flat with other immigrants, visiting girlfriends in Denver, or spending a night in an Oakland jail. Every time Pancho came, he recounted a new adventure, with a smile and dimple which softened his otherwise hard look.

Fiercely independent and loud, he yanked my brother and me into his world of James Brown, Jackie Wilson and Sam

Cooke, of barroom dances, Old English 800 Malt Liquor Beer and weight lifting. He seemed to have seen it all before his 20s.

"*Please, please, please...baby, please don't go,*" he sang to a James Brown classic. On James' quicker-paced record cuts, Pancho would imitate the man's steps, forcing Rano and me to loosen our feet and try it. Pancho taught us soul, from the ruptured streets of Ciudad Juarez to every city ghetto he ended up in. He tutored us to the latest "hip" songs, the latest dance craze, the coolest what-to-say.

My mother and father tolerated Pancho, the son of my mother's only sister Chila, although I guessed they weren't too sure about what he was teaching us. But Rano and I were ecstatic whenever Pancho sauntered through the door. We tried to soak up Pancho's leanness, his half-smile and tight eyes that made him look so knowledgeable, unafraid and wary.

Right away he detected how skinny we were.

"You guys could be runned over by spaghetti," Pancho said.

One day Pancho came to the house with a set of weights. He coerced my brother and me to pump them day after day, eating loaves of bread for bulk and tons of eggs for protein. I strained and pulled and heaved and hauled the weights with my ten-year-old's body, until one day in school I felt a sharp pain below my abdomen. The nurse checked it out and then had me taken to a doctor for more exams. It turned out I had ruptured myself, the sac that held my bottom intestine had a slight rip and threatened to spill its contents, and my life along with it.

My parents took me to White Memorial Hospital in Boyle Heights where surgery had been scheduled to repair the rupture. While they were at it, they decided I should get circumcised.

In one of those peculiarities of life, the ritual circumcision was somehow overlooked at Saint Joseph's Maternity Hospital in El Paso where I was born. Being born to a non-citizen, I could see how. They threw the illegals over the border as soon as the babies emerged. Mama apparently thought of taking care of it later, but there wasn't much time — what with moving to L.A. and all. Just one of those things that got missed, I guess.

I could survive without the circumcision, of course, but I wasn't doing a good job of cleaning myself and had developed some sores. So the call was "off with the foreskin."

The hospital could have been a medieval castle, filled with shrieks, broken bodies, smells of illness and medicines and grim, cruel faces everywhere. At the children's ward, there were kids worse off than me, with horrific diseases, defects and traumas. The crying all night, the hurried staff, the worried parents — I thought maybe I had died and this was hell.

One night after the surgery, a pain crept up in my newly-rearranged member — a slow throbbing at first, soon it became intolerable. I hollered and evoked my mother's name. Nurses swaggered in, bothered and tired. They looked at the wounds, the stitched flesh below the abdomen — then my penis. A shadow seemed to cross their faces. They muttered something to themselves. Somehow the circumcision had gone wrong. What? I exclaimed. Isn't this a hospital? Weren't these trained doctors? *How difficult could a simple circumcision be!*

Later orderlies pushed my bed into a surgery room; someone gave me a local anesthesia with a shot to my penis that seemed to penetrate my spine. A doctor came and began to undo the stitches, then cut and pull. I could see everything. Blood sprayed onto the front of his white coat. *I'd never be a man now!*

Days later, I came home in a wheelchair, unable to move or even sit on a toilet. Eventually all would turn out okay, though, including my manhood. Pancho was there as Rano maneuvered the wheelchair up the steps and through the front screen door into the living room. Pancho flashed me a dimpled smile, called me a "dish rag," then shook my hand.

"Get better, *trapo*," Pancho said. "When you get rid of the machine, we're going dancing."

Clavo healed pretty well after the shooting, but he lost an eye, and I'm sure his nerve. The pellets, some unable to be removed, left unsightly scars on the right side of his face. Chicharrón and Wilo sensed he wanted out. We understood his dilemma, yet we didn't want him to leave us. We couldn't be *los cuatro*. It wouldn't be the same. So the first real good weekend for Clavo, we decided to organize a trip to a "real" beach.

This didn't happen too often. Although L.A. hugged the Pacific coastline, the beaches were still many miles away for neighborhood people to get to. There were families then, in and around L.A., who never visited the beach. Most of the time the barrio people from around the San Gabriel Valley went to an area along the Río Hondo in Whittier Narrows. We called it *Marrano Beach*.

In the summer time, Marrano Beach got jam-packed with people and song. *Vatos locos* pulled their pant legs up and waded in the water. Children howled with laughter as they jumped in to play, surrounded by bamboo trees and swamp growth. There were concrete bridges, covered with scrawl, beneath which teenagers drank, got loaded, fought and often times made love. At night, people in various states of undress could be seen splashing around in the dark. And sometimes, a body would be found wedged in stones near the swamps or floating face down. The place stunk, which was why we called it what we did. But it belonged to the Chicanos and Mexicanos. It was the barrio beach. Ours.

This one time, to celebrate Clavo's coming back, we decided to go instead to what we recognized then as the *Gabacho* beaches, or white people's beaches. Why not? It was an important occasion.

Chicharrón, Wilo and I were in on this trip. We invited a few of the "homeys," including Black Dog, who was called that because he was so dark. We had qualms about inviting Black Dog as he was known to be trouble, but he had just bought a "bomb," a 1950s car cut low and sleek, and we needed the ride.

And we invited *rucas*. There were the Acuña sisters, Herminia and Santita — pretty and shapely girls who lived just below the Hills. We invited Canica and La Smiley. And they brought Elaine Palacios and Corina Fuentes. We gathered at Garvey Park, two carloads full. We scored on cases of beer and some *grifa*. A few *colies*. Everything was ready — but no Clavo.

"Where's the dude, man," I asked.

"Wilo went to get him. They'll be here soon," Chicharrón said. But it was a lie. Clavo wasn't ready. I knew, somehow, he never would be.

As soon as Wilo came with his *jaina* Rita, sans Clavo, we decided to go.

We caravaned to Huntington Beach in Orange County — "whitebread" country — which was a straight drag south on the San Gabriel River Freeway, the 605, then a spell on Pacific Coast Highway. The sun bore down on our rides; we opened windows and drank and toked and laughed. Already the dudes without girls were scoping out who they would be with. I always did terribly when it came to this kind of thing. I liked Hermie Acuña, but I never let on. Yet I couldn't help but sneak a look at her cute face as she gazed out the window at the sights off the freeway. Hermie had lips like car bumpers, wide and swollen, but perfectly shaped, with thin creases. Looking at them conjured up a daydream of lips licking my mouth, whispering into my ear, becoming her lips. I fell into a dream of me and her, embracing, our mouths joined. She opened them slightly and my lips slowly mimicked hers — but suddenly a tractor-trailer rumbled by and I careened to backseat reality.

Crowds filled the beach area. Chicharrón knew of a place called "the coves," further down, less peopled and scenic, and he suggested we go there.

To get to it we had to park away from the beach and walk down several rocks and boulders. The water came up to the rocks, a sandy area nearby. Chicharrón buried several six-packs in shallow water to keep them cold. Black Dog began to roll reefer and pass it around. Wilo and Rita placed a blanket in the sand and lay down, beer and chips nearby. The rest of us decided to play a loose game of beach football.

The girls and guys split up into teams. We threw the ball around. A few of us got tackled. Then we threw the girls around, mostly into the water. None of us had bathing suits or trunks. We were just too cool. We had cutoffs, T-shirts, overalls, sandals and such. Some of the guys removed their shirts to reveal teen muscle, and maybe show off a tattoo or two. Chicharrón and Black Dog moved from one girl to the other, except Rita who adhered to Wilo like skin. They picked up the girls as if they were sacks of *masa harina* and threw them into the bursting waves.

Hermie got thrown in last, mainly because she kept running away and hiding in the rocks. I just watched. Chicharrón, Black Dog and this dude from Mexico named Félix crept up behind her, several-sized hands reached for her arms, her legs — I saw one hand hold up her butt. They took her to the ocean's frothy edge and threw her in, squealing and kicking. Hermie rose quickly — rivulets of water falling from her once-teased hair, her face a flood. Hermie's blouse clung to her body, revealing hard nipples through soaked bra and top. She feigned anger, while the others laughed and laughed. Her sister Santita, who had already been dunked, looked pleased.

Strangely, we were all alone there on that short stretch of beach. Black Dog got bold and brought out some mescaline. Félix took a hit and before long he was tripping, falling all over the sand and bumping his head on rocks and shit. Canica and Smiley took some hits too. Before long Black Dog maneuvered Canica over to a cave section of the coves and I knew what he was doing, copping feels and such.

Wilo and Rita lay back on the blanket and enjoyed the sun. The rest of the pairing happened by mid-day. Félix stood beside Santita, or I should say she held him up a lot. Chicharrón and Elaine were together, holding hands and sloppy kissing on top of some rocks. Corina and Hermie sat apart from everybody, as I did. Black Dog, however, left the cave area and took Smiley back there with him. I only guessed what was happening there with all that reefer, mescaline and partying with Canica and Smiley.

Corina sat down near me and started a conversation. She was the least good-looking of the girls who came that day, but she was good to talk to.

It was Hermie who I kept eyeing, whether I was alone or with Corina, as she tried to stay dry. The brownness of her nipples which had shown through her blouse earlier was lost from view as it dried.

By the afternoon, we spied a van of white dudes, looking like surfers, parked above the coves near our rides. They stared in our direction, dressed in sunny beach wear, noticeable by their blonde hair and eye shades. Chicharrón stood up to see them better.

"What's with the paddies, man?" he yelled out to me.

"¿Qué sé yo?" I responded. "Maybe waiting for a 'bitchin' wave'."

This was a tiny dig into the beach culture that Anglos had created in California. There were constant battles between the barrio people and the beach people, who were mostly whites or *engabachados* — Mexicans trying to pass as white, even when some were dark as night. As far as anyone could remember, it was "surfers" against "beaners."

The van didn't move, nor its occupants. Then after a few minutes, we heard shouting from the parking area.

"Fuck you, beaners!"

"Mexicans suck!"

Black Dog emerged from the cave, shirt off, muscles wet and rippling on mahogany-tinged skin. He looked at the white dudes, and then yelled back.

"*Putos*...come get some of this," as he squeezed his crotch. Félix livened up all of a sudden, and in accented speech he yelled out "modder fockers."

Chicharrón also got into it, shouting out "Animal Tribe" and "*¡Qué Viva South San Gabriel!*"

The white guys challenged us to come up there. It didn't take much to get us going. Chicharrón took off his belt, Black Dog picked up a bottle. Soon everyone followed behind them, even the girls.

"I don't like this," Corina said. "I don't like this at all."

"*Híjole*, we can't go anywhere without some *plato*," Hermie responded in disgust.

There were about six white dudes, and as we got closer, we saw they weren't teens but grown men.

"Come on greasers," one tall dude said. "Who wants to go first?"

"Fuck you," Black Dog shouted and then charged them. But what should have been a good old ass-stomping, to talk about later, turned out to be something completely different.

The white dudes pulled out guns. Then one of them flashed a badge.

"Everyone line up. This is the Huntington Beach Police Department."

They were *chota*!

"*Puta madre*," Chicharrón said, as the cops turned him around and had him place his hands against the side of the van. Then the rest of us, even the girls, were forced to kneel and keep our hands on our heads. Corina started to sob, but I could tell she tried not to. Hermie looked scared as did Santita. Canica and Smiley swaggered and acted cool, but I knew the mescaline had a lot to do with it.

They separated the guys from the girls. After a quick search, the girls were allowed to stand by the side. But the guys were told to squat on the asphalt and not move. One of the cops radioed in some information. Another proceeded to harass us.

"Tough guys, eh? Gonna take us on. You don't look so tough now."

I went to move my leg over to another, more comfortable, position. But the cop yelled at me, his hand still palming a .38 revolver.

"Don't fuckin' move," he said, coming up to my face, eyeball to eyeball. "Did I give you permission to move? Don't do anything unless I say — you fuckin' greaser asshole!"

They had us squatting there for five, ten, then fifteen minutes. We couldn't stand up, kneel or sit. The circulation in my legs felt blocked. The muscles cramped and ached. But we weren't supposed to do anything but squat. After several long minutes more, one of the cops started throwing sand in our faces.

"Hey!" we all yelled at once.

"Don't move, I said," the cop continued. "Don't understand English or what? I don't want to hear anything, don't want to see anyone lift a finger."

They were getting us to do something stupid in anger, an excuse to knock us around. One of the cops came up to the parking area with Wilo and Rita, who had been down below trying to keep quiet. They brought the beer cans.

"This is a violation," a cop said.

Then another cop turned around smiling. He had Black Dog's jacket and had found caps of mescaline and some joints.

"All right, now we got some felonies."

The cops were ecstatic. They had something good to book us for.

They dragged us handcuffed to the local jail, and took us into a small interrogation room. By now Corina cried. Black Dog talked back, acting up even as the cops poked blackjacks into his ribs. They separated him from the rest of us and took him first.

The police called our parents. Chicharrón's father said he'd take me home. After several hours, they finally released us. Only Black Dog didn't go home. The officers transported him to a juvenile facility. Besides the drugs they found, Black Dog had several prior arrests. It didn't look good for Black Dog.

I said goodby to Corina, and nodded a goodby to Hermie and Santita whose mother came in ranting about us troublemakers and how she'd never let the sisters go anywhere with us again. For a second, in the midst of her mother's squabbling and hands flying, I thought Hermie smiled at me.

✝ ✝ ✝

"You have to work, to help us out here," Mama said. "You're a big man now. There's got to be something you can do."

We had just moved to South San Gabriel. I was nine years old — a good working age, as far as my mother was concerned;

she had picked cotton at the age of nine in South Texas. But looking for work at nine is not easy in a city. We weren't fruit pickers, which were often children as young as three. In a city, a child had to find people to work for — cleaning up for them, doing deliveries or tending lawns. I did a little bit of everything. Mowing lawns with Rano, picking up boxes and cleaning out people's garages. I even did housework like my mother had done when we were younger. I vacuumed, wiped windows, scrubbed floors on my knees and used tooth brushes to clean the edges. The homes I went to were in Alhambra, a mostly white area then with some homes sporting swimming pools. I learned how to vacuum the bottom of the pools, and how to use the pumps and the chemicals to keep them clean.

My brother also worked, finally landing a job as a newspaper boy. In those days, it meant delivering papers door-to-door on bikes. At the age of 12, I started working a paper route too. I found an old beat-up ten-speed and delivered around our neighborhood, tossing a local daily called The Post-Advocate. Every day after school, our crew manager dropped off bundles of unfolded newspapers and bags of rubber-bands. On rainy days we used plastic covers.

We had to fold all the papers, place the rubber bands or plastic over them and then stuff them into double cloth bags we draped over the handle bars. Our hands and faces got blackened with newsprint. We had a list of subscribers and we had to make sure they received their newspapers in or around their porches. This was the trick of the trade.

Fíjese: I got good at it. It was the first important accomplishment I remember as a child. I couldn't exactly talk with any coherency, or do sports, or show any talent for anything. But, man, I could deliver newspapers! I got so good, I built up a route system which at its peak included four different routes. I received awards. I won recognition in the Copley Newspaper magazine (Copley owned the Post-Advocate then). The routes wound around city blocks for several miles and often took until after midnight to complete. On that old ten-speed, I pedaled through street, alley, boulevard and back road, past vicious dogs and hobo nests, past the *vatos* who chased me for my bike or change. But I made my deliveries, always on time. On the mark.

Selling the newspaper was the other trick. On weekends, the crew manager would take his den of newspaper boys and drop us off in various neighborhoods to sell subscriptions, what we called "starts." Mainly he had us cover the well-groomed suburban streets because he figured they were more likely to buy subscriptions. Man, I was lousy at it. Door after door slammed in my face. We had free gifts — pot holders, TV trays, things to hang on the wall. But where people had money, this had little effect. They usually received the bigger papers like the Los Angeles Times or the Herald-Examiner. The Herald-Examiner deliverers, in fact, often sneered at us because they took in more pay and the better clientele.

One day the crew manager, at a point of desperation, dropped me off in the Hills.

"Go up this road," he said, sounding unhopeful of my prospects. "I'll meet you down below in about an hour."

I climbed up a sidewalkless street and entered the foliage which shielded the shacks and houses on stilts and cars being worked on. I walked up a cluttered dirt driveway. Children played in and around a mud puddle without shoes. Mexican music burst out of a kitchen window. The porches were old, unpainted, sunken wood planks. I knocked on a torn-screen door nearly off its hinges. A round woman peered from inside. Instead of sofas or end tables, crates furnished her bare living room. There were palm-leaf crosses tacked on cracked sheet rock.

"¿Qué traes tú?" she inquired.

I didn't believe I'd sell any subscriptions — most of these people didn't even know English. But as soon as I talked about the free gifts, they signed up. So simple. Shack to shack. Off-hinged door after off-hinged door. I tried to explain they were required to pay a monthly fee. But here they were, watching *telenovelas* on beat-up TV sets, those who had them, their children running around in rags and bare feet, and still they ordered the Post-Advocate for the free gifts. In time they'd never pay. They'd never be part of anyone's route. But I got the starts. I became the hero for the day. The crew manager patted my back and announced to everyone the record number of subscriptions I obtained.

The people of the Hills vindicated me.

Work took other turns. At age thirteen, I was hired at a car wash with my brother. We were the cleanup crew. We came to work in the evening after the undocumented guys finished washing cars and had gone home. Rano and I swept, mopped, and picked up around the small office, waiting area and parking lot. We picked up all the dirty rags and threw them into massive washing machines. Then near the end of the evening, we hooked up a monstrous hose and watered down the place. Rano, who was 16, actually washed cars during the day and learned to drive almost every make and model.

"You should have seen the Mustang I pulled out today," he said, excited.

"Oh, listen," he'd tap my arm. "Then there was this Firebird!"

I came along to help him in the evening to make more money for the family. Everything we made went to Mama — and we always needed more.

But soon after I started working there, I picked up a foot fungus. I often worked in sneakers and I couldn't help but get them soaked every night in the soap and water we used to hose down everything. Terrible flowery lesions sprang up on the soles of my feet and through my toes. I also had an ingrown toenail that produced a painful redness on my left toe, forcing me to place steaming hot towels on it every night to lower the swelling.

A foot doctor prescribed medication, but nothing lessened the sores. And surgery on my toe was out of the question. I couldn't even go to gym classes, which I missed for the rest of junior high.

One day, the sores worsened and I refused get out of bed. My mother dabbed ointments on them but they were of no use.

Then Tío Kiko came over. He examined the sores, staring intently at the petals that seemed to be growing from my feet. Tío Kiko knew a little of the Mexican healing arts, the use of herbs and incantations from old Indian traditions used to treat most ailments. In desperation, Mama asked her brother for help.

"This will hurt you," Tío Kiko told me in Spanish. "But be brave. It will be over soon."

He pulled up a chair and directed my mother's hand.

They sliced each of the milky sores. Blood and pus streamed out. I screamed. I didn't believe in witchcraft or chants or herbs. I felt I would die. Tío Kiko had boiled water and put together some herbs he had brought from a *botánica*. Mama covered each open wound with leaves and concoctions as Tío Kiko prayed over my feet.

Was there a God for feet? Would the proper words be strung together to wake it from its sleep? Would the magic of the herbs, the spirit evoked, seep into the sores and bring the feet back to me? These were the questions.

Days passed. I lay in bed as the daily rituals worked their wonder. The sores started to disappear. Soon I hobbled around in slippers. Even the ingrown toenail slid back into a somewhat normal shape. Tío Kiko, this border priest, this master of snake and siren, did what the Anglo doctors could not. Who knows if it's real magic? There was another kind of magic which made me feel special, to look at my Indian-descended mother and uncle and believe in the power of civilizations long since written off, long since demeaned and trampled. Jesus Christ was a brown man. A Mexican Indian. A *curandero*. Not a stringy blond-haired, blue-eyed icon. He was like me, like my Tío Kiko. He lived in the earth, got drunk, inhabited the leaves and herbs, not a sanitized doctor's office — or a church of spires and colored glass and elaborate carvings. He lived in my feet, and with the proper calls and enticements, made them whole again. This is the Christ I wanted to believe in.

✢ ✢ ✢

Through the bars of a cell, I talk to a deputy as he sits behind an immense wood desk in the Temple City sheriff's station, the station responsible for Las Lomas. He's Chicano like me, but I know how much he hates everything I am, as if I represent all the scorn, venom and fear instilled in him since a child.

"We have a plan here," the *hura* says. "We detain every seven-year-old boy in your neighborhood."

"Detain them for what?" I ask.

"It doesn't matter. Curfew, loitering...whatever we can," he replies. "Then we keep their names. Keep track of them over the years. Soon we've picked them up for other things — stealing, fighting, mischief..."

"And that's how you get a hold of 'em," I continue for him.

"That's right — hey, you've got half a brain, huh?"

"It ain't hard to figure out that by the time some of the boys do something serious, they have a detention record a mile long and end up hard time — juvey or camp."

"You guys just don't know," he says with a smirk. "You just don't know what you're dealing with."

In the barrio, the police are just another gang. We even give them names. There's Cowboy, Big Red, Boffo and Maddog. They like those names. Sometimes they come up to us while we linger on a street corner and tell us Sangra called us *chavalas*, a loose term for girls. Other times, they approach dudes from Sangra and say Lomas is a tougher gang and Sangra is nothing. Shootings, assaults and skirmishes between the barrios are direct results of police activity. Even drug dealing. I know this. Everybody knows this.

ᵼ ᵼ ᵼ

Yuk Yuk became one of *los cuatro* after Clavo disappeared. No one knew exactly what happened to Clavo. There were rumors his parents sent him to Mexico. Others said he was in a youth prison camp, although we couldn't substantiate this. Chicharrón, Wilo and I went to his house. Nobody there. For Rent signs everywhere. He had already dropped out of school and left no forwarding address.

Yuk Yuk lived in the Hills, in one of the gullies. He had been a member of the Tribe for a couple of years, but spent most of that time in juvenile hall. He had two teardrops tattooed below his left eye, signifying two years lost in the hall. Sometimes the teardrops stood for the members of one's family fallen in street warfare or the number of people one had killed. Anyway it started off as a Chicano thing, like most of the street and *pinto* traditions, but later other dudes picked up on it.

Yuk Yuk's real name was Claudio Ponce. But he had this funny laugh, see, and this is why we called him Yuk Yuk. Barrio names usually came from the obvious. Chin came from my deformed jaw. Chicharrón because he had skin the color of Mexican pork rinds. Clavo because he was thin and hard, like nails, and Wilo because he was skinny as a pole. The girls had similar designations. In the Hills there were *rucas* called Seria (serious) or Chatter (because she talked too much). Sometimes the *placas* came from corruptions of real names: Chuy from Jesus, Chi Cho from Narciso, Nacho from Ignacio, Yogi from Olga, Beto from Roberto and Nando from Fernando.

And then there were names that were simply made up: Fuzzy, Toots and Baba.

Tribe members carefully placed as many names as could fit on a wall, a means to identify individuals, not just the group. More and more the lists would end with "Animal Tribe/Lomas." Lomas became increasingly prominent. There were dudes like Yuk Yuk coming out of juvey, the youth camps, or prisons who insisted Lomas, the barrio, be on every marking, on every wall.

Then there were dudes who didn't even claim the Tribe anymore. Just Lomas.

Yuk Yuk got us involved in organized stealing. Up until then, we stole here and there without much planning or thinking. At seven years old in Watts, I remember going into corner grocery stores every day after school and stuffing my Roy Rogers Lunch

Box with toys and candy. I took the loot home and hid it in the closet. Mama eventually found some, carved into my flesh with a leather belt, and made me return it. I remember throwing it over a bridge which crossed a sewer tunnel.

At 13 years old, a record shop owner caught me stealing records. Rano had stolen some records earlier and bragged about it. I decided to try it myself. I went back to the same store, a stupid thing to do, and stuffed a few 45s into my jacket. But a store guard stopped me as I walked out of the store, pulled the records out of the jacket and dragged me back in. My mother had to come get me.

Later various combinations of *los cuatro* stole food, vodka and beer from markets, and gas from service stations so we could cruise in Wilo's *carrucha*.

Once we decided to rip off the *gabachos* leaving a Kentucky Fried Chicken stand. Chicharrón, Wilo and I waited outside the joint. As some dude came out with a bucket or two, we ran up to him and snatched the buckets from his arms, then took off like we were ravaging coyotes on *yesca*, chicken parts flying everywhere.

Another time, after a night of heavy-duty drinking and partying, hunger called out to us. Wilo waited in the parking lot of a 24-hour market nearby, the car running and in gear. The rest of us scurried through the store and packed our pockets, coats, shirts and jackets with chips, baloney, soda cans, bread, and canned hams. Then bursting with merchandise, we walked out at the same time. It was harder to catch three of us than just one.

Clavo was still with us then. I managed to make it to Wilo's car. But one of the store employees ran up behind me and insisted I come back with him — they had spotted me stealing food. I discreetly placed the food under the car seats and walked back in. Of course, they had no evidence of stolen food and had to let me go. But the commotion around me allowed Clavo and Chicharrón to walk out with the items they took.

When I finally left the store, I saw Clavo running across the parking lot as store employees chased him. The *pendejo* couldn't find Wilo's car! Clavo ran down the street, through some alley, dropping packages of lunch meat as his long legs loped over the asphalt, four or five store employees at his heels. Wilo came by and picked me up and then sped off.

Later we roamed the streets looking for Clavo. Sure enough he evaded his would-be captors and we found him hiding behind some trash cans in an alley — an opened can of tuna in his hand and a huge grin on his face.

But this was all lightweight.

Yuk Yuk introduced us to two key figures in the stealing business. One was Jandro Mares, a 30-year-old budding entrepreneur. Jandro owned a large Victorian-style home in Alhambra. He had a large driveway and a huge garage. He "commissioned" teenagers like us to steal certain cars he needed, on order, then drive them to his garage. He taught us how to strip them down in a matter of minutes. With *un chingo* of dudes, this was easy to do.

"*De volada*," as Yuk Yuk always said. Just do it without thinking; on impulse.

The other guy was Shed Cowager. He was a junk man who had a huge building on Garvey Boulevard full of metal, antique, and wood items. Shed usually sat in the back of the shop and you had to get through a long stretch of metal files, TVs, chairs and desks, and every hubcap known to humanity, to get to him. He didn't tell us what to do or not like Jandro. He was just a guy who bought bikes, TVs, stereos, cameras, guns — whatever we could bring to him — and paid us cash on delivery.

Yuk Yuk had us walk around the malls scanning for bikes, good bikes, ten-speeds mostly. Many of the *gabacho* kids used to lay them down without locks when they entered a store. We walked up cool, got on the bike, and then took off. Wilo or Yuk Yuk followed near us in a car as we rode the bicycles to Shed's business. The bikes were probably worth several hundred dollars. Shed gave us between $15 and $25 each.

Soon Yuk Yuk had us scoping out the good homes in Alhambra, some of which I cleaned when I was younger. He showed us how to find signs of nobody home. He also had us spot ways to enter them. For example, a lot of the homes had louver windows in bedrooms, kitchens, or bathrooms, which were easy to remove from the outside.

We were told to take only things we could walk out with, such as money, jewelry and guns. For bigger jobs, we'd pull up in a VW van Yuk Yuk had borrowed and then we'd take bigger items like TVs, cameras and stereos. Before long, Yuk Yuk started to hijack trucks, mainly from warehouses or appliance stores, and then sell the electronic equipment in parking lots and drive-ins. The truck stops leading into L.A. were particularly lucrative. Yuk Yuk would pull a gun out on a driver, force him out of the truck, take his money, and if the truck was maneuverable enough, his keys too.

From there, armed robberies included the newly-sprouting convenience stores we called "shop and robs". If we worked in teams, somebody stayed in the car, another held a gun, and another walked the aisles loading up on whiskey and food.

Placing a gun to a man's head took some doing at first. We often took turns because Yuk Yuk didn't want any *lambiches* going with him. If you could pull a gun on someone, with only a heart pulse holding the trigger, than you can do just about anything, Yuk Yuk reasoned. *De volada.*

But to me, stealing and taking someone's life were two distinct capabilities. You can kill for a lot of reasons, or no reason at all, but killing for stealing didn't sit well with me. This was a problem. A big problem, Yuk Yuk pointed out.

"You better get used to it," Yuk Yuk would say. "Or you'll find yourself at the other end of a gun and be dead, like real quick."

I don't remember whose idea it was to rip off the drive-in. We usually sneaked in there through several holes we created in the corrugated steel fence alongside the Alhambra Wash, a concrete tributary of the Río Hondo which snaked through here. We built ourselves a makeshift hangout among the bushes and weeds that lined the fence, the hideaway for *los cuatro*. We used wood planks for a roof. We found old carpet and metal siding to cover the ground and sides. We used banana leaves to cover the entrances. It wasn't easy to find.

One night, as we relaxed on an old sofa watching the drive-in movie, it was decided we would go in after the cars left and rob the concession stand. Many times we would break in there for food, but this time it was for the night's receipts.

"Chin, I want you to hold the *cuete*," Yuk Yuk said.

"¡*Chale, ése!*" I exclaimed. "I'm not up to it today. I don't feel good about it."

"What's this feel shit," Yuk Yuk said. "I'm not asking for a temperature."

Then he gave out his yuk yuk laugh.

I had on a long black trench coat. The others were in their *cholo* attire. We peeled back a section of fence and walked through. The march to the concession stand was sustained and arduous. I held the small caliber handgun in my hand through the long pockets of the trench coat. Sweat smeared on the handle.

Chicharrón walked in first, then signaled the rest of us to follow. The concession stand looked empty. Wilo walked up to the cash register and rang it up to check for money. Nothing. Yuk Yuk probed around while I stood there, wishing the night would end, hoping nobody would be there.

Then an older fat white-haired guy walked in from another room.

"What the fuck is going on here?" he said as we ransacked the stand.

I thrust out the gun and yelled, "Freeze, motherfucker!" It had so much conviction, I failed to recognize the voice.

Tension sizzled in the air. He stood there, just staring. I stood there, gun pointed in his direction. Yuk Yuk walked up to him and demanded money.

"It's in the safe," the man said. "You can't get to it."

"Fuck you!" Yuk Yuk exclaimed. "You can open the safe."

"No, I can't," the man continued. "The only one who can get to it is the owner. And there's no way he would be here tonight."

Yeah, let's leave, I thought. Before the police came. Before somebody with a bigger weapon than mine showed up.

"I don't believe you," Yuk Yuk said, and me thinking: Believe him, believe him.

Yuk Yuk yanked the man down on the floor, and walked into the adjacent room where presumably the safe was stashed.

I continued to point the gun down on the man as he lay on his belly like a beached whale. Then Yuk Yuk pushed open the door and ran out of the room. Gunfire blasted a hole in the wood, splinters sailing around us.

"Get the fuck out of here!" Yuk Yuk yelled.

I supposed I could have fired the gun, but I took off just behind Chicharrón and Wilo. Whoever it was who fired ran out of the concession stand and shot into the dark toward us. We bobbed and fobbed, zigged and zagged.

"Shoot at him," somebody said.

"What?" I responded in between breaths.

"Shoot at him," everybody chimed in unison.

I turned around and saw a shadow highlighted by a fluorescent lamp above his head. He continued to hold a gun in two hands. I aimed at him, but then he fired again and I swear the bullet brushed my eyebrow, that's how close it felt. Fuck it — I ran.

Unfortunately, we went in a direction away from the section of fence where we could exit from. Yuk Yuk looked lost for a moment, then began to climb. It's not easy to scale a corrugated steel fence. But Chicharrón and Wilo followed suit. I dropped the gun into my trench coat pocket and climbed also. Suddenly everything slowed down. I just couldn't do anything fast enough. The dude shooting at us appeared closer and fired another round.

"¡Chingao!" I yelled as a bullet struck the fence, resounding in a metal-echo peal next to my ear.

I tried to get over fast. I hoped I wouldn't lose my grip and fall back down. There's nowhere to position your sneakers when you climb corrugated steel. It was muscle and hustle all the way.

I reached the top. I could hear Chicharrón, Wilo and Yuk Yuk yelling at me, like a squad of cheerleaders.

"*Orale, ése,* you can do it!"

"Come on, Chin — jump, man, jump!"

I pulled myself over and then leapt, the trench coat like a huge cape fluttering around me. A bullet ripped through the air I had been occupying just seconds earlier. I encountered the ground, then took off like a desert rabbit. *De volada.*

CHAPTER FOUR

"Oh, you'll get over it...eventually."
— La Payasa de Lomas

"Hey Louie, get up!"

Gloria's voice swept across the small room. Through sleep-drenched eyes, I barely made out the outline of my sister's body, framed by a clutter of boxes, clothes and opened dresser drawers. Unable to move out of the way, I felt a shoe bounce off my head. Gloria ran out of the room in fits of laughter. Another morning after.

It appeared to be a special morning with a sort of pleasing compassion. The tree leaves against the window glimmered green with veins of chlorophyll blood. Birds chortled in the branches, sounding like laughter. Sunlight oozed through window blinds.

The room, the size of a jail cell, was separated from the rest of the garage by unfinished sheets of wallboard. On every section of wall space were murals painted in acryllic and spray-paint, with fiery colors and images of *vatos locos*, three-dimensional crosses and serpents writhing through dripping syringes. Various scribblings covered the door and table tops.

I arose from a bed of old blankets on the floor, bumped a toe on the bottom of the dresser and almost stepped into a pail of piss. Somehow, I made it outside, greeted by the moist dawn air.

Limping toward the back porch, the smell of *huevos estrellados* (two grade double-As, looking at you) cleared the tangle of thoughts which lingered from the night's turmoil of dreams. I made it across the back yard to my mother's house and entered through a wrought iron door.

"Sorry about the shoe, "bro," Gloria said as she glanced up from the dining table with a grin. "Couldn't help myself."

"Just like I won't help myself when I shoot you in the head, *pinche*," I replied.

"Is that any way to talk to your favorite sister?"

"No, that's the way I talk to my pain-in-the-booty, so-called sister."

Mama leaned over the stove, preparing corn tortillas to go with the eggs.

"*Hablen en español*," she said. "*Ya saben que no entiendo inglés.*"

Mama kept telling us this. And we kept talking in English.

The night before I was in combat with myself, against a dark side, poised for destruction, with death about to tap my shoulder. I tried to commit suicide. I had come home in a stupor from pills, liquor and from sniffing aerosol can spray. I had slithered into the house around 3 a.m. and made it to the bathroom. Everyone else slept. Leaning on a wash basin, I looked into the mirror and stared into a face of weariness, of who-cares, of blood-shot eyes, prickly whiskers poking out of the chin, an unruly mustache below a pimpled nose, a face that much as I tried could not be washed away.

I staggered out of the house and crossed into a backyard with lemon trees and decayed avocados on the ground, and a tiled ramada with hanging vines. I entered my room in the garage, grabbed the pail I used to pee in, and filled it with water from a faucet on a rusted outdoor pipe. I planned to thrust my arm into the water after I cut an artery (I didn't want any blood on the floor — even at this moment I feared Mama cursing about the mess).

I pressed my street-scarred and tattooed body against the wall and held a razor to my wrist. Closed my eyes. Hummed a song — I don't know what song. But I couldn't do it.

Prior to this I had been exiled to the garage for months. My mother had thrown me out of the house and afterwards the garage became the compromise between coming back and the street. She was just too tired: pulling me out of jail cells, of getting reports from school about the fights I'd been in, of expecting a call from a hospital or morgue.

One day, I made 100 bucks working a weekend on the graveyard shift at one of the docks in the warehouse district. I took it home and placed it on the dining table in front of my mother. But Mama stood up, took the $100 and threw it in my face. Dollar bills, fives and 20s fluttered around me like green-and-black birds.

"¡Hipócrita! You can't buy my love," she yelled in Spanish. "You can't show respect with this money. I don't want it — I don't want anything from you!"

That night I slept in the "fields." The next evening Yuk Yuk took me in, but after three days his mother demanded I leave. I then took a bus to downtown L.A. and walked the streets of Spanish Broadway — what the Mexicans called El Centro — assaulted by the lights of the movie marquees, the sleaze bars and liquor stores. I spent about 75 cents in an all-night movie house, which featured continuous showings of three or four movies. There I slept with the winos and the other homeless, and woke up to ushers throwing us out at daybreak.

The sunlight invaded my eyes, forcing me to squint. Office girls whisked by on their way to work, their fragrance awakening my senses, and then my loins. Iron enclosures were thrown open as brick-and-stone stores began selling clothes freshly sewed from the nearby garment plants, as well as appliances and food items. The traffic up my nose.

This part of Broadway, from First Street to Olympic Boulevard, was where the Latino people shopped, roamed, explored. Norteños and salsas blared out of stereo shops and open-air fruit stands rippled with the breakneck bargaining and accompanying hand gestures of the Spanish tongue. On weekends, that stretch of Broadway must have had a million people or so.

On other nights, I stayed with homegirls who knew I needed a place to crash, crawling through windows left slightly opened for me. Also in abandoned cars. By the railroad tracks. Finally, I came home and negotiated an arrangement with Mama.

She laid down the rules: I couldn't set foot in the house unless I had her permission. And I could stay in the garage room, which barely held blankets, some drawers and a card table. It had no toilet, no closet space, no heating. At night, when the desert temperatures fell to almost freezing, I could use a small electric heating device which would only keep me from becoming a block of ice.

I accepted.

⁜ ⁜ ⁜

I began high school a *loco*, with a heavy Pendleton shirt, sagging khaki pants, ironed to perfection, and shoes shined and heated like at boot camp.

Mark Keppel High School was a Depression-era structure with a brick and art-deco facade and small, army-type bungalows in back. Friction filled its hallways. The Anglo and Asian upper-class students from Monterey Park and Alhambra attended the school. They were tracked into the "A" classes; they were in the school clubs; they were the varsity team members and letter men. They were the pep squads and cheerleaders.

But the school also took in the people from the Hills and surrounding community who somehow made it past junior high. They were mostly Mexican, in the "C" track (what were called the "stupid" classes), and who made up the rosters of the wood, print and auto shops. Only a few of these students participated in school government, in sports, or in the various clubs.

The school had two principal languages. Two skin tones and two cultures. It revolved around class differences. The white and Asian kids (except for "barrio" whites and the handful of Hawaiians, Filipinos and Samoans who ended up with the Mexicans) were from professional, two-car households with watered lawns and trimmed trees. The laboring class, the sons and daughters of service workers, janitors and factory hands, lived in and around the Hills (or a section of Monterey Park called "Poor Side").

The school separated these two groups by levels of education: The professional-class kids were provided with college-preparatory classes; the blue-collar students were pushed into "industrial arts."

The Mexicans assembled beneath the big, gnarled tree on the front lawn next to the gym and shop area. The well-off students usually had cars and hung out in the parking lot or the cafeteria. Those who were in between or indifferent couldn't help but get caught in the crossfire.

By the time I went to Keppel, I had become introspective and quiet. I wanted to be untouchable: Nobody could get to me. I walked the halls facing straight ahead, a saunter in my step, only slightly and consciously glancing to the sides.

Keppel had a rowdy reputation among San Gabriel Valley schools. Fights all the time. I believe it related to the ingrained system of tracking and subdivisions. The teachers and administrators were overwhelmingly Anglo and whether they were aware of it or not, favored the white students.

If you came from the Hills, you were labeled from the start. I'd walk into the counselor's office for whatever reason and looks of disdain greeted me — one meant for a criminal, alien, to be feared. Already a thug. It was harder to defy this expectation than just accept it and fall into the trappings. It was a jacket I could try to take off, but they kept putting it back on. The first hint of trouble and the preconceptions proved true. So why not be proud? Why not be an outlaw? Why not make it our own?

☩ ☩ ☩

I often lay back in my garage room, listening to scratchy records of Willie Bobo, Thee Midniters, War, and Miles Davis. Sometimes oldies; the "Eastside Sound" revues, old Stax and Atlantic rhythm & blues: Wilson Pickett, Rufus Thomas, Solomon Burke and The Drifters. And of course, Motown.

For the most part, the Mexicans in and around Los Angeles were economically and socially closest to blacks. As soon as we understood English, it was usually the Black English we first tried to master. Later in the youth authority camps and prisons, blacks used Mexican slang and the *cholo* style; Mexicans imitated the Southside swagger and style — although this didn't mean at times we didn't war with one another, such being the state of affairs at the bottom. For Chicanos this influence lay particularly deep in music: Mexican rhythms syncopated with blues and ghetto beats.

My brother Joe once played bass in a band of mostly black musicians called "Taboos Children." Although only 17, Joe played with the band in bars and after-hours clubs in South Central Los Angeles. They had one original song, a local club hit called "Young Lovers." The other Chicano in the band was a San Gabriel guitarist named José Palmas who had these magical fingers and could play anything from Wes Montgomery to Jeff Beck to Delta Blues to raunchy *norteñas*.

I myself picked up a saxophone, a used brass tenor. I saved the money over the years, dollar by dollar, from whatever Mama would let me keep from the jobs I held. I managed a couple of lessons at a local music shop to learn the fingering, scales and some basic chords. But I tried to learn to play the saxophone by listening to records.

A few times I went with Joe and Palmas to see Taboos Children perform in some bar or dance hall, paying strict attention to the sax player. I got stinking drunk once, throwing up in the car to an eight-track guitar slice of Hendrix, and recall cruising down Hollywood Boulevard and taking a piss in the middle of the block with traffic lined up on both sides of me.

Mama later blamed Joe for making me an alcoholic.

When I finally mastered about two or three saxophone riffs, such as those like "Sad Girl" which the East L.A. band Thee Midniters made popular, I started jamming with a couple of local garage bands.

The Animal Tribe also had a band which went through several changes according to the currents in the music scene. First it was called Thee Occasions which mirrored what Thee Midniters were doing in the early to mid-60s. Then when the music started taking a blues turn, it became the Coyote Blue Hemp Boogie Band and Joaquín López learned to play a mean harmonica, as penetrating as any original blues man. Later still, the band became Agua Caliente (Hot Water) when Latino-rock fusion like Santana, El Chicano and Malo permeated the airwaves in the early '70s.

The saxophone meant everything to me. When I needed time to myself, I locked the room and played it. I didn't really know how, but I envisioned myself offering melodies which screeched of back roads and wet sidewalks and Spanish Broadway night stalkers. I felt like I had this brass throat, moaning like Billy Holiday, shrieking like James Brown. Colors swirled around me. Faces. Notes. A rhapsody pressed out from a sultry furnace somewhere inside — a cacophony of crippled cries.

One day, Joe knocked on the door. I stopped bellowing on the sax, put the instrument down and peered out the window. He looked angry. For years, this look would prompt a flow of blood from the pit of my stomach. It meant I would be accused, abused, pushed around, and ordered to do something to make up for some perceived wrong.

But I was 14 already. I had grown stronger. I had been in many fights. I opened the door.

"What you want Joe?"

"You took some of my records, and I want them back."

"Don't worry — I was going to return them."

"Listen, don't take anything from me unless you ask me. Understand?"

"No you listen, you come and take my things all the time. You're always picking up my stuff and walking out. You want me to ask you, then you better ask me!"

"Fuck you!"

"No — fuck you!"

I never told Joe this before. His nostrils flared and his face flushed with red. He pushed himself into the room and stared into my eyes as I returned the look without flinching. For a second, he looked like he didn't know what to do. He couldn't just slap me down like we were kids. But he couldn't be challenged that way either. He had to do something.

Joe turned toward the saxophone on the bundle of blankets, and in two shakes, stomped on it — his boots crushing in sections of brass.

"Stop!" I yelled. "Stop, or I'll...!"

Joe stopped.

"You'll what?"

I looked at the saxophone as it lay beaten, bent. Then this fury quivered through every vein, flamed through the skin, stormed out my eyes. Everything became a flash of lights. I pounced on Joe, swinging away, punching and gouging. Years of rage erupted out of me. Joe fought back, but I kept at him, like a panther. He was getting the better of me, but I wouldn't let up — flailing away at his head and body.

My sister Ana heard the bodies slammed into the wall, the dull thuds of fists on a face, and rushed to get Mom and Dad.

When our parents came in, Joe was on top of me, mostly trying to protect himself. My dad held Joe by the chest and pulled him off. I jumped to my feet, balled fists ready to continue firing. Joe looked exhausted and shamed. I'm sure he never expected this of me — or perhaps he always wondered about that dreaded day when I would stand up to him.

Dad let go of his grip. Joe shoved him aside, almost knocking him down, and ran out the room. He didn't return home for three days.

All I could think about was my saxophone; I couldn't afford to fix or replace it. All I could think about were the lost melodies.

Ϯ Ϯ Ϯ

The San Gabriel Mission held an annual "Fiesta Days" celebration to honor the Spanish-Mexican heritage of the area. There were parades, speeches, carnival rides, directed for the most part at the Anglos who commemorated a past they were never a part of, as if the Mexicans were long dead and mummified, while in the present they'd rather spit on a Mexican than give him the time of day.

During the daytime the *gabachos* put on phony *sombreros*, rode rhinestone-garished horses, and applauded one Hat Dance after another. But at first hints of nightfall, they skulked back to their walled estates in San Marino or Pasadena, to Spanish-style mansions and the melancholy of manicured lawns.

At night, the fiesta belonged to the Mexicans.

The Sangra barrio surrounded the Mission. But the dudes from Lomas often showed up, prepared for anything. Families also arrived, by the carload.

One summer during the "Fiesta Days," Chicharrón and I hitchhiked to the edge of the Sangra neighborhood. Instead of crossing through it, we meandered over to the railroad tracks and walked the wood ties to the Mission. We slipped past some Sangra Diablos loitering at the entrance to the carnival by sprinting through the cemetery next to the Mission church and scaling an old stone wall.

Once inside, we strolled among mothers with carriages, lovers holding hands, and children darting past while the colored lights of the Ferris wheel, "the hammer," and miniature roller coaster flickered across our faces.

Then I met Viviana.

She stood in line for the Ferris wheel, looking like delicate earthenware, glazed in honey. Endless, silky hair framed her face, hair as black as those in velvet paintings people sold at swap meets. Lashes like paint brushes encircled her eyes, which were immense and bursting with brown. I wanted to climb into them.

"*Trucha*, homes, what do you call them?" Chicharrón remarked after he spotted Viviana and another *ruca* standing next to her.

"It looks like heaven's missing a couple of angels," I declared, echoing a popular song by the Tavares Brothers.

We elbowed our way through the line of people, closer to the girls. Once behind them, Chicharrón turned on his charm and started a conversation.

"Hey babes, what do ya say?"

Well, it wasn't much, but the girl next to Viviana lit up and pursued it. Viviana appeared distant, subdued. I felt like leaving. I didn't deserve to breathe the same air as her. The thought of her looking at me and saying "Ugh!" was killing me.

"What's your name, *ésa?*" Chicharrón asked.

"I'm Eva, and this is Viviana."

Viviana pushed Eva slightly with her arm when she said this. Eva smiled.

As we waited in line, Chicharrón and Eva talked and talked. I could hear Eva rambling: "Me and this *vato*, eh, we've been seeing each other, eh, but it's no big thing, you know? He wants to get married and all that, but I don't want no part of that *pedo*, eh. I don't want to be tied down, you know..."

Chicharrón rapidly lost interest. I managed only slices of sentences with Viviana before our turn came to get on the Ferris wheel. So there we were, Viviana and I, stepping onto a carriage and sitting down together. I didn't know what to say. The carriage moved upward. We remained at the top for a spell and Viviana moved close to me. My heart felt like it had been stuffed into my ears. Then the Ferris wheel spun and Viviana placed her arm around mine and snuggled up, closing her eyes and smiling. I didn't want to breathe for fear she would let go.

"*Híjole*...I think I lost my breakfast," I finally said.

She laughed.

"There goes lunch," I continued and she squealed with abandon.

I wasn't funny, but she made me feel like I could've said anything and she would consider it brilliantly clever. The carnival noises, the colored tents and streams of light, the faces of the people on the ground, first clear and distinctive, then distant and dull, all this surged toward us. I wanted to rotate there forever, chuckling and clutching with Viviana. I didn't want the ride to end because on the ground, I didn't think she would be so generous.

But it did end. We emerged from the carriage and I felt clumsy toward her again. By then Eva's yapping was long gone, although leaving a trail of "ehs" like a far-off echo in my head. I couldn't find Chicharrón, so Viviana and I took a walk through the midway where hawkers challenged passersby to try their luck at the coin tosses, rifle shoots and dart throws.

"You want a stuffed animal, *ésa?*" I asked.

"*Órale*, whatever," she said coolly, in a way that suggested she knew exactly what she was doing.

We went through several games, losing a small fortune, before I hit pay dirt at the baseball toss. Viviana selected a panda bear and I wondered if I could have bought a real one with all the money I threw away.

We walked some more, not many words between us, but I sensed Viviana felt safe with me. I think she wanted to hang out. I thrust my hands into my pockets, then let them hang awkwardly, feeling like two-ton steel beams. Soon Viviana pushed her arms around mine — probably in empathy with my plight — and I eased.

By the midnight hour, summer winds slipped softly through the carnival grounds. The odor of tacos, cotton candy and *churros* saturated the air, along with tension.

Lomas and Sangra soldiers began to congregate in different sections of the enclosed area. Sangra dudes, in particular, moved in large numbers from the entrance area to the other side of the cemetery. A scattering of Lomas dudes pushed through the crowd from the other end, each crew heading toward a collision on the midway. By then papas gathered their small children and mamas yelled out for their older sons and daughters to go home. Police officers, some in uniform and others in plainclothes with walkie talkies, walked two abreast down the aisles of booths. The terror-struck rushed to their cars.

"You know where I'm from?" I asked Viviana.

"*Simón*," Viviana said. "I knew all the time. I know all the Sangra dudes — my brothers are Diablos. You and the other *vato* I'd never seen before. Besides, Lomas dudes look a certain way."

"What do you mean?"

"Well, the dudes from Sangra look like the old days, you know: small hats, long coats, baggy pants. But you guys from Lomas look like summer — white T-shirts, starched Levis with royal cuffs and bandannas. I kinda like that."

"I don't care about this Sangra and Lomas stuff," she continued. "Why this war? Aren't we the same? I don't care about *de donde eres* — where you from? My brothers do, they're all-the-way gangster lean. What I care about is the kind of person you are."

As we talked, in front of us appeared five girls with blazing red peroxided hair. They were *cholas* from Sangra. The hair color served as their mark. These girls were known to start many of the fights which their homeboys inevitably had to finish. They were led by Cokie and Dina.

They looked agitated, talked loud — as if they could taste the coming battle, able to sniff the blood in the air.

"Hey Viviana," one of them said. "*¿Qué hubo?*"

The others quieted down as we walked past, looking at me hard — knowing I wasn't from the neighborhood, but not sure where I came from.

"Let's get out of here," I said while taking Viviana's hand and leading her toward the kiddie rides. Already the place swelled with activity; even the carnival hands sensed the impending storm: They gathered their stuffed toys and closed their booths.

"Where we going?" Viviana asked.

"I don't know," I said, looking around. "How about up there?"

I pointed to the rooftop on the Mission school building. I also felt something tug at me, the feeling I should be with my homeboys, that I should be marching with them tonight. But I wanted to be with Viviana, away from the war cries, the bloodshed, away from the adrenalin pumping up our speech and walk.

"Be serious, I can't go up there."

"Sure you can."

I moved some trash cans and wood crates beneath a fire escape. I ascended a couple of steel rungs and then grabbed Viviana's hand, her other hand grasping the stuffed bear. Together we climbed three flights to the roof. Jumping over the roof's edge, I reached down and pulled her over. Long wavy black hair fell across her face. Something warm moved inside me as I fingered the tousled strands.

"Don't look down," I said.

"Why not?" Viviana retorted. "I ain't scared. I've worked with my dad and brothers fixing houses. I'm used to it."

I placed my arm around her waist and directed her toward the roof's edge.

"Well, we've come this far, now what are you going to do with me?" Viviana inquired.

"You mean before or after I suck your blood."

Again she laughed. And me, the one who can't tell a joke!

"See all the people," I said. "I like looking at them this way. You see things about people you wouldn't see if you were there with them. Like a God?"

"Man, you're crazy," Viviana said.

"Yeah, that's true."

Soon we spotted a flurry of activity at the far end of the church yard. Several dudes had surrounded a *vato* whom I recognized as Enano from Lomas. Chava, in a small brim hat and leaning on a cane, led the group. One of them swung a steel-studded belt in his hand. I knew him as Turtleman from Sangra.

"Hey, I gotta go," I told Viviana.

"No, don't Louie," she said while pressing me to her. "Don't go, stay here with me."

I felt a tightening of muscle and beads of sweat forming on my forehead, the way I usually got before fights. Viviana dropped the panda bear and stroked my head and back, loosening the tightness, and moved her hands up my chest.

"Don't go down there. It's not your fight. They're always going at it. Don't be a part of that tonight. I'm from Sangra. You're from Lomas. So what? ¿Me quieres?"

I saw the dudes from Sangra move closer to Enano, the girls with the red hair laughing nearby.

"I can't let my homeboy duke it out without me," I said. "I can't let him down, man."

I moved away from Viviana. But from the other side of the carnival, I saw about 15 Lomas dudes — armed with sticks, chains and bumper jacks — rushing to Enano's aid. Chicharrón was among them, his shirt adorned with blood stains. No doubt, he had already gotten into some *guantes* with Sangra.

"It's started," I shouted.

People ran in all directions. Screams pierced the night. Shouts of "Lomas Rifa" and "Sangra Controla" bellowed as *vatos* clashed in senseless fury.

"Don't go *prieto*," Viviana repeated as she turned my head toward her. "Stay with me."

I felt torn. There I was, a *vato* from Lomas staring into the eyes of a Sangra girl. This made me a traitor. But at the same time, all I could think about was her touch, her scent — those eyes.

Viviana stroked my face with a fingertip. *Voices heightened below. Footsteps cracked on cement.* I nuzzled my face against Viviana's; her lips parted and the eyes closed. *Bottles crashed. Trash cans tumbled over.* Viviana breathed into my mouth and I licked her lips lightly with my tongue. *Sounds of shooting. Strained shouts.* She placed her hand against the back of my head as we kissed, and reached deep inside my mouth as a sweet burning crawled over me. *Sirens wailed in the distance. A child cried.*

✝ ✝ ✝

José Palmas strums at a six-string as fluid fingers move across its neck like a warm wind across one's brow. Every note sweating. Palmas often practices on his porch, swaying by an old eaten-up tree; sometimes his brother Bobby accompanies him on a conga and Joe on bass. He sits in for local bands who call out his name from the stage. Blues, jazz or a *huapango* — he can play almost anything. One Christmas, Palmas, Bobby, Joe and I jam in my room, whiskey bottles at our sides, and record it on a hand-held tape recorder. We call it "Latin Christmas '69."

The Palmas brothers are Joe's best friends, even as Joe continues to do well in high school as a gymnast who practices karate, and turns in homework and thumps a bass on weekends.

There comes a time, however, when Palmas fails to venture too far beyond his rickety porch. He stops showing up for gigs. Sometimes he sits alone in his room, the guitar on a corner of an unmade bed.

The last I heard, he plays only when the heroin in his body gives him a booking.

ϒ ϒ ϒ

At Mark Keppel High School there was an annual observance: the battle between the Mexicans and Anglos. We called it "The Tradition." It usually started soon after the new school year. When I became a sophomore, the spark which set it off occurred during a football game between Mark Keppel's Aztecs and a predominantly white school called Edgewood. Bus loads of whites from Edgewood came to Aztec Field to see their boys play. A few of us from Lomas decided to crash the game.

When I arrived at Keppel that evening, the football field was lit up; the bleachers were covered with people on both sides. Almost all of them were white, including those on Keppel's side. My homeboys were loitering in the parking area. They were Enano, Santos, Midnight (the only black guy in the gang: One night the homeboys found him AWOL from the army, homeless and sleeping in the fields. The next day they initiated him into the 'hood and he's stayed ever since.), Carlitos,

Baba and Lencho; some of the homegirls included Payasa, Trudy and Chata. We shared a bottle of T-Bird.

Dressed-up, prim students from Edgewood walked past. We called out to them.

"Hey, got any change *lambe?*" Santos queried.

"What's your name baby?" Lencho asked one of the girls.

"¡*Chúpame!*" Baba added.

They looked scared, walked around us. One guy got huffy: "Hey, can't you see we came to see a game? I'm sure you have something better to do."

"As a matter of fact," Santos said, "we don't, so come over here and hand us your money — you butt-on-the-back, paddy motherfucker."

They started to run, but we surrounded them and forced them to fork over some bills. As they ran off, Lencho kicked one of them in the ass.

Nothing would have come of any of this. We were bored. Everyone else soon watched the game, the cheering and roaring — something we weren't a part of.

"Let's squint to the Hills," Santos suggested.

We turned and walked down Hellman Avenue. Suddenly a Monterey Park police car drove by and stopped. Two uniformed officers rushed out.

"Hold it right there," one of them ordered.

This became a routine with us. Whenever the people from the Hills made it down to Monterey Park, San Gabriel or Alhambra, the police departments in those communities made it a habit to roust us out.

We placed our arms on a chain-link fence and spread our legs. One officer searched us while another radioed in. They asked for identification. Where did we just come from? Where were we going? The regular.

Carlitos questioned why we were being stopped and searched.

"We didn't do anything. We just walking, man."

One police officer told him to shut up. But Carlitos kept on.

"Why are we always being harassed?"

The police didn't want to hear it. Before long, an officer struck Carlitos with a baton on his knee. He buckled and fell. We turned around but the other officer pulled his gun out on us. Two more cops arrived. One of them put a choke hold on Carlitos as the other struck his legs. Payasa yelled out: "Leave him alone — he ain't doing nothing, man!"

Carlitos looked like he lost his breath. His face turned blue as the officer behind him put pressure on his neck.

"He can't breathe!" Trudy yelled "You're killing him!"

They knocked Carlitos to the ground and held onto his head. He looked bad — slobbering from the mouth, his pupils turned up. More officers came. Carlitos was out cold. The paramedics arrived, but the police refused to let them do anything. They left Carlitos lying in the street. By that time more Lomas people had arrived, including some older ones who had come to watch the game. Anger flowered among the crowd as word spread about what had happened. A bottle struck one of the police cars. Then another. And another.

Things soon exploded. More cops came but they too were pelted. A major confrontation erupted just above where the two high schools were playing their game, oblivious to what was going on. Soon the police pulled out. The ambulance took Carlitos and sped off, but not before receiving a barrage of rocks, bottles and debris. We assumed more police and firepower were coming. The only path out was toward the football field.

Santos led the way. A car with a local resident drove by. Santos picked up a trash can and threw it in front of the grill — it rolled beneath the car, slowing it down. Then people threw rocks, smashing windows. Whoever drove the car pulled it out and took off, dragging the trash can bunched up under the car, sparks flying everywhere.

We pushed our way through the entrance, some tore down part of the fence surrounding the field. We pulled white guys from out of the stands. Some of them tried to fight back. Even older men, probably war vets and construction workers, got into it but we thumped on them as well.

The game continued for a few more plays before the realization set in a battle was raging out of control in the stands. We rushed into the grandstand, smacking people around. The rage from seeing Carlitos being choked and the cops pushing us around had been building up for years. Spectators tried to flee, a number of cars were smashed. The crowd with us grew larger. More homeboys were involved, ready for *plato*.

I removed my belt and walked down the street with Santos, Lencho and Midnight, who had experience with racial violence among Blacks, Whites, and Latinos from his time in Army boot camp. Skirmishes popped up in the middle of the streets, in alleys and on front lawns. Whites got together and attacked as well. They found isolated groupings of Mexicans and pounced on them.

At first we avoided jumping on the Asians, even if they were with the Anglos and had lettered jackets and were members of the teams. Maybe the whites didn't care for them either, but at least they had their money, status and grades. But one Asian guy got into our face. It wasn't so much he thought he was white. It was more in defense of what was "right." It was wrong to jump on innocent people. It was wrong to focus on the color of skin. It was wrong to throw rocks at cars, police and homes.

"You can't do this," the Asian guy clamored. "We didn't do anything to you!"

Five guys jumped on him.

A group of whites from Edgewood came by our way. We confronted them in the street in front of the school. Everybody started throwing blows. I held on to one guy's shirt, tight, and punched him repeatedly in the face. He tried to kick and hit and block my hands, but I just held on, pulling him to the ground while hitting.

Some other guys jumped on me, but I continued clutching this guy's shirt and watching my fists beat his face, making deep cuts and welts. They tried to pull me off, and I even felt some blows, but I wouldn't let go.

Assistance came from various police departments. Streets were blocked off to keep the disturbance from moving to the main business section on Garvey Avenue. One white guy found himself surrounded by a large group of us. I felt sorry for him for some strange reason. I walked up to him.

"Get the fuck out of here — now!"

"Fuck you beaner," he responded and hit me square on the jaw. I fell back onto the asphalt. I looked up and saw a swell of guys on him.

"Get off him," I yelled.

Then I rushed up and struck the guy. He fell back too, but got up and ran through the crowd.

The Mexicans moved toward Garvey Park, armed with hand-held weapons as we pushed ourselves out of the flat land area toward the Hills. I found myself walking with Payasa, Trudy and Chata to get them home. As we turned down one desolate street, a car pulled up. I swung my belt, ready to strike. It turned out to be Mexicans.

"¿Qué pues, compa?" one of them greeted.

"Shit, I almost went after you guys."

I didn't recognize them, but they offered to take the girls home. Just then the white guy who I struck earlier showed up in a car and pulled out a gun.

"Hey, you fuckin' spic," he said. "Come get some of this!"

I looked at the barrel of the gun. His taut finger encircling the trigger. The flash of his blue eyes and his clenched teeth.

"Go ahead, puto," I said. "But make sure you kill me, or I'll come after you."

The white guy looked at me, and then the others, who just stood around not knowing what to expect. The tension lasted for a long minute. But his threat was a bluff; he put the gun down and took off.

Although I didn't really know her, Chata gave me a wet, desperate kiss, as if it were our last moment on earth. We had to go in opposite directions. I lived past the tunnel and they were going up into the hills. She wished me luck and went with the dudes in the car. I found myself alone in hostile terrain.

The night blazed with car fires, and the whirling lamps of police and fire vehicles. The Sheriff's department blocked off all entrances to the Hills, stopping people and cars before allowing them to go in or out.

I continued toward home on the other side of the San Bernardino Freeway, where I would be safe.

Suddenly a jeep came screeching down the road, its headlights blinding me as it approached. It went past me, then stopped. I saw about 10 guys crammed inside. White guys. With baseballs bats. ¡Qué desmadre! I was going to get it good!

The jeep turned back and came at me. I took off. I heard yelps and hollers, like cowboys do on TV shows, as the vehicle closed in. I propelled my legs through several yards, leapt over fences and hid next to some trash cans in an alley. I heard the peeling of rubber and the yelling as the jeep circled around to locate me. It entered the alley and I ran again. Somehow I made it over to the underground tunnel which led into my neighborhood: Various colored markings located its entrance. The jeep came up to its mouth. I could see the headlights beam through the darkness. After a few moments, it turned around and sped off. This was one Mexican scalp these cowboys wouldn't get.

The next Monday at school the fights continued. The Tradition for that year had started. Mexicans roamed the hallways, beating on any white guy they could see. Girls got into it too, ripping the blouses of the prim and proper "society" girls and wreaking havoc in the gym area. Parents came to pull their kids out of school.

Some whites gathered in the parking lot behind the school and began an offensive. The fighting would last for two or three weeks, tapering off for the rest of the year with only isolated incidents. But during the heat of the Tradition, classes were canceled. Police brought in. Ambulances summoned.

The whites in school brought in dudes from out of the area. They were tall, wide with long blonde hair. Two carloads cruised by where the Mexicans assembled by the gnarled tree. Santos, Chicharrón and Tiburón were there to challenge them. The white dudes got out of their cars, armed with bats. But it didn't stop the homeboys from Lomas. I saw them attack the dudes while I looked out the window of a classroom. I rushed out with a few others, even though the class was still in session.

As one white guy swung his bat to strike Santos, Chicharrón came from behind and hit him over the head with a tire iron. Lencho and Wilo also showed up and went blow to blow with the others. I jumped on one guy. Soon the police came. As usual, they went after the Mexicans. The white dudes got into their cars and split without any trouble. But the rest of us were pulled to the ground, hands forced behind our backs. Guns pointed at our heads.

School officials had the police take us to the office. The police left after they had resumed some order. Santos and Tiburón, who were drop-outs, were dragged to the police station. Those of us still in school were expelled. This was fine with me. I hated school. And I loved fighting.

I worked as a bus boy in a Mexican restaurant in San Gabriel when I was 15 years old. My hours were in the evening until closing, which kept me up until 2 a.m. most nights. The father of a former Southside Boy managed the restaurant, which is how I got the job. It was kicking, hard work. Sometimes I'd be practically asleep while walking the dining areas — but we had to keep moving. We carried thick plastic trays heaped with dirty dishes, cleaned up tables, poured water into glasses, provided extra coffee — and took abuse from the well-to-do people who came there.

"Hey boy, clean up this mess."
"Hey boy, how about some more water."
"Hey boy, this steak is too well done."
Hey Boy became my new name.

The clientele arrived in suits and evening dresses. They ordered the margaritas, considered the best in "aallll Caliiforniaaa." They ordered and ordered. Even before dinner arrived, they were already pushed back against the chairs, ties undone and stupefied.

Before the night finished, white-haired women tried to do Spanish fan dances on the dining floor as businessmen called everyone "pancho," holding dollar bills in our faces for more service.

We had our ways of getting back. The usual: putting snot and piss in their food before it got to their tables or "accidentally" spilling ice cold water on their laps or backs.

"So sorry, *señor*. How clumsy of me. A thousand pardons."

But there were some fringe benefits. These people would order the best steaks, lobsters, and Mexican specialties and leave almost everything when they left. We stuffed the food in bags and later had feasts. Every once in a while I took home cooked lobsters and two-inch thick prime ribs!

My best friends were the waitresses and waiters. One waiter, a gay dude from Mexico, actually protected us younger guys from the cooks who ordered us around. I always thought it was because he wanted to get to me, but even so I must say he never raised this issue. One time he let us borrow his X-rated 16-millimeter films. After work, the bus boys got together for a marathon viewing of his films while dropping pills and chasing them with tequila.

The waitresses were cool and understanding, considering they had to endure even more abuse since they were women — dressed in peasant blouses which had been plunged down to reveal their shoulders and short *poblana* skirts with ruffles. They helped make sure I didn't get cheated on the tips, something the waiters were less inclined to do.

But the most interesting part of the job involved the raids. Almost everyone who worked in the restaurant was an undocumented immigrant. Every so often, the immigration authorities assaulted the place. They would close doors and pull out badges.

"This is the United States Border Patrol," they'd yell. "Nobody move...*nadie se mueve*."

Cooks flew out of kitchen windows.

They tried to pull me into their detention vans, but I carried a food-stained and slightly torn copy of my birth certificate in my pocket. It saved me from being deported, although there were times I thought it wouldn't matter and I'd have to call home from Tijuana.

After about a week, the ones they threw across the border were back at work.

✝ ✝ ✝

Not going to school meant a lot of free time. Sniffing became my favorite way to waste it. I stole cans of anything that could give a buzz: carbono, clear plastic, paint or gasoline. Sometimes I'd mix it up in a concoction and pour it on a rag or in a paper bag we sniffed from.

Behind the school, on the fields, inside the tunnel, at Marrano Beach and alongside the concrete banks of the San Gabriel River: I sniffed. Once I even climbed on top of a back hoe at a construction site, removed the lid off the gas tank and inhaled until somebody checked out the noise and chased me away.

Spray was dangerous; it literally ate your brain. But it was also a great escape. The world became like jello, like clay, something which could be molded and shaped. Sounds became louder, clearer — pulsating. Bodies removed themselves from bodies, floating with the sun. I sought it so desperately. I didn't want to be this thing of bone and skin. With spray I became water.

Once I sniffed with Chicharrón and Yuk Yuk behind the "Boys" Market in San Gabriel. I don't remember the trip, but they told me I suddenly stood up and proceeded to repeatedly bang my head against a wall. Pieces of hair and skin scraped on the brick. Chicharrón walked me home; refused to give me any more spray.

While on spray I yelled. I laughed. I clawed at the evening sky. I felt like a cracked egg. But I wouldn't stop.

Then another time Baba, Wilo and I gathered in the makeshift hideout we had alongside the Alhambra Wash, next to the drive-in. We sat ourselves down on the dirt, some blankets and rags nearby to lie on. We covered the entrance with banana leaves and wood planks. There were several cans of clear plastic — what we called *la ce pe* — around us. We each had paper bags and sprayed into them — and I had already dropped some pills and downed a fifth of Wild Turkey. I then placed the bag over my mouth and nose, sealed it tightly with both hands, and breathed deeply.

A radio nearby played some Led Zeppelin or Cream or some other guitar-ripping licks. Soon the sounds rose in pitch. The thumping of bass felt like a heartbeat in the sky, followed by an echo of metal-grating tones. I became flesh with a dream. The infested walls of the wash turned to mud; the trickle of water a vast river. The homeboys and I looked like something out of Huckleberry Finn or Tom Sawyer. With stick fishing poles. The sparkle of water below us. Fish fidgeting below the sheen.

Dew fell off low branches as if it were breast milk. Birds shot out of the tropical trees which appeared across from us. Perhaps this trip had been the pages of a book, something I read as a child. Or saw on TV. Regardless, I was transported away from what was really there — yet it felt soothing. Not like the oil stains we sat in. Not like the factory air that surrounded us. Not this plastic death in a can.

I didn't want it to end. As the effect wore thin, I grabbed the spray and bag, and resumed the ritual. Baba and Wilo weren't far behind me.

Then everything faded away — the dew, the water, the birds. I became a cartoon, twirling through a tunnel, womb-like and satiated with sounds and lines and darkness. I found myself drifting toward a glare of lights. My family called me over: Seni, Mama, Papa, Tía Chucha, Tío Kiko, Pancho — everybody. I wanted to be there, to know this perpetual dreaming, this din of exquisite screams — to have this mother comfort surging through me.

The world fell into dust piles around me. Images of the past pitched by: my brother tossing me off rooftops, my mother's hearty laughter, my father's thin and tired face, the homeboys with scarred smiles and the women with exotic eyes and cunts which were the churches I worshipped in. Everything crashed. Everything throbbed. I only knew: I had to get to the light, that wondrous beacon stuffed with sweet promise: Of peace. Untroubled. The end of fear. *Don't close the door, Mama. I'm scared. It's okay, m'ijo. There's no monsters. We'll be here. Don't be scared.*

No more monsters. Come to the light. I felt I would be safe there — finally. To the light. The light.

Suddenly everything around me exploded. An intense blackness enveloped me. A deep stillness. Nothing. Absolute. No thinking. No feeling. A hole.

Then an electrified hum sank its teeth into my brain. Hands surrounded me, pulled at me, back to the dust of our makeshift hideaway.

A face appeared above me. It leaned down and breathed into me. Images of leaves, crates, stained blankets came into view. Wilo pulled back and looked into my eyes. A haze covered everything. I felt dizzy. And pissed off.

"Give me the bag, man."

"No way," Baba said. "You died Chin — you stopped breathing and died."

I tried to get up, but fell back to the ground. A kind of grief overwhelmed me. I was no longer this dream. I was me again. I wished I did die.

"You don't understand," I yelled to the homeboys. "I have to go back."

I crept toward a paper bag but Baba kicked it out of my reach. Later I found myself stepping down a street. Baba and Wilo had pointed me in the direction of home and I kept going. I hated being there. I didn't know what to do. God, I wanted that light, this whore of a sun to blind me, to entice me to burn — to be sculptured marble in craftier hands.

ϯ ϯ ϯ

Wilo's sister Payasa liked me and told him. She was okay, I guess, a real *loca* when it came to the 'hood. She had the high teased hair, the short tight skirts, the "raccoon" style makeup and boisterous presence. I ended up going with her. Mostly for Wilo's sake at first.

After I got expelled from school, Payasa and I spent time together during the day since she refused to go to classes herself. We'd walk to Garvey Park. She would hand me some *colies* which I'd drop and soon start to sway, talk incoherently and act stupid.

"Oh, you'll get over it," Payasa said. "Eventually."

She always said that.

After a time, whenever a car crashed, a couple argued or somebody tripped and fell, we'd look at each other and say at the same time: "Oh, you'll get over it...eventually."

When Wilo and I sniffed aerosol spray, sometimes Payasa joined us.

"Why do you let your sister do this?" I asked.

"That's her," Wilo shrugged. "I can't stop her."

Payasa was always high. The higher she got, the more bold she became. One time we were sniffing in the tunnel beneath the freeway. I started tripping: Snakes crawled from the sides, as well as melted faces and bolts of lights and a shower of shapes. She brushed up to me and pulled off her blouse. Erect nipples confronted me on firm breasts. I kissed them. She laughed and pulled me away.

"Oh, you'll get over it," she said. "Eventually."

I was too fucked up to care.

One time in the park she said she wanted to take her pants and underwear off.

"Right here? Right now?...in front of everybody?"

"Yeah, why not?" she responded. "You dare me."

"Sure — I dare you."

She did.

Sniffing took the best out of her. Sometimes I'd walk through the tunnel and she would be there, alone, with a bag of spray, all scuffed up, her eyes glassy.

Payasa became a *loca* because of her older brothers. They were Lomas *veteranos*, older gangsters. Because Wilo and Payasa were younger, they picked on them a lot; beating them to make them stronger.

Payasa fought all the time at school. Whenever she lost, her older brothers would slice her tongue with a razor. She wasn't ever supposed to lose. This made her meaner, crazier — unpredictable.

As a girlfriend Payasa was fun, but she couldn't be intimate unless she was on reds, spray or snort.

I had to break with her. I loved the spray and shit but Payasa became too much like the walking dead. So I told her I didn't want to see her anymore. She didn't say anything, just turned around and left. I faintly said to myself, "Oh, you'll get over it...eventually."

She was later found in a daze, her arms with numerous deep cuts all the way to her elbows. Nobody would let me see her after she was taken to a rehabilitation hospital for teenage addicts. Wilo suggested I let it go.

"That's Payasa, man," Wilo said, and shrugged his shoulders.

✝ ✝ ✝

I sank against the wall, my naked back splattered with grit. A razor glistened in my hand. A pail of water sat next to me. The room was stuffed to the top with junk I had accumulated, including stolen stereos and car radios which Yuk Yuk had stashed there for safekeeping.

The blade touched the skin and each time this song became louder in my head, a song which wouldn't let up, as the melody resonated through me and the emptiness inside compressed into itself. Soon I filled up with a sense of being, of worth, with a clarity that I belonged here on this earth, at this time. Somehow, some way, it all had meaning. I made sense. There in the garage. Alone but alive. I barely made it. I almost got to the light. And somehow I knew the light wasn't all the great feeling, hope and desire I thought at the time it would be. I stumbled upon the blackness; I had dared to cross the light, to enter the other side, beyond the barrier, into the shadow. But I had been yanked back just in time. Wilo and Baba for some reason were able to respond fast as I lay unconscious, unbreathing, there by the wash.

I put the blade down, peed into the water and fell asleep.

In my mother's kitchen, I tried to recall the song of the night before, the one which stopped me from wasting myself, that said it was all right, but I couldn't. I walked up to Mama. She refused to turn around and face me, although she knew I was there.

"Can I stay here and eat this morning?" I asked her in Spanish.

She turned around, hard eyes encircled by wrinkled skin. Then a smile filled her face and she became like a young woman again.

"Of course, *m'ijo*," she said as she turned back to the stove to toss over a tortilla. "When you're ready to visit, with respect to our house, you can come to eat."

I kissed her on the neck.

I went to the dining table where Gloria sat, stuffing her mouth with food. I pulled out a chair and looked down at a plate resting on a tablecloth.

"Hey — do these eggs have anything to do with me?"

CHAPTER FIVE

"It is the violent poetry of the times, written in the blood of youth."
— Linda Mendoza, Chicana poet from South San Gabriel

The Animal Tribe practically died with the death of one of its last presidents: John Fabela.

17-year-old John — whose girlfriend had just given birth to his infant daughter — succumbed to a shotgun blast in his living room as his younger brother watched from beneath a bed in an adjacent room. About 13 members of the Sons of Soul car club, made up of recent Mexican immigrants living in East L.A., were rounded up by the police.

By then Joaquín López was already in prison for a heroin beef. Many of the older Tribe members were also incarcerated or hard-core *tecatos*. As the Tribe's influence diminished, Lomas initiated Tribe members into the various sets based on age groupings: the Pequeños, Chicos, the Dukes and the Locos. Lomas was reorganizing and recruiting. No longer could one claim Lomas just by being there. Chicharrón invited me to get in.

"They beat on you for about three minutes — that's all," Chicharrón urged. "You get a busted lip. So what? It's worth it."

So later I decided to go to a party in the Hills, fully aware I would join a Lomas set. Like most barrio parties, it started without any hassle. *Vatos* and *rucas* filled every corner in the small house; some ventured outside, smoking or drinking. The house belonged to Nina, this extremely pretty girl whom everyone respected. Nina's mother shuffled in the kitchen, making tacos from large pots of meat and beans simmering on low flames.

The dudes were polite; dignified. *Señora* this and *Señora* that. You couldn't imagine how much danger hung on their every breath.

As the night wore on, the feel of the place transformed. The air was rife with anticipation. Talk became increasingly louder.

Faces peeled into hardness. The music played oldies we all knew by heart, and *gritos* punctuated key verses. Fists smashed against the walls. Just as the food simmered to a boil, the room also bubbled and churned. Weed, pills and hard liquor passed from hand to hand. Outside, behind the house, a row of dudes shot up heroin. In the glow of the back porch light, they whispered a sea of shorn sentences.

A crew of older, mean-eyed *vatos* arrived and the younger guys stacked behind them. Nina's mother showed concern. She pulled Nina into the kitchen; I could see her talking severely to her daughter.

I didn't know these dudes. They were *veteranos* and looked up to by the homeys. They had just come out of the joint — mostly Tracy, Chino or Youth Training School, known as YTS, a prison for youth offenders. Chicharrón pressed his face close to my ear and told me their names: Ragman, Peaches, Natividad, Topo...and the small, muscular one with a mustache down the sides of his mouth was called Puppet.

I then recalled some of their reputations: Natividad, for example, had been shot five times and stabbed 40 times — and still lived! Peaches once used a machine gun against some dudes in a shoot-out. And Puppet had been convicted of murder at the age of 16.

"Who wants in?" Puppet later announced to a row of dark, teenaged male faces in front of him. Chicharrón whispered something in Puppet's ear. Puppet casually looked toward me. They designated me the first to get jumped.

Topo walked up to me. He was stout, dark and heavily tattooed. He placed his arm around me and then we marched toward the driveway. Chicharrón managed to yell: "Protect your head."

I assumed when I got to the driveway, a handful of dudes would encircle me, provide me a signal of sorts, and begin the initiation. Instead, without warning, Topo swung a calloused fist at my face. I went down fast. Then an onslaught of steel-tipped shoes and heels rained on my body. I thought I would be able to swing and at least hit one or two — but no way! Then I remembered Chicharrón's admonition. I pulled my arms over my head, covered it the best I could while the kicks seemed to stuff me beneath a parked car.

Finally the barrage stopped. But I didn't know exactly when. I felt hands pull me up. I looked back at everyone standing around the driveway. My right eye was almost closed. My lip felt like it stuck out a mile. My sides ached. But I had done well.

Hands came at me to congratulate. There were pats on the back. Chicharrón embraced me, causing me to wince. I was a Lomas *loco* now. Then a homegirl came up and gave me a big kiss on my inflamed lip; I wished I could have tasted it. Then other homegirls did the same. It didn't seem half-bad, this initiation. Later they invited me to pounce on the other dudes who were also jumped in, but I passed.

As the night wore on, Puppet, Ragman and Nat had the initiates pile into a pickup truck. I was already quite plastered but somehow still standing. Puppet drove the truck toward Sangra. Elation rasped in our throats.

"Fuck Sangra," one of the new dudes chimed in, and other voices followed the sentiment.

We came across a cherried-out 1952 DeSoto, with pinstripes and a metal-flake exterior. Puppet pulled the truck up to the side of it. There were four dudes inside drinking and listening to cassette tapes. We didn't know if they were Sangra or what. We followed Ragman as he approached the dudes. One of them emerged from the passenger side. He looked like a nice-enough fellow.

"Hey, we don't want no trouble," he said.

I knew they weren't Sangra. They looked like hard-working recreational lowriders out for a spin. But Ragman wouldn't have it. He punched the dude down. A couple of other guys came out of the car, and they too tried to salvage the night, tried to appeal for calm.

"Listen, man, how about a beer," one of them offered.

Nat grabbed his neck from behind and pulled him to the ground, then beat on him. Ragman looked at the other guys who were clearly scared.

"Who don' like it?" he demanded. "Who don' like it...you?"

Ragman hit another guy. By then the dudes in the truck had climbed out and bashed in the car, breaking windows and crunching in metal with tire irons and two-by-fours which had been piled in the back of the truck. One dude tried to run off, but somebody chased him down with a wine bottle and struck him on the head. The dude fell down and I saw the wine bottle keep coming down on him, as if it was supposed to break, but it wouldn't.

The driver of the DeSoto tried to pull out, but somebody threw a brick at his head. For a long time, I observed the beatings as if I were outside of everything, as if a moth of tainted wings floating over the steamed sidewalk. Then I felt a hand pull at my arm and I sluggishly turned toward it. Puppet looked squarely into my one opened eye. He had a rusty screwdriver in his other hand.

"Do it, man," he said. Simply that.

I clasped the screwdriver and walked up to the beaten driver in the seat whose head was bleeding. The dude looked at me through glazed eyes, horrified at my presence, at what I held in my hand, at this twisted, swollen face that came at him through the dark. *Do it!* were the last words I recalled before I plunged the screwdriver into flesh and bone, and the sky screamed.

Within a year, the local headlines' business boomed:

"Gang Violence: Teen Wars Bring Death To Two"
"Valley Teen Gangs Flourish"
"Three Wounded By School Intruders"
"Youth, 17, Murdered: Victim Shot In Chest"
"Five Hurt, Two Arrested In Rosemead Party Crash"
"Three Still Held In Gang Deaths"
"San Gabriel Teenager Shot In The Face"

> *"Rosemead Youth Gunned Down: Murder Said Gang Related"*
> *"Shooting Victim Critical"*
> *"Fired From Car: Four Wounded By Gunshots"*
> *"Rosemead Boy, 17, Shot By Deputy, Dies"*
> *"Deputy Escapes Sniper"*
> *"Slaying Suspect Bound Over To Superior Court"*
> *"Sheriff Moving On Gangs"*

Committees, task forces, community centers, born-again store-front churches and behavior guidance counselors proliferated in response. Rosemead's South Side, South San Gabriel and San Gabriel's barrio became targets of programs, monies and studies. Local reporters drove along with law enforcement officers through Lomas and Sangra to get "the feel" of these misaligned and misunderstood communities. Gang members were interviewed and news photographers worked the Hills to depict the poverty — usually of children playing in mud next to rusted cars, trash cans and pregnant mothers peering out of makeshift sheds.

La Casa Community Center served the needs of Sangra; Bienvenidos Community Center and its John Fabela Youth Center covered Lomas; and the Zapopan Center catered to the southside of Rosemead. The centers offered dropout programs, welfare assistance, federal job placements, teen mother day care and places for young people to hang out.

The people who worked at the centers put in 80-hour weeks, covered weekly funerals and had to enter the doors of domestic conflicts armed with nothing but a prayer. Some were ex-gang members who ventured back to help. Or they were the first wave of minority college students who entered institutions of higher learning through special scholarships and economic opportunity grants.

At La Casa and Zapopan, community activists made the payroll. The triumvirate of community centers began to play a leading role in the struggles which emerged out of the Mexican sections here. Besides the gang killings, there was widespread drug use. Police beatings and killings became prominent. And the battles in the schools for decent education intensified. Because the three centers were dealing with similar crises, their staffs often met together to consult on strategy.

By 1970 I felt disjointed, out of balance, tired of just acting and reacting. I wanted to flirt with depth of mind, to learn more about my world. My society. About what to do. I became drawn to the people who came to work at the community centers; they were learned. Full of ideas and concepts; they were, I realized, similar to my father, this former teacher and biologist, who once labeled all the trees and plants in the backyard so we would know their scientific names.

Amid South San Gabriel's hottest summer, the Bienvenidos Community Center hired Chente Ramírez. His credentials included a lifetime in the White Fence barrio in East L.A. — known as the oldest "street gang" in the country. But Chente managed to avoid gang involvement, went to school, worked in industry, helped his father with his trucking business and pretty much took care of his mom, six sisters and a brother while his dad traversed the land in a tractor-trailer rig.

Chente, in his late 20s then, had already gone to a university, been a founding member of the United Mexican American Students (UMAS), helped organize the East L.A. school walkouts of 1968, participated in forming MEChA (Movimiento Estudiantil Chicano de Aztlán) and the Brown Berets. Later still he put together a number of East Los Angeles study groups engaged in revolutionary theory. He was also a martial arts expert.

I had certain yearnings at the time, which a lot of us had, to acquire authority in our own lives in the face of police, joblessness and powerlessness. Las Lomas was our path to that, but I was frustrated because I felt the violence was eating us alive.

Chente impressed me as someone I could learn from. He was calm, but also street enough to go among all those crazy guys and know how to handle himself. He didn't need to act bad to operate. He could be strong, intelligent, and in control. He was the kind of dude who could get the best from the system — education, karate training — without being a snitch or giving in. I wanted to be able to do this too.

I was in my mid-teens and Chente was about twelve years older. I looked up to him, but not as a big brother. He was someone who could influence me without judging me morally or telling me what to do. He was just there. He listened, and when he knew you were wrong, before he would say anything, he would get you to think.

✝ ✝ ✝

The cue ball rolled across the tattered green felt and struck an odd-numbered striped ball like a firecracker, the violence sending it twirling into the corner pocket. Smoke curled through the luminance of the fluorescent light hanging by wires over the billiard table. Puppet gazed momentarily at the remaining balls which lay scattered on the playing field as he contemplated the next move. Across from him stood Toots, aware of Puppet's every gesture. Puppet placed a well-worn piece of chalk and twisted his cue stick into it for several seconds, all the time deducing the trajectory of the cue ball for his next stroke. Next to him in leather blouse and tight denim jeans stood Pila, Puppet's squeeze.

Puppet's forearms were a canvas of extremely elaborate, interwoven and delicately-pinned tattoos that danced on skin with *cholo* images, skulls, serpents and women's faces. On his neck was a stylized rendering of the words *Las Lomas*. At 20 years old, he was a *veterano* and just out of YTS.

Along with a handful of other *pintos* — like Ragman, Peaches, Natividad and Topo — Puppet ruled the 'hood with fear. Soon the *veteranos* took over the John Fabela Youth Center, along with its pool and ping pong tables.

Puppet bent low, closed an eye, and with the other followed the length of the stick, which rested on the skin between his thumb and forefinger, all the way to the cue ball.

"Eight ball in the corner pocket," he announced, as if he had sawdust in his throat.

He waited, breathing easily, then he pumped the stick, the cue ball sliding toward the side of the table, then back down in an angle and striking the eight ball into another corner pocket. The game belonged to Puppet.

Pila placed her arms around Puppet's shoulders. Toots pulled out some bills from his pocket as his *jaina*, Lourdes from Mexico, looked hard in Pila's direction.

"What you looking at, *puta tijuanera?*" Pila responded.

Lourdes walked up, placed her arms out wide and replied: "Fock you — *quieres algo conmigo, pues aquí estoy.*"

Toots rushed up between them and pushed Lourdes back into the dark. He knew what messing with Pila meant — a rip across the belly or face. But he also knew it might involve crossing Puppet, and he wanted to avoid this more than anything.

Fuzzy then called out for other players and more bets.

Puppet looked intently at everyone, especially Toots in a corner with Lourdes. He neither disciplined nor encouraged Pila. She took care of what she had to take care of. Puppet didn't like people from Mexico anyway. For that matter, he didn't like blacks, whites or other barrios. In fact, Puppet didn't care about anybody.

✝ ✝ ✝

La Casa Community Center occupied a two-story, former warehouse building with Mexican motifs on the outside, a gym and a recreation area with a single pool table. For a few weeks I took karate lessons there until I decided to leave before anyone discovered my ties to Las Lomas. Sangra members roamed in and out of the center nightly, planning battles, drug deals, or just to get high. Cokie and Dina would practically live there, along with the other girls in the flaming red hair. Sal Basuto was the community organizer, playing the role Chente had at the Bienvenidos/John Fabela Center. He walked through the T-shirted and muscular Sangra dudes, with combed-back short hair or bald heads.

"¿Qué hubo?" Sal greeted.

Some gave him Chicano-style handshakes while others responded with hand signs signifying Sangra. Boy, Hapo, Night Owl, Tutti and Negro were there, sort of hanging and barely acknowledging Sal's enthusiastic approach.

"Hey, homes, you got a *frajo?*" Hapo asked.

"Lung cancer kills," Sal said and handed him a cigarette.

"Don't worry," Hapo smiled. "I don't inhale."

Sal entered the pool table area, a small room which once held books and tables and a record player but which were taken during a break-in by unknown persons who also vandalized the place, tore shelving off brackets and ripped away chunks of wallboard.

Blas played a solitaire game of pool. Blas had a birth defect in which his right arm came out missing and only a rumor of fingers pressed out of his shoulder. But he trained himself to play pool with one arm and became a leading player, often beating those with two good arms.

Sal looked weary. Once, he told me he always tried to put on a face of interest. He felt a lot depended on his mood. There were days he didn't know what else to do with these young people. There were no jobs for them. The schools surrounding the barrio catered to the affluent whites who lived around Sangra, so they all dropped out. And Sangra and the police were in a constant clash.

Appropriately, the initiation for new Sangra members involved jumping a cop. Ambushing police car units in any of the narrow alleys here became a common occurrence. The city of San Gabriel had its own police force and jail house, which lay on the outskirts of the barrio. Every homeboy knew the inside of those cell walls. It was home.

Sal often returned to his cluttered office inside La Casa's main building. He would sink down in an ancient metal chair, and stare out the window at the small, well-kept homes in front of the center. He felt sorry for Sangra. They were a small barrio. The leading section, Los Diablos, had no more than 100 members. Lomas, on the other hand, had several hundred. Sangra was constantly under fire: Monte Flores, 18th Street and El Sereno were some of the other barrios at war with them — and each of them as big as Lomas. In the first year Sal worked at La Casa, he attended nine funerals of Sangra warriors.

Yet in many ways this made Sangra more vicious. Because they were small in number, they made up their strength with guts, intensity and uncompromising *locura*.

Cokie and Dina made sure the Sangra girls were intimidating and feared. The leader of Los Diablos, Chava, did the same thing with his stylized dress and ever-present small felt hat and cane. Also their style of graffiti, quite colorful and cryptic — and their ability to sneak into the Hills unnoticed and cross out Lomas *placas* — brought much ire upon them.

Sal knew one day they would pay a heavy price.

✝ ✝ ✝

Many nights in the garage, while in the throes of sleep, I heard knocking and voices. They appeared to be woven into the dreams. But I'd wake up and realize it was no dream but Chicharrón or another homeboy or homegirl needing a place to crash, to party or just hang.

On such a night, I woke up to raps on the window. I yanked myself out of the blankets and opened the door. Santos, Daddio and Pokie, three of the Lomas crazies, were standing there.

"*Qué hubo*, homes?" I greeted.

"Chin, we need to do something tonight," Santos responded. "You with it man."

I already sensed what they meant. They wanted me to do a *jale*, a hit against Sangra. The night before Tutti from Los Diablos had gotten into a big argument with his long-time girlfriend, Cokie. In anger, Tutti drove up to Las Lomas and shot Little Man, killing him instantly. The police had already busted Tutti, but Lomas needed to exact some revenge. I knew the whole story. What I didn't know was Puppet, Ragman and the other main dudes had decided I needed to help "take care of it."

"*Orale*, let me get ready."

I put on dark clothes and my trench coat. It became a habit for me to take the trench coat whenever I did jobs like this.

We climbed over fences behind the garage and emerged onto Ramona Avenue. A car was there already. I entered, sitting in between Pokie and Little Man's brother, Beto, who had been sitting, deathly still, in the car. Santos and Daddio sat up front.

"What we got to do?" I asked.

"Look under the seats," Santos casually suggested.

I looked down with my eyes, without moving, and could see the edges of bottles and some rags. Shit, I thought, they want to firebomb a house. This meant somebody's mother, little sister or brother could be hurt or killed. But this is how things had gotten by then. Everyone was fair game in barrio wars; people's families were being hit all the time.

We cruised toward Sangra. Santos knew the police would be extra heavy the night after a shooting. But if we didn't move in a timely manner the impression would be anyone could hit us, anytime.

"Where we going?" I asked.

"We're going to Chava's *cantón*."

This was heavy. We were going after Sangra's main warrior. Who knows how they found out where his family lived, because Chava had moved in with Dina somewhere else. But the idea was to make him pay dearly, going after his mother's house, and if need be, anybody who might have the misfortune of being there.

I felt edgy, my muscles straining, my leg striking a beat against the back of the seat. I didn't want to do this. But once you're asked to do a hit, you can't refuse, can't question or even offer an excuse. Since I was easily accessible in the garage, I became a good candidate for these undertakings.

We pulled up to a quiet, suburban-looking street. Chava's family actually lived outside the barrio, in a better part of San

Gabriel, pretty much like me. We parked down a ways and climbed up an embankment behind a row of houses.

Pokie brought up a bag filled with the bottles and rags. Daddio had cans of gasoline. We squatted in weeds behind a brick-fenced house with a back yard full of flowers and exotic plants, the way of many Mexican homes. A back porch had leisure chairs and gaily-painted rubber tires filled with soil and topped with purple, red and yellow petals.

It looked similar to my mother's back yard.

Santos poured gasoline into the bottles and stuffed the rags at the top, leaving a section hanging over. We each had a bottle. We were to toss them at the back porch, then run like hell to the car where Beto kept the engine running.

I didn't want to do it, but I couldn't stop. I felt trapped. I knew the only thing for me was to go through with it, and get out of there as fast as possible. I felt excitement. And an ache of grief.

A news account reported five people ran out of a house in San Gabriel after four molotov cocktails struck its back porch. Everybody got out safely, but the back of the house went up in flames and the rest of it sustained irreparable water damage from the fire hoses.

Little Man's death and the firebombing were part of a series of violent incidents between Lomas and Sangra which stretched back generations. Dudes had fathers and even grandfathers involved in the feud.

Of course, word got around about who did Chava's house. I don't know how this happened. But it soon involved my family.

By then my sister Gloria, 13 years old and a student at Garvey, looked up to me. To her, I was independent, in starched khaki pants, tattooed, with an earring in one ear before anybody did this kind of thing; always full of stories and good times. Her inexperienced mind soaked it all up.

Gloria joined a younger set of Lomas girls called United Sisters or US, and called herself Shorty. Sometimes I hung out with them, just for the kicks. I didn't see Shorty becoming a crazy Lomas girl. I saw it only as something she would get over as she matured.

One night she attended a dance at the San Gabriel Mission sponsored by Thee Prophettes, another girl's club. I didn't go, so Shorty played it smooth, hanging with her homegirls Cece and Huera from US.

Sure enough, Cokie and Dina showed up at the dance with a few Sangra girls. One of them was Spyder, who knew me from Garvey before she moved to Sangra and became one of the *locas*. When Spyder first noticed Shorty she felt a tug of recognition.

The Sangra girls gave everyone hard looks. US and Thee Prophettes kept cool, not wanting anything to undermine the benefit dance. Later that evening, though, Spyder figured out Shorty was my sister. I was "marked," meaning Sangra members were obligated to shoot Chin from Lomas. But a sister would do as well, Spyder reasoned.

Spyder relayed the information to Cokie and Dina. They had small caliber handguns. They discussed how they would corner Shorty and then let her have it, possibly in the girl's restroom.

Sometime later, my brother Joe received a phone call.

"Pick us up Joe," Shorty whispered in a frightened tone. "There's something happening here — and I'm scared."

Shorty told Joe to drive around the dance hall to a back entrance. Shorty, Cece and Huera planned to be there and get into the car. Timing was everything.

Joe didn't know what the problem might be. He got into his car and proceeded to do as Shorty asked.

He drove to the side of the dance hall where a door entrance was located, but Shorty and her friends weren't around. He waited. Suddenly the doors burst open. Shorty, Cece and Huera ran out, almost tripping as they held their heels in their hands.

"Joe, get the car going — hurry!"

"What the..."

But Joe couldn't get the final words out. A volley of gunfire came toward him. My sister and her friends rushed into the car, piling on top of one another. Joe pressed the accelerator, forcing the car to peel across the asphalt. Shorty didn't quite get inside but she held on as the car sped off; Cokie and Dina stood in the entranceway, and, firing from the shoulder, continued to pump .22 bullets toward the car as it vanished into the fog-drenched distance.

☥ ☥ ☥

Sheriff's helicopters were a nightly annoyance. It could have been Vietnam, only we were the enemy. They hovered above the slopes and ravines, covering the ground with circles of lights. Deputies drove by often, pushing dudes against walls, detaining them and dispersing crowds of two or more. The homeboys shot out the few lampposts to keep the place in darkness. We hid in bushes, in basements and abandoned buildings. We were pushed underground. Codes, rules and honor became meaningless.

Rapes became a common circumstance in the Hills. They began as isolated incidents, then a way of life. Some believed this ritual started with outsiders, not from within the Hills. Others said it began with one guy who happened to be crazy, but the rest followed suit as the attacks signified a distorted sense of power. One dude was said to have raped 17 girls one summer.

Enano once pulled up in a four-door green Chevy as Chicharrón and I lolled around on Teresa Avenue. He climbed out of the car, opened the back door and invited us to "get in on this." A naked girl, passed out, lay in the back seat. A black patch of pubic hair stood out on a shock of white skin which looked as if she had been immersed in flour.

"*Chale*, homes," I responded. "I ain't with it."

Chicharrón nodded the same sentiment.

Without hesitation, Enano closed the door, entered the front seat and took off, perhaps looking for somebody else to approach.

A rainy evening greeted Yuk Yuk, Fuzzy, Ernie López and me as we left a *quinceñera* dance in the Avenues, a barrio northeast of downtown Los Angeles. We jumped into Ernie's lowrider van. Paco and two girls were inside the van. Ernie put on some music which rattled the brain cells through speakers in the front and back of the van. Fuzzy and Yuk Yuk talked with the girls as I took swigs of Silver Satin wine and snorts of heroin. Mellowed and mumbling, we drove through the wet side streets toward the Hills.

The girls were loaded; incoherent and sleepy. Makeup smeared their faces. Paco groped through the blouse of one of the girls, who faintly tried to pull him off. Fuzzy held the other girl up as he smiled at Yuk Yuk and me. I nodded off, and then woke, nodded off and then woke. Soon I noticed Paco on top of the girl he had been manhandling. Her legs were spread outward, and a torn underwear twisted around an ankle. Paco's pants were below his knees and I could see his buttocks rise up and down as he thrust into her, her weak moans more from the weight of the body than anything else.

Ernie pulled up to Toll Drive. Yuk Yuk and Fuzzy pulled the other girl out and down the slope to the field. Paco kept at it with the girl in the van. I clambered out, the cold humid air jolting me to my feet. Ernie passed me the bottle of Silver Satin as he wobbled down to where Yuk Yuk and Fuzzy were already situated. I looked back. I could hear Paco coming, scratchy noises rising from his throat. The girl, who was somewhere between 12 and 14 years old, had her arms laid out over her head, her eyes closed, her mouth opened — unconscious, but as if in a silent scream.

I made it to the field and saw Yuk Yuk kissing the other girl on a section of cinder-block wall while Fuzzy opened her legs with his hand to get a better feel. Ernie looked at me and motioned me to come over. I didn't want any part of it.

Something filled my throat and I puked around my shoes. Yuk Yuk by then had thrown the girl to the ground. I knew what they were going to do, and wandered off.

I walked up the slope, saw Paco pulling his pants up through the slightly-opened van doors. As before, I found myself ambling along a dirt road.

✝ ✝ ✝

Wilo and Payasa moved to El Monte to live with an aunt, partly to remove themselves from the violence surrounding the barrio. Their older brothers stayed and continued to carry on the fight. Glad my friends were not to be in the line of fire, I went to say goodby on the day they were leaving.

They lived on Berne Street, a section of Lomas called "Little TJ," which consisted of a road which flowed in mud on rainy days, making it difficult to get in and out. Makeshift stucco, brick and clapboard shacks clawed the hills on either side of the road.

Payasa looked different, following several months in rehab hospitals and half-way homes. Her hair was back to its normal luster, short and combed straight down instead of teased. She had on no makeup and thus seemed a stranger, although we were so close at one time, sleeping together on park benches, sniffing and groping in the tunnel or in my garage room. I no longer knew this person in front of me.

Payasa didn't smile. Yet she acknowledged me rather sweetly.

"Oh my Chin — you'll miss me?" she asked, more a statement than a question.

"Depends," I replied. "Just keep in touch."

"I'll always remember you, homes," she said and placed her hand on my face; meandering scars across her arms. "We've seen things most people never see. We've seen death. And here we are, still able to say goodby. I don't know if we deserve this."

"*Orale*, sure we deserve it. Don't ever forget that."

"I mean, we haven't done anything really decent," she said, then paused.

"You know," she continued. "I've forgotten what it is to cry. I don't know why."

"Me neither, but I know one thing, we better find out."

Wilo came by with a medium-sized bag of his belongings, but then he wasn't one for possessions.

"Hey, *ése*, what's up?" he said.

"*Aquí nomás*. You got everything?"

"You pack for where you're going, and where I'm going there's nothing to pack for."

"Are you sure you want to do this?"

"I'm sure I don't want to do this," he answered, then looked back toward his former home. "But there's nothing I can do about it. Even my *carnales* want us to leave. And I do what they say."

I helped Payasa and Wilo put their things into their father's beat-up station wagon which had a side door held on by twine and good wishes. I would miss them but it was best they leave, maybe start fresh again if this were possible.

"I owe you man," I finally said, something I never told Wilo about his role in my near-death experience. "You saved my life."

"*Chale, ése* don't put that on me," he said. "You don't owe me nothing. Just pay yourself back."

I hugged them both and proceeded down Berne Street to the nearest fields. It would be the last time I ever saw them again.

Later I found out Payasa ended up pregnant and in a prison of matrimony somewhere. But 10 days after they moved, dudes from the Monte Flores barrio would shoot and run over Wilo several times; his body discovered wedged between metal trash bins in an obscure alley. Payasa called me one day to say she hadn't heard from Wilo for a day or so. Then she called back to tell me she heard of his death while listening to the radio. Wilo was 15 years old. Payasa didn't cry.

✝ ✝ ✝

Everything lost its value for me: Love, Life and Women. Death seemed the only door worth opening, the only road toward a future. We tried to enter death and emerge from it. We sought it in heroin, which bears the peace of death in life. We craved it in our pursuit of Sangra and in battles with the police. We yelled: *You can't touch this!*, but *Come kill me!* was the inner cry. In death we sought what we were groping for, without knowing it until it caressed our cheeks. It was like an extra finger in the back of our heads, pressing, gnawing, scraping. This fever overtook us, weakening and enslaving us. Death in a bottle. In spray. In the fire-eyes of a woman, stripped of soul and squeezed into the shreds of her humanity.

✝ ✝ ✝

I stopped spray soon after my near-death experience. But I needed something else. At first, the dudes in the Animal Tribe used to go off somewhere and shoot up smack. At 13 years old, they shooed me away.

"This is not for you," Joaquín used to say.

Still, I fooled with all kinds of pills, with mescaline and meth. I sought the death in Silver Satin and muscatel, and then pure tequila and vodka. I snorted heroin and PCP with Payasa. By the time I turned 15, smack was everywhere. The epidemic followed a pattern in the barrio. It began with the *pachucos*. Most of the old-timers in prison, the *pachucos* of the 30s and 40s, were incarcerated because of *chiva*. Then every ten years or so a generation of ex-gang bangers became hooked. Now it was our time. Already, the older dudes in the Tribe were hypes, most of them behind bars.

Chicharrón went with me the first time I tried it. For this maiden trip, we skin-popped it in our forearms, a few "cents" worth. Lencho, who had marks up and down his arms, only gave us a taste until we could score with more money. Because Yuk

Yuk turned us into a stealing organization, this became the basis for scoring heroin.

Chicharrón and I often cruised Whittier Boulevard. Every weekend, the 14-block stretch between Atlantic Boulevard and the Long Beach Freeway became the cruising capital of the world. Lowriders from every barrio in Southern California, and often from places throughout the Southwest, congregated there. Girls sat on car tops, dressed to impress, while dudes piled into dancing "shorts" as speakers blared the latest street beat. Some of the corners were taken over by different barrios. Lomas controlled the corner of Clela Avenue and the Boulevard. The lowrider club, Groupe, allowed us use of the parking lot there. In our finest *cholo* attire, we drank, laughed, and challenged. We picked up women and fought with other barrios. Sometimes we had shoot-outs with the dudes from 18th Street who controlled the corner across from us.

So on weekends, Chicharrón and I went out on excursions, looking for good times. Being out of school, and up to our eyeballs with time to kill, this also involved hitchhiking throughout East L.A. and the San Gabriel Valley and pretending to be incoming students at local high schools for a day. It proved to be easy: We told school officials we were new students and our parents would come in the next day to sign us up. Some of the schools allowed us to figure out our courses and start attending classes. We met more girls this way. We also got into fights with the local *vatos*, one time being chased by a mob of irate boyfriends in La Verne.

Soon we had girls to visit with in Pomona, Pasadena, Norwalk, in Boyle Heights, and El Monte.

So there we were, cruising the boulevard and pulling into a side street crowded with girls. We offered them booze or pills and then slid around an alley, behind a brick wall. We drank, staggered about and had a taste of some of them by pushing a finger around the crotch of their panties and into their vaginas, then continued on our way.

Around two in the morning, we passed Atlantic Boulevard when we spotted two girls sitting at a bus stop. We pulled over. Many times girls would shine us on when it got to be this late, but one of them came up to the car. She was big, but not fat, in tight jeans. She had kinky hair and *chola*-style makeup. The other girl was thinner, cute like a china doll, with short straight hair and a party dress.

"You want a ride?" I asked from my shotgun position in the car.

"Sure, you know where there's a party?" the kinky-haired one inquired.

"No, but I'm sure we can find one."

They climbed into the car, almost too easy, and we sped on looking for some "haps." The big one was named Roberta, the cute one was Xochitl, a Nahuatl name which sounded like Shoshi, so that's what we called her.

We ended up in Legg Lake along Whittier Narrows. The park was closed but we snuck in and ran around the swing area, having our own party with the pills and booze Chicharrón had left over from before. Police cruised by and we fell to the ground, quiet as the grass, until they passed by.

That night we drove Roberta and Shoshi to barrio La Rock Mara in the Maravilla Housing Projects. Roberta said she lived in one of the duplexes there with a 21-year-old sister named Frankie, which stood for Francisca. Frankie also happened to have five children. Shoshi was a runaway who stayed with them for a while. They were both 15 years old, like us.

We sat in the car until the dawn swam in orange-red colors across the horizon. I moved over to Roberta and kissed her, while Chicharrón made out with Shoshi in the front seat. After that night, Chicharrón and I practically made this our second home.

"Oh, Louie, touch me there...*simón*, just like that...ummm."

Sweat roamed down the side of my face. The car windows steamed. I broiled, as if working in a foundry, while Roberta lay there in the back seat with her blouse open and ample breasts wet with my saliva.

"Don't stop...ummmm, don't stop."

My tongue drew circles around her nipples, which were on a dark patch over honey-brown skin. My hands rubbed her cunt from the outside of her pants. Her hips moved in waves, pushing harder and harder into my hand. She groped for my zipper, tugged and slid it down. Her fingers kneaded the top of my penis, hard and wet with anticipation.

"*Eso, así*...oh baby, lick me."

Roberta pushed me up, my back arched and my head scraped the top of the car. Then she held on to my penis with both hands while her lips smothered it and her tongue lightly flickered over the tip. After a moment, she pulled at her pants, pushing them off with her hands and feet. I looked down and saw the tuft of wild hair at the crotch, her legs spread and nearing my shoulders, inviting me to enter.

She grabbed the back of my neck and then pressed me down to her. The penis sank into the bristle of pubis, then slid into the oiled vagina, covering it in flesh and juice and rhythm of pelvis. Roberta's mouth sucked at my chest, my neck and shoulders as her fingernails scraped tracks into my back. The scent from her hair and neck filled my head as I moved and quivered inside of her.

Night after night, I stayed over at Roberta's place. Because there were many children in her house, who never appeared to fall asleep, we made love in the car, beneath the staircase, or fondled in the driveway. Chicharrón and Shoshi found their own spots. At four or five in the morning, Chicharrón and I left, grabbing some *huevos rancheros* at a 24-hour Mexican restaurant on First Street.

Sometimes Fermin, Frankie's wino husband, would show up and the fights would start; the yelling and plates being tossed against a wall, and then the poor bastard being thrown out on his ass. Frankie was one tough East L.A. mama.

But other times we had to hassle with Smokey, Roberta's brother and a member of La Rock. I stayed cool with him and he pretty much left me alone. But Chicharrón and Smokey didn't get along. I believed Smokey also liked Shoshi.

One night, after Roberta and I lay back in the car seat, following a fevered bout of lovemaking, Chicharrón rapped on the car window.

"What's up homes?" I yelled out.

He opened the door. A lead pipe filled his hand.

"I'm waiting for Smokey," he said. "He's after me. You got to back me up, *ése*."

"Ah, just leave it alone, he's only testing you," Roberta responded. "He does it to everyone — to see how tough you are."

Chicharrón didn't like being around there though. Often he took Shoshi away from there while I stayed with Roberta.

There were a few nights when I came over to see Roberta and she wasn't there.

"Man, where does she go?" I once asked Frankie.

"You don't want to know," she said.

"What do you mean, I don't want to know," I replied. "Of course I do."

"Listen, I like you Louie," Frankie confided. "So it's better you just don't ask."

But I insisted. And it was true. I shouldn't have asked.

It happened that Roberta turned tricks. This is how she could pay for staying with Frankie, and sometimes to help pay for her sister's habit. Frankie had marks on her arms — but she was careful not to get popped because she didn't want the children taken away. In fact, her husband Fermin had been an old hype who turned to the bottle. To Frankie, this was worse, and she threw him out.

A fever of emotion swept through me. The thought of Roberta selling herself to other guys for money choked on me. Frankie told me Roberta worked the Boulevard, the same place I met her.

"How come she didn't ask me for money?" I yelled. "How come she didn't even come off like a whore then?"

"Maybe she liked you from the start," Frankie submitted. "She's only a teenager, Louie. She still has feelings for men — but I don't know how long this will last."

I didn't know what to do. I wanted to rush out of there. But I felt I had to wait for Roberta to come home. I wondered if Shoshi also sold her sex and if Chicharrón knew.

"Oh, yeah, her too," Frankie said. "Not only does Chicharrón know, but he's out there pimping for her."

"Are you fucking with me!" I yelled. "How come he never told me?"

"You're a sweet dude, Louie," Frankie said, coming up to me and kissing me softly on my lips. "There's not too many of you out there. We told him not to tell you."

I started to feel tears beneath my eyes, but I wouldn't let them fall. Frankie pressed her finger on my eyelids and a drop traced down my cheek. She kissed me again. Told me how much she liked me, how she had liked me from the first day, then led me into her bedroom and closed the door.

Later that morning Smokey came by and invited me to a house across the street, situated on top of another one. We climbed a section of unkept stairs. Smokey knocked, said a few words to the door before it opened and we entered. The place had no electricity or gas. Candles were situated around a kitchen table. Hypodermic needles, spoons, matches and bags of powder were on the table. I looked around and saw about five people, including two women. They had dark circles beneath their eyes, tattoos like old *pachucas*, and collapsed veins along the inside of their arms.

Smokey was also a *tecato*, although he looked fit and muscular; if you know what you're doing you can actually live well on heroin for a while.

My head swarmed with tortuous thoughts of Roberta in somebody else's arms, but it was also my fault. I fell in love with a prostitute. Although she never asked me for money, indicating perhaps I was special, I still felt hollow inside. Smokey prepared a kit while I tightened a belt around my upper biceps. I watched the needle enter a bulging vein that Smokey brought up through the skin by slapping it with two fingers. I saw the tinge of blood enter the needle, indicating it had punctured the vein, then watched the clear liquid get pushed into the bloodstream. The sensation began like a pinhole glow at the inner pit of my stomach and then spread throughout my body. There was nothing like it, this rush, and here I was on the edges of a new fraternity which crossed barrio and sex lines, this fellowship of *la carga*, so integral to "la vida loca."

CHAPTER SIX

"There are choices you have to make not just once,
but every time they come up." — Chente

It starts with a dream. This dream creeps beyond others of sinuous ordeals, beyond demons throwing side-glances, beyond falling out of the bed and into an abyss of molten stone, beyond slipping in traffic and being unable to get up as headlights swim toward me. Then one night, a variation of the dream:

I'm in front of a house situated in a clearing among tall, moss-infested trees. The house is enormous, Gothic in style. I see myself walking toward it, leaves and branches lightly scraping the sides of my face.

I step up a creaky set of stairs with marble railings and emerge on a large empty porch. Through a walnut door, which opens without my assistance, I go through a dimly-lit hallway, the walls breathing. There are rooms on either side of me, but I venture on, ignoring them. I continue past a row of doors without doorknobs. Out of a smoky haze, another room comes into view. The door of this room opens, slowly, as I stand transfixed in front of it. The breathing walls now follow the cadence of a heartbeat.

I enter the room, a chill dampens the beads of sweat above my brow. In the center of the room is a baby's bassinet, washed in orange-red and draped in lace with ruffles along the edge, like something out of a Sears catalogue. I move toward the bassinet, deliberate, as if rehearsed. Lying there among the lace is my long-dead sister Lisa in a white baptism dress, her face in tranquil sleep like the way she looks in a picture my mother keeps in an old album.

This is where the dream usually ends, with Lisa in a death-bed of bliss.

But this time, the dream advances. This time I keep looking at the child. This time Lisa opens her eyes, so suddenly I jerk back. Only blackness stares out of them. Then the baby's mouth opens and a horrendous scream fills the room, distant yet distinct. The scream echoes through the walls, the hallway, the doors. I wake up with my hands to my ears. I enter consciousness. But the scream does not stop. It isn't in my head. It comes from the next room, where my sister Gloria sleeps.

I get up from bed and stagger into Gloria's room; she is screaming in spurts and talking nonsense. I wake up Mama, who's in the living room asleep. Soon Dad is rushing about, looking for the car keys. Gloria is dangling in Mama's arms, fading in and out of delirium. My brother Joe and sister Ana are also up, Ana in tears.

"What's wrong with her?" she cries.

No one offers an answer.

My parents take Gloria to the hospital. I look out into the early morning dark as the car speeds off. A call later informs us Gloria had ruptured her appendix and the poison had begun to invade her body. The doctors say if she were brought in only minutes later, she'd be dead.

✝ ✝ ✝

Mama gazed out of the back porch window to the garage room where I spent days holed up as if in a prison of my own making.

She worried about me, although not really knowing what I was up to; to protect herself from being hurt, she stayed uninvolved. Yet almost daily she offered quips and comments about me not attending school.

Mama called on the former principal of my elementary school in South San Gabriel to talk to me. This was the same school where Mrs. Snelling performed seeming miracles for my brother. While Joe amounted to something, to Mama I turned out to be a smudge on this earth, with no goals, no interests except what got puked up from the streets.

Bespectacled and bow-tied, Mr. Rothro wore unpressed suits which hung on his tall, lean frame. Mama knocked and I invited them in. Mr. Rothro ducked under the doorway and looked around, amazed at the magnificent disorder, the colors and scrawl on every wall, the fantastic use of the imagination for such a small room. Mama left and Mr. Rothro, unable to find a place to sit, stood around and provided an encouragement of words. Some very fine words.

"Luis, you've always struck me as an intelligent young man," Mr. Rothro said. "But your mother tells me you're wasting away your days. I'd like to see you back in school. If there's anything I can do — write a letter, make a phone call — perhaps you can return at a level worthy of your gifts."

I sat on a bed in front of an old Royal typewriter with keys that repeatedly got stuck and a carbon ribbon that kept jumping off its latch. My father gave me the typewriter after I found it among boxes, books and personal items in the garage.

"What are you doing?" Mr. Rothro inquired.

"I'm writing a book," I said, matter-of-factly.

"You're what? May I see?"

I let him glimpse at the leaf of paper in the typewriter with barely visible type, full of x's where I crossed out errors as I worked. I didn't know how to type; I just punched the letters I needed with my index fingers. It took me forever to finish a page, but I kept at it in between my other activities. By then I actually had a quarter of a ream done.

"What's the book about, son?" Rothro asked.

"Just things...what I've seen, what I feel, about the people around me. You know — things."

"Interesting," Rothro said. "In fact, I believe you're probably doing better than most teenagers — even better, I'm afraid, than some who *are* going to school."

He smiled, said he had to go but if I needed his help, not to hesitate to call.

I acknowledged his goodby and watched him leave the room and walk up to the house, shaking his head. He wasn't the first to wonder about this enigma of a boy, who looked like he could choke the life out of you one minute and then recite a poem in another.

Prior to this, I tried to attend Continuation High School in Alhambra — later renamed Century High to remove the stigma of being the school for those who couldn't make it anywhere else. After a week, they "let" me go. A few of us in Lomas fought outside with some dudes from 18th Street who were recruiting a section of their huge gang in the Alhambra area. But Continuation High School was the last stop. When you failed at Continuation, the only place left was the road.

Then my father came up with a plan; when he proposed it, I knew it arose out of frustration.

It consisted of me getting up every day at 4:30 a.m. and going with him to his job at Pierce Junior College in the San Fernando Valley — almost 40 miles away on the other side of Los Angeles. He would enroll me in Taft High School near the college. The school pulled in well-off white kids, a good number of whom were Jewish. My father felt they had the best education.

I didn't really care so I said sure, why not?

Thus we began our daily trek to a familiar and hostile place — the college was located near Reseda where the family once lived for almost a year. The risk for my father involved me finding out what he really did for a living. Dad told us he worked as a laboratory technician, how a special category had been created at Pierce College for him.

My father worked in the biology labs and maintained the science department's museum and weather station. But to me, he was an overblown janitor. Dad cleaned the cages of snakes, tarantulas, lizards and other animals used in the labs. He swept floors and wiped study tables; dusted and mopped the museum area. Dad managed some technical duties such as gathering the weather station reports, preparing work materials for students, and feeding and providing for the animals. Dad felt proud of his job — but he was only a janitor.

I don't know why this affected me. There's nothing wrong with being a janitor — and one as prestigious as my dad! But for years, I had this running fantasy of my scientist father in a laboratory carrying out vital experiments — the imagination of a paltry kid who wanted so much to break away from the constraints of a society which expected my father to be a janitor or a laborer — when I wanted a father who transformed the world. I had watched too much TV.

One day I walked into the college's science department after school.

"Mr. Rodríguez, you have to be more careful with the placement of laboratory equipment," trembled a professor's stern voice.

"I unnerstan'...Sarry...I unnerstan'," Dad replied.

"I don't think you do, this is the second time in a month this equipment has not been placed properly."

I glanced over so as not to be seen. My dad looked like a lowly peasant, a man with a hat in his hand — apologetic. At home he was king, *el jefito* — the "word." But here my father turned into somebody else's push-around. Dad should have been equals with anyone, but with such bad English...

Oh my father, why don't you stand up to them? Why don't you be the man you are at home?

I turned away and kept on walking.

The opportunity for me to learn something new became an incentive for attending Taft High School. At Keppel and Continuation, I mainly had industrial arts classes. So I applied for classes which stirred a little curiosity: photography, advanced art, and literature. The first day of school, a Taft High School counselor called me into her office.

"I'm sorry, young man, but the classes you chose are filled up," she said.

"What do you mean? Isn't there any way I can get into any of them?"

"I don't believe so. Besides, your transcripts show you're not academically prepared for your choices. These classes are privileges, for those who have maintained the proper grades in the required courses. And I must add, you've obtained most of what credits you do have in industrial-related courses."

"I had to — that's all they'd give me," I said. "I just thought, maybe, I can do something else here. It seems like a good school and I want a chance to do something other than with my hands."

"It doesn't work that way," she replied. "I think you'll find our industrial arts subjects more suited to your needs."

I shifted in my seat and looked out the window.

"Whatever."

The classes she enrolled me in were print shop, auto shop and weight training. I did manage a basic English literature class. I walked past the photography sessions and stopped to glimpse the students going in and out, some with nice cameras, and I thought about how I couldn't afford those cameras anyway: *Who needs that stupid class?*

In print shop I worked the lead foundry for the mechanical Linotype typesetter. I received scars on my arms due to splashes of molten lead. In auto shop, I did a lot of tune-ups, oil changes and some transmission work. And I lifted weights and started to bulk up. The one value I had was being the only Mexican in school — people talked about it whenever I approached.

One day at lunch time, I passed a number of hefty dudes in lettered jackets. One of them said something. Maybe it had nothing to do with me. But I pounced on him anyway. Several teachers had to pull me off.

They designated me as violent and uncontrollable; they didn't know "what to do with me."

After school, I walked to Pierce College and waited for Dad to finish his work so we could go home, which usually went past dark. I spent many evenings in the library. But I found most books boring and unstimulating.

I picked up research and history books and went directly to the index and looked up "Mexican." If there were a few items under this topic, I read them; I read them all.

Every day I browsed, ventured into various sections of shelves; most of this struck me with little interest. One evening, I came across a crop of new books on a special shelf near the front of the library. I picked one up, then two. The librarian looked at me through the side of her eye, as if she kept tabs on whoever perused those books.

They were primarily about the black experience, works coming out of the flames which engulfed many American cities in the 1960s. I discovered Claude Brown's *Manchild In The Promised Land*, Eldridge Cleaver's *Soul On Ice*, and the *Autobiography of Malcolm X*. I found poetry by Don L. Lee and LeRoi Jones (now known as Haki R. Madhubuti and Amiri Baraka, respectively). And a few books by Puerto Ricans and Chicanos: Victor Hernández Cruz's *Snaps* and Ricardo Sánchez's *Canto Y Grito: Mi Liberacion* were two of them. Here were books with a connection to me.

And then there was Piri Thomas, a Puerto Rican brother, *un camarada de aquellas*: His book *Down These Mean Streets* became a living Bible for me. I dog-eared it, wrote in it, copied whole passages so I wouldn't forget their texture, the passion, this searing work of a street dude and hype in Spanish Harlem — a barrio boy like me, on the other side of America.

I didn't last long at Taft High School. My only real friend was Edwin, a black dude who lived at the Pacific Boys Home. During lunch hour, we "worked" the neighborhood: breaking into the nearby fancy houses. Edwin eventually got popped stealing a car and ended up in youth camp.

There were a few Jewish lowriders I talked with in auto shop. We shared ideas about hydraulic lifts and pinstripe body designs. They even sported *cholo*-style clothes, slicked their hair back, and learned a few street songs and dances. But nobody else dealt with me.

One day I came in slightly late to my English Lit class and sat down; I placed a book on top of the desk. The teacher walked up to me and picked up the book.

"*American Me* by Beatrice Griffith," he said. "Where did you get this book?"

"It's a library book — it's about the *pachuco* experience in the 1940s."

"Sounds good, but the book you were to bring here today was Wordsworth's *Preludes*. That is your assignment, not *American Me*."

"This book is something I'd like to read. I can even do a report on it."

"Young man, you don't decide your assignments in this class. If you can't participate like the rest of us, I suggest you leave."

"Fine — who gives a fuck what I want!"

I stormed out of there. Needless to say, this was my last day in the English Lit class.

But the teachers' strike of 1970 was the real reason I stopped going to Taft. The strike lasted a couple of months. But when the teachers settled with the Los Angeles School Board, I stayed out; I felt the school district hadn't settled with me yet.

I ended up back in the streets. Somehow, though, it wasn't the same as before. A power pulsed in those books I learned to savor, in the magical hours I spent in the library — and it called me back to them.

Sometimes I roamed the street with nothing to do and ended up in a library. Later on my own I picked up Wordsworth, Poe, Emerson and Whitman. Chicharrón and the others noticed the difference. Chicharrón even called me the "businessman" because whenever he'd ask me about the books I carried, I would say: "Just taking care of business."

I also learned not to be angry with my father. I learned something about my father's love, which he never expressed in words, but instead, at great risk, he gave me the world of books — a gift for a lifetime.

ᛉ ᛉ ᛉ

I lay, sprawled on the bed. Jazz sounds emanated from a stereo player, saxes everywhere. Loud knocking picked up the beat. They were Chicharrón's knocks; I could tell.

"Get in here," I yelled, bothered for being bothered.

"What's up homes?" Chicharrón greeted. Somebody walked in behind him, some *lambe*, who tripped on the threshold.

"Who's the shadow?" I asked.

"This is Arnie," Chicharrón said. "Arnie, meet Chin."

Arnie stuck his hand out. I ignored it. I gave Chicharrón a look like "what gives here?" Chicharrón grinned and shrugged his shoulders.

"Arnie? What kind of name is that?"

"It stands for Arnulfo."

"*Qué jodida* — that's even worse."

I grabbed a bottle of Silver Satin wine and offered it to Arnie.

"Take a *trago*, man."

"What...what's a....I don't understand."

"What's the matter, don't you know anything?"

"I don't speak Spanish."

"It's mostly English, poop butt," I responded, then looked hard at Chicharrón. "Man, where did you find this dude?"

I handed Arnie the bottle. He took a swig, swallowed it as if it were a ball in his throat, then just about fell down on the floor.

"Whew, is that strong!" Arnie finally said through a shriveled face.

"Yea, it packs a punch."

"Hey homes," Chicharrón clipped in. "How about getting some *refín*?"

"You're all the time eating."

"I know and so what — let's make our squints."

I left the sounds on the stereo, and together we walked into the night. We made it to a big boulevard in Rosemead. Faces, gestures, street signs came and went. We infiltrated a packed sidewalk, winding through Christmas shoppers, above us multi-colored lights, in front of us a mall resounding in chorales. Suddenly neon, on top of a stuffed restaurant.

"This looks like the place," Chicharrón suggested.

We made our entrance. Waiters and busboys were dressed up in white shirts, black vests and bow ties; the counter girls were in pleated, plaid skirts with ribbons on their hair. Arnie looked uncomfortable, but I got the feeling he always did.

A hostess approached and offered us a table.

"Hey, we must rate around here," Chicharrón said.

"Yeah, we rate all right," I said. "They'd like us to get through as fast as possible so we can get the hell out."

At our table, surrounded by family-type folk, I ordered the largest cheeseburger with fries and the biggest tastiest milk shake on the menu. Chicharrón, not to be outdone, asked for a bacon, lettuce and tomato sandwich, with all the trims, and a super-duper banana split. Arnie looked amazed at us, and ordered a tuna sandwich.

"Hey Arnie — *homeboy*," I responded with a furrowed brow. "You don't go to a fancy place like this and order a tuna sandwich. Go for the works, *ése!*"

Conceding, Arnie added a pie a la mode. I nodded approval. Once the food came, we got down to some heavy-duty chowing.

We rushed through the orders, then the time came to consider the bill. I looked at it, then moved my eyes toward Arnie.

Arnie looked at me, smiled, but — catching on — changed into a frown.

"Now, don't look at me," he said. "I, I didn't bring any money."

Not the right response.

"No money, what's with you man?" Chicharrón scolded.

"I thought you guys were inviting me. How was I supposed to know..."

"Forget it, dude," I said, already planning the next move. "Listen, it's no problem. We'll just take the long walk to the exit — and then run like your mother made you."

"What are you saying? Just walk out and not pay?" Arnie asked.

"Shhhh! You want to make an announcement or what?" I said. "Listen, I ain't got no *feria*, Chicharrón and you ain't got none. There's only one thing to do."

I motioned my head toward the door.

"¡A la brava! Understand?"

"Yeah, sure," Chicharrón agreed. "There's a lot of people in the place. There's a line at the cash register. It's a good time to esgüintar."

"I don't know about this you guys," Arnie protested. "I never done this before."

"It's no big deal, a piece of taco," I reassured him. "You guys just get up and walk out like nothin' is happenin'. I'll go to the head, to distract them, but we all can't go — that's a sure sign we're walking. I'll be right behind you."

"I don't know about this, you guys," Arnie repeated.

"Well, Arnie, you can stay here an' wash dishes, cuz we is jammin'."

I got up and shuffled cool-like to the restroom. Once inside, I combed my hair. Scraped at a hang nail. Checked out a blemish. Then I straightened up and pushed out the restroom doors, heading toward the exit. I didn't look around, just straight in front of me. People appeared too busy talking, eating and having a good time to notice a cholo make his way out the door.

Almost outside, I took in a deep breath, stepped onto the pavement and tried to walk away when two Frankensteins came up from behind and intervened. I went to hit one, but the other grabbed my arm and pulled me to the ground. A woman shrieked. I could see faded images of people who stopped to look on as we battled on the sidewalk. I punched and pulled, but the dudes held me there on the ground. As soon as I calmed, they lifted me up as if I were a trapped rat and dragged me through the restaurant. Some people were already on their feet, others stunned in their chairs, all looking at me in a hush. I felt like I should get applause.

The Frankensteins pushed me through a storage area behind the restaurant and into a small office. A partly-bald man with a loosened tie over a wrinkled white shirt sat there, looking tired.

"Go ahead, sit down," he told me, then turned to the Frankensteins. "Thank you. You did good."

The dudes gave me a last look, like maybe they should've broken my arm or something.

"Just called the police," the baldy said. "They'll be here any minute."

I sat there expressionless.

"What's your name, kid?"

I looked at him.

"What's *your* name — kid?" I answered.

Surprisingly, he laughed.

"The name is Kearney — Charles Kearney."

Kearney looked at me with some interest behind a pile of papers.

"May I ask why you did it?"

"I was hungry."

"Don't you have food at home?"

"Sometimes, but I don't live at home."

"You've been arrested before, I gather."

"Here and there — lightweight stuff."

"Well, what you did was wrong," Kearney explained. "It's against the law to order food, eat it and not pay for it. It's stealing!"

"I know."

He shuffled one pile of papers to another.

"How old are you?"

"Going on sixteen."

He shook his head.

"And you don't have a home to go to, huh?"

I crossed my right leg over my left, placed my arms across the legs, and looked straight at Kearney.

"Listen Mr. Kurley — or whatever your name is. I was hungry. I don't have no money. So I got something to eat. My moms works hard for the family. She don't like me doing this, and I know she feels bad 'cause she can't get enough for us. It's not her fault. She threw me out of the house for being an asshole. So I can't cry about it. I just have to make it on my own, do what I can to keep the pressure off moms and the family. You know what I'm talking about?"

"But stealing is against the law."

"I understand I did wrong. I'm not making excuses. You caught me, up and up. I'll go to jail."

I paused, looked around the place a little, then back at Kearney.

"Don't get me wrong, I don't like jail. They beat you in jail, but like I said: No excuses."

"What do you mean — they beat you in jail?"

"Yeah, man, the cops," I responded. "They beat on us all the time. Especially them sheriffs. They're the worst. They don't care if you're hungry, if you have a job or not, or anything about hurting your moms who works so hard. They want control over you, including over your life. That's a fact. That's the way of the neighborhood."

Kearney looked intently at me.

"I don't know about any of this, all I know is you did wrong. You stole from me. You have to pay something for it."

"I don't mind that. The problem is we end up paying more for the same thing than other people do. On this side of town, the cops don't beat up people. On this side of town, the cops don't stop you for no reason. They don't be hitting you in the head, trying to make you mad so you do something you'll regret later."

"I don't mind paying for my mistakes," I added. "But it seems like we're paying for everyone else's mistakes too. Sometimes we pay even when there's been no mistake. Just for being who we are, you know what I mean? Just for being Mexican. That's all the wrong I have to do."

Kearney mulled over my words in silence. Soon a sheriff's deputy entered the office. I recognized the ugly scar across his cheek. It belonged to Cowboy.

Kearney looked up at Cowboy, then at me. Cowboy recognized me too.

"What do we have here!" Cowboy exclaimed. "Chin, my man. Yeah, this is going to be fun — right Chin?"

"You know him?" Kearney asked me.

"Sure," I said with disgust. "He's one of those sheriffs I was telling you about."

"Listen, Mr. Kearney, don't let these punk kids con you into anything," Cowboy said. "If you ask me, they all need a swift kick in the behind."

Cowboy pulled out a note pad and prepared to ask Kearney questions. But Kearney did a most startling thing.

"It's okay, officer, I don't want to press charges."

Cowboy smiled and removed a pencil from his jacket.

"I know how it looks, but don't feel sorry for these clowns," Cowboy responded. "They'd just as soon shoot you as steal from you."

"I understand, but it's all right," Kearney persisted. "I don't want you to take him. I'll take care of this."

"Are you nuts?" Cowboy lost his patience. "This guy is bad news. I know him. He's been arrested so many times, his record could cover the floor."

Man, I thought, Cowboy wants me so bad he could taste it.

"No, officer, I'm sorry for having called you and making you come all the way down here," Kearney insisted. "But this is my final decision. I'm not going to let you take him."

Cowboy's face turned red, infuriated. He jammed the pencil back into his jacket and stuffed the note pad into his back pants pocket. He turned toward me, fire in his eyes and a tremble in his lip. Then, without a word, he swung around on his boots and left, slamming the door behind him.

What a relief! I already imagined the beating Cowboy had in store for me.

"Look kid," Kearney said. "I want you to get out of here. Don't misunderstand what I've done. I don't want to see you in my restaurant ever again, you hear?"

"That's fine with me — and thanks."

Kearney allowed me to leave out the back door. I cross-looked down the alley. I sensed Cowboy lurking around somewhere, waiting for me.

I sprinted up the alley.

"*Orale*, homes," a voice came at me from some bushes. I looked over and saw Chicharrón emerge through the branches with a piece of pipe in his hand.

"*Chingao*, am I glad to see you," I said. "You been here all this time?"

"Sure, man, I saw them get you," Chicharrón explained. "So I hid back here and then Cowboy parked and went inside. I figured as soon as he brought you out, I'd bash him over the head with this pipe. But he came out alone. What the hell happened?"

"You'll never believe it," I said. "I can't hardly believe it myself. I'll tell you later."

Then I looked around for Arnie.

"What happened to the *lambe*."

"Arnie — that *puto*! As soon as I get the pipe and tell him what we're going to do, he babbles some nonsense about us being crazy and takes off running."

"No matter," I said. "Let's get out of here before Cowboy finds us."

✞ ✞ ✞

Chente entered the John Fabela Youth Center, the place dense with smoke, and the slow-talk and laughter of *vatos* and *rucas*. As director of the center's activities, Chente played administrator, father-figure, counselor and the law. But he had to do it through strength of character. With style. He knew these teenagers didn't respect imposed authority.

Chente opened up classes at the center such as martial arts, arts & crafts and photography. New government programs existed then for agencies like the Bienvenidos Community Center, which ran the youth center; Chente tapped into some of these funds to provide Lomas its first and only recreational facility.

Chente eyed me standing with Chata and Trudy, and came by.

"Luis, I'd like to ask you something."

"Go ahead dude."

"In my office, it's a little quieter."

I followed Chente to a small room with ancient metal files and a carved-up desk. I stood next to a window which overlooked the billiard-playing area.

"I got a job for you," he said. "It's part of the Neighborhood Youth Corps. We got funded for several slots. I'd like for you to have one of them."

"What do I have to do?"

"Well most of the jobs involve cleaning up parks, painting, carpentry and alley maintenance," he said. "I want you to run one of the crews. We'll be hiring next week, but you have to sign up. It's for families below the poverty level. What do you say?"

"Sure, you know I ain't working right now."

"There's one catch though," Chente said, looking intently at me. "I want you to consider going to school next semester — to Keppel."

"What for? I've had it with school. Anyway, they don't want me at Keppel."

"Listen, there's going to be some changes," Chente informed me. "Keppel is getting a new principal, Mr. Madison. He says he wants to meet with the students from Lomas. We're working on this now. Some of the community have already met with him and he's agreed to provide a Chicano Student Center, a full-time Youth Adviser and — get this — a school club for Chicano students."

"No! What a change, man."

"I'd like for you to go back and get involved. We need strong leaders. We need intelligent voices. We're going to make deep changes and you're one person who can help make them."

"Are you sure?"

"Believe me, I'm sure — what do you say?"

"I don't know, man. Let me think about it."

"Okay, all right. You have a whole summer still," Chente said, shaking my hand. "And don't forget to come back next week for the job."

By summer, I worked on an NYC crew. We took an old flatbed truck with wood planks on the sides to use on the various cleanup sites. We piled up the back of the truck with junk which had been dumped on the roadways, parks, empty lots, and abandoned buildings. From there we trekked over to the dump to unload it. We also hung wallboard, did light carpentry and some electrical, and helped build the new day-care and student dropout center next to the John Fabela Center.

Community projects popped up all over. The government brought out a number of teen programs and job placements. Activists came into Lomas with various ideas. They opened up a food co-op run by the Lomas mothers. They hired consultants, grant writers and fundraisers.

I became deeply involved at the center. On weekends, I woke up at 3 a.m. to go with some parents to the farmer's market in downtown L.A. and pick up crates of fruits and vegetables for the food co-op. During the week, I worked a regular day shift cleaning up the neighborhood. Then in the evenings, I hung around the youth center, often volunteering for various programs, including giving out bags of groceries for families without food.

One time a man named Daniel Fuentes came in to sign up dudes for amateur boxing. There were a number of tournaments opening up: the Junior Olympics, the Junior Golden Gloves, the Golden Gloves and Olympics. I decided to try boxing. Fuentes ran the boxing club out of his house in the Hills. We used the almost-collapsing auditorium of the elementary school just below Graves Avenue to work out. We ran laps around the school's play yard.

On the days we sparred, Fuentes piled up all the guys into his hand-painted black station wagon and had us ply the rings at the Main Street Gym in downtown L.A. or at a makeshift gym in a South El Monte warehouse.

Fuentes demanded so much of us. He knew he had mostly undisciplined, could-give-a-fuck street dudes to shape up. He had to make skilled boxers out of some difficult, raw material. But he had one thing in his favor: We had guts.

The first days of training, we tried to look like bad-ass dudes with our high fists and our bouncy stances. Fuentes had his son Steve go a couple of rounds with us. At 18, Steve was an experienced amateur, having won a few local titles with almost 100 fights under his belt. He didn't look like a homeboy. But when he got us in the ring, he tore us to pieces. We had no defenses. We had no combinations. We understood nothing about balance, footwork or even where to place our eyes when we fought.

"You guys think you're the toughest people around," Fuentes said. "Well, you wouldn't last a round in an amateur fight. But this is going to change."

Every evening we did our laps around the elementary school. On certain occasions, Fuentes dragged us to East L.A. College where we ran our butts off around a large track field. Fuentes taught us how to hit the heavy bags, use the speed bag and jump rope, and he helped build up our shoulders and chest areas.

"The power doesn't come from your arms," he said. "It comes from your shoulders. You put the force of your whole body into a punch. This way, you make every punch count."

Rubén Navarro — also known as The Maravilla Kid — was then a contender for the world's featherweight title. The Maravilla Kid became our sponsor. We were then known as the Maravilla Kid's United Teen Pugs.

The Maravilla Kid would pay a visit every other week or so. He drove up in a classic 1930s motorcar, all stocked and shiny. He emerged in a long wool coat, silk shirts and fedora hat. A lot of the dudes lit up at the sight of him. Sometimes a blonde woman sat beside the Kid as he watched us work out.

One day, I sparred with this dude we called Left Brain. The Maravilla Kid looked at us for a while, then got up and stopped us.

"What do you think you're doing?" he demanded.

We didn't have any words.

"Tell me, I want you to explain what you're doing."

"I'm trying to protect myself and wait for an opening," Left Brain offered.

"Protect yourself?"

Then the Maravilla Kid threw a slap from his left side and smacked Left Brain solid on his cheek. Everybody else stopped what they were doing. Left Brain stood there, embarrassed and hurt.

"I didn't see you protect yourself," The Kid said. "This is what happens when somebody really hits you. I want you guys to go at it for real. Not this paddy-cake shit. When you're in the ring, nobody is going to play paddy-cake with you."

The Kid turned toward me, a look of disdain on his face.

"And you, I want you to go at him like he just spit on your mother."

Whenever the Kid came, everything turned up a few notches. Sometimes Fuentes got frustrated. He had his own way of training. But the Kid wanted some trophies. He wanted our names to spell fear for the other amateur clubs. He wanted us to take the Golden Gloves and Olympic championships.

The competition between the various boxing clubs in and around L.A. was fierce, almost deadly. A lot rode on the boxing business for Chicanos. Fuentes argued long and hard with the Maravilla Kid about funds. We needed gloves, we needed bags, we needed so many things, but the Kid would only say "in time."

Soon I came home with the whites of my eyes glazed in red because of broken blood vessels; bruises and welts on my nose, cheeks and mouth. After a heavy night of working out, I'd still work the next day at my Neighborhood Youth Corps job, all beat up and sore.

I had a few fights for trophies with clubs from East L.A., Pomona, Azusa, the L.A. Harbor and South Central L.A. They consisted of three torturous rounds. We put so much into each round, so many blows and energy, that most of us practically died of exhaustion by the end of a bout.

My skills weren't very good. But I had what they called heart. I came to kill. I rushed up to my opponents and mowed them down. Not much of the sweet science, I must say. The Maravilla Kid didn't mind, as long as I won fights.

Fuentes asked me to try for the Junior Olympics tournament. I had bulked up to middleweight. The dudes in this division were harder-hitting but not so big they weren't able to move around and rouse up excitement. The competition proved stronger and better trained. Most of the boxers came from clubs with more money and prestige. The Maravilla Kid's United Teen Pugs were like everybody's sick stepchild. Because of our lack of resources, we had this added pressure to be better.

My big chance to make the top of the tournament came with a bout at the Lorena Street Gym in the basement of a church in East L.A. Fuentes worked to build up my confidence.

"This is your big break," Fuentes said. "If anyone can make it, you can."

In my enthusiasm, I invited my whole family to see me: My mother, my brother and sisters showed up for the match; the first time they had anything to do with me in months.

The place was packed with spectators. Clubs from all over L.A. came to box. Most of the clubs' fighters consisted of blacks or Latinos, boxing for us being the proverbial way out.

Fuentes and his assistant, this old pro named Winky, who had slurred speech and the cartilage removed from his nose from being battered so many years ago, gathered the Teen Pugs in the back of the gym for a pep talk. I sat there along with the others — in maroon boxer shorts, shoes, a towel around my shoulders, and Winky going through the ritual of wrapping tape around my hands to protect them from getting broken.

"This is a big fight for you guys," Fuentes said. "But I believe there's no better fighters in the world than those sitting right here. You've trained hard, considering the conditions we have to work under. But remember the one who wins is the one with the most *jaspia*. If you guys don't have this, I don't know who does."

Jaspia meant hunger and Fuentes often yelled it at us from the corner to remind us of our motivation.

Hector Sorillo came in, late as usual, with the arms of a pretty, light-skinned Chicana named Delfina around his shoulders. The club's best fighter and Steve's former stable mate, Hector obtained most of the trophies and glory. I believed Fuentes hated him because Hector threw his weight around, but the Kid praised him to the gods.

"Hector, you're looking too pretty," Fuentes said. "This is a fight. Get your gear on. You're good, but not that good."

Delfina sat next to me while I waited my turn to enter the ring. She had on a going-out lavender dress which crinkled when she moved; her light-brown hair piled up nice around her flawless face. I sat there relaxed, gloves on hands and sweat dripping on my lap.

"How you doing Louie?" Delfina asked. She never talked to me before.

"Not too bad — I got my family out there."

"You nervous."

"All the time. But Fuentes thinks I'm going to do good here."

"What do you think?"

"I think I better think what Fuentes thinks."

Our team went about half and half with losses and victories. Hector and Steve won their bouts, and even Left Brain managed a victory. But the other dudes were losing. There were some great teams out there. Winky then came in, gestured to me and said: "You're next."

I stepped up to the ring. People were sitting on fold-up chairs scattered throughout every corner of the gym. As I climbed the ring, I saw my pudgy mom at ringside, Joe and my sisters around her. I could tell she wasn't enjoying herself. But she came out for me and I felt I had to win this one for her.

Fuentes climbed up with me. The referees gave both fighters the rules. The rounds were three-minutes long. We had on safety helmets and mouthpieces. The judges were officials of the Junior Olympics tournament. The winner of this bout would move up to the next level of tournament, leading to finals at the famous Olympic Auditorium in downtown L.A. As everybody left the ring area but the fighters and referee, I heard Fuentes say: "¡*Jaspia!*"

The bell rang. My hands flew up. I rushed to the middle of the ring. *Aquí estoy* — come and get me! The other warrior came up to me. Despite the crowd's yelling and the countless faces turned toward us, I never felt more alone with another human being than in a boxing ring.

We rattled each other with blows. I came at him the way I usually did, throwing fists from all directions. I pushed the dude around the ring. He tried to get out of the way of the onslaught, dipping and pivoting. I followed his movement by looking straight at his chest, to tell which direction his arms were coming from.

Whenever I entered a boxing ring, I became obsessed. I threw so many blows, most people couldn't get out of the way. But this dude in front of me proved no sucker. He knew how to get away from many of the punches, gliding and slipping beneath my gloves. He threw only enough at me to keep himself in competition — a clever ruse. I needed to really box him, not just throw blows; otherwise I would find myself punched-out.

The first round ended. People were on their seats and clamoring for more. Fuentes gave me a smile and said: "You got him. He's yours."

I peeked over to my mother who just sat there, very still. My sisters whooped and hollered. My brother flashed a grin. I felt great. I must win; so many people depended on it.

The bell rang and I jumped up — ready for my last dance. I jabbed and jabbed.

"¡*Pégale, pégale!*" somebody yelled from my corner.

But halfway through the round, my arms became impediments. The weight of the gloves brought my hands below my waist. I wanted to yell as I used every ounce of strength to keep them up, but this took away from my ability to hit. My opponent's ruse worked: I tired.

There is no pain like being exhausted in the ring — except labor pains, but this explains what I mean. Professionals know this feeling in later rounds; it's as close to dying as one can get while alive. Every blow opens up something inside, tearing at your resolve while tearing up skin.

The weight of my gloves became intolerable. Amateurs wore heavier gloves than professionals, weighing eight ounces, but in the ring they might as well be anvils. I heard *pégale, pégale*, but I just couldn't. The dude in front of me backed up and jitterbugged. He threw clean shots — on my arms, my kidneys, through the safety helmet. I cringed with every blow I returned. *When is the bell going to ring?* Everything took forever. The hand motions, mouths and voices around me were all in an aggravating slow motion. ¡*Jaspia, Jaspia!* I ducked and swayed. I backed up and felt a barrier of ropes push me back in. *Where the hell is this bell!*

Finally the bell exploded in sound, and the round ended before a merciful knockout. It ended and I wanted to go home. Suddenly regret overcame me. I knew then, the dude had me. I went back to my corner, barely able to sit down. Fuentes showed concern but only said *jaspia*. I did not look over to my family.

After a minute's rest, another bell signaled the coming agony of the last and third round. This is the one where you're supposed to give it all you've got. *Lo chingaré.* I rushed out as in the first round. I let the excitement of the yells and screams around me pull the strength to give my opponent the best blows I had. I pushed him around the ring again. It looked good for me. In a glimpse, I saw Fuentes and Winky with their arms in the air, shouting in delight. Then out of nowhere, like a hammer, a fist struck me square in the nose. I flew back, and down on one knee. Blood came out in globs from my nose, a sign it was fractured.

The referee pushed the dude back. I heard my opponent say: "¡Ya estuvo, ése!"

I made it to my feet. The referee asked me something. I just nodded. Everything looked fuzzy in front of me. The referee looked hard at me and asked me something again. I only remembered an incoherent whisper. Then the referee went over to the other dude and raised up his arm in triumph. Not even an eight count. I stood there, a hero of disgust, a fallen warrior. Fuentes came up to me and untied my gloves.

"You did good. We'll get him next time."

Winky brought a towel and crammed a section of it up my nose.

"It's got to be looked at, Dan," he said to Fuentes.

I saw Delfina peering at me from behind Hector, who stood all showered and smug in his clothes. It looked like Delfina tried to tell me something with her eyes, something to ease the loss.

My eyes crossed over several rows of faces to the direction of my family. They were all on their feet. My sisters had their hands up to their mouths. Joe looked awkward, like he didn't know whether to congratulate me for trying or to give his condolences. And Mama — I could see Mama had been crying.

☦ ☦ ☦

Jorge's Junk Yard on Garvey Avenue shone like a metal-and-glass city beneath the sun's afternoon radiance; automobile carcasses piled on top of one another, all symmetrical and sloping as if rusty mountain ranges galloping through a desert plain. We curled our fingers through a section of mesh fence and stared at the steel, paint and rubber wreckage of a 1969 Chevrolet sedan.

The day before, Yuk Yuk and Daddio had chug-a-lugged several pints of tequila, as in the old country where men of leather tamed the wilds of land and animal only to be enslaved by the maguey's juice, fueled by the residue of herbs, the ferment of harvests — quenching a deeper thirst.

Later the sky brought down a stinging rain, and Yuk Yuk and Daddio stole a car and then strolled into a convenience store on San Gabriel Boulevard. But something went wrong. There was shooting. They ran out the glass doors, climbed into the car and took off toward the Pomona Freeway — sheriff's units and a helicopter gave chase as Yuk Yuk pushed the *ranfla* some 120 miles per hour on a down slope and failed to make the upturn. According to the medical examiner, the sedan rolled over so many times that Yuk Yuk and Daddio "practically disintegrated" before the car lodged near an abandoned warehouse, across from a hobo's nest with spiritless bodies loitering by the railroad tracks.

The next day people visited the wrecking yard, taking turns examining the jagged monument to our homeboys and paying their respects before the car's remains are removed and crumpled into a rectangular object, to be feed for a blast furnace somewhere; the steam of their being becoming water, becoming what is expelled from our breaths, becoming what keeps us alive.

✢ ✢ ✢

I sat among learners and teachers in our fourth or fifth study session — I had already lost track — with a group Chente called "the collective."

I came once just to check it out, perhaps to get Chente off my back. But after the first time, I kept coming. The group studied politics, philosophy, economics — the dynamics of social revolution. There was something about the way Chente and the others made sense; the way they made dead things come alive — how they took what seemed obvious and proved the direct opposite. The words were a fascinating revelation for me. Another culture. I had never experienced anything like it. Here all perceptions were challenged. Here knowledge, this elusive dove which had never before found a landing near my grasp, could be gently held — where it would not fly away.

The sessions also involved Sergio, his wife Ofelia, Octavio and Skin. They were activists and students. They were sons and daughters of factory hands, mechanics and truck drivers who lived in and around East Los Angeles. They met weekly in a house in the Hills where Sergio, who was studying to be a doctor, lived. We kept the location a secret; real names and places could not be uttered over the telephone.

From one of the readings came a statement which stayed in my mind: *"An invitation to abandon illusions about a situation, is an invitation to abandon a situation in need of illusions."*

But on that particular day everything felt in disarray. I did not participate in my usual manner. The constant questioning, inquiries which entertained but also had something daring — or foolish — in the asking, failed to materialize. The others were there with me, but I was not with them. They sensed something was wrong.

The group delved into the social processes governing events in the world and the United States. But I looked strangely at the book in front of me as someone read a passage out loud. I only saw contorted faces on the pages. Between the lines of type, I saw mouths wailing and eyes filled with terror. I saw what I was living. And although I tried to participate, that night I only saw my homeboys and homegirls dying.

I laid my head back, distracted. The fascinating prose turned ethereal — the profundity lost on an empty field somewhere in the barrio.

"I think we should call it quits for tonight," Skin said, her eyes aimed at me. I looked down to a pattern on a rug which covered a section of hardwood floor and appeared to flow with rivers and birds and tropical scents.

Chairs were pushed back. Coffee cups gathered. Dishes clanged in the kitchen.

I slowly stood up. Everything around me spun. Voices melted away. I plunged back into the sofa's softness. Ofelia's voice broke through a din in my head.

"Luis, what's the matter. You messed up or what?"

Yeah, I'm messed up. Good and messed up, in some cloud, a voyager on a misty ship, floating through the lamp shades, the pots of greenery by the sunlit window — through the forest of a woman's hair.

Others gathered around me, staring at me; waiting for me to say something. But my voice stayed in my head. I looked at Sergio's bearded face, at Ofelia's concerned eyes, at Chente — good ol' Chente, calm as ever — and Skin, with a flowery Indian blouse from Mexico which made her look like what I imagined a Mayan princess to be.

Warriors would die for you, Skin. They would climb steep mountains, swim vast seas and destroy armies for you, deity of sauntering, Goddess of aura and bloom.

But soon, I felt shame. I couldn't tell them what I had done. Why I felt like running and running, without ever stopping.

The others picked up their materials and left. But Chente stayed to walk me out. We went outside; the fresh air slapped me across the face.

"All right Luis," Chente demanded. "Tell me what's going on."

"It's nothing, homes."

"Then let me tell you," Chente said, his voice firm. "You're on something again. I've seen it many times. Only now there is no turning back for you."

"Listen, I know I did wrong. I didn't want to do it. But ever since Yuk Yuk and Daddio got killed, the rest of us have needed to get high. And Santos and Lencho came across some good shit — "

"Where were you?"

"In the fields, *ése* — I know, I know, I should never have gone there," I said. "But, it's my neighborhood, man. I'm there bulljiving, just passing the time. And they had a little bit of *la carga...*"

"¡*Hijo*!" Chente interrupted. "You said you'd stop taking dope to study with us. You know what it does: dulling your thinking, your actions. What are you going to do when it makes mincemeat out of your brains?"

"Don't get *escamao*," I replied. "I didn't take a lot — just took a taste, you know."

"Sometimes you need it," I added, looking into the distance. "Sometimes you can't always be on top of things, Chente. You ever think about that, *ése*?"

"Sure, Luis, I think about it all the time."

Chente turned away and walked toward the car parked in the alley. He gazed at the wood fences and brick walls with markings that have been there for 30 or 40 years. Names upon names. Nobody ever erased them. The graffiti stayed and every new generation just put their *placa* over the old.

Chente surveyed the walls, tired of what they represented: pain, a mark in this world, often death. He then turned toward me.

"I'm sure it feels good to get messed up once in a while," Chente said. "To let it all go. But the fight for a better life won't stop just because you aren't ready. What we're doing is not something you decide to do when you feel like it. Whether you're ready or not, this struggle will go on. You're a *vato loco*. For you the world is one big *chingaso* after another — and some good dope. But you have to make a choice now. Either the craziness and violence — or here, learning and preparing for a world in which none of this is necessary."

Chente reached for the keys in his pocket and opened the car door. Just before stepping inside, he threw me another look; I could see he didn't want to give up on me yet. But he always told me: People give up on themselves first.

"Luis, you don't have to study with us to make me happy or the collective proud of you," Chente explained. "There are a lot of people involved in your life now. When you win, we win; but when you go down, you go down alone."

Chapter Seven

"When the hanging's done and the embers at the burning stake are grayed and cold, the conquered bodies of martyrs become the unconquerable ideas."
— Nelson Peery

August 29, 1970: Tens of thousands gathered in East L.A.'s Belvedere Park to protest the Viet Nam War. The organizers placed flyers on lampposts and bus stops with the following statistics: 22 percent of the war's casualties came from Spanish-speaking communities — although this population made up less than six percent of the U.S. total!

The ensuing march and demonstration — called the Chicano Moratorium Against The War — became the largest anti-war rally ever held in a minority community.

I jumped on a bumpy bus from South San Gabriel and exited on Beverly Boulevard and Third Street, toward Belvedere Park. When I arrived, people carried signs denouncing the war, including a few which said "Chicano Power." The Brown Berets, both men and women, in military-style tan, fatigue clothing, marched in cadence on Third Street. A man with a bull horn shouted slogans: "No More War," "¡Chale! We Won't Go" and "¡Qué Viva La Raza!"

The slogans incited the crowd to chants. Signs and fists pierced the sky. Conga drum beats swirled around a grouping of people at one end of the park. I melded among the protesters, dressed in street attire and my favorite blue Pendleton shirt. When the marching started, I threw a fist into the air.

We advanced down Atlantic Boulevard, past stretches of furniture stores, used car lots and cemeteries. Store owners closed early, pulling across rusty iron enclosures. Young mothers with infants in strollers, factory hands, gang-bangers, a newly-wed couple in wedding dress and tuxedo — young and old alike — strolled beside me.

We snaked around to Whittier Boulevard where people from the neighborhood joined in the march; some offered us water and food. Battles between police and young dudes flared up in alleys and side streets. Thrown bottles smashed the windshields of squad cars.

The protesters pulled into Laguna Park in the heart of the largest community of Mexicans outside of Mexico. A stage thundered with speeches, theater and song. Music permeated the air. I spotted Cuervo and Eight Ball from Lomas. They had reds and we dropped a few. There was a liquor store on the corner of Indiana and Whittier where we scored on some brew. But Cuervo and Eight Ball stole a case, forcing the store owner to close up shop. Soon a crowd gathered outside the store demanding to get in. Somebody banged on the glass door. Suddenly a shotgun pressed against my skull.

"Move or I'll blow your fuckin' head off," a sheriff's deputy ordered. I returned to the park, wandering through feet and bodies, coolers and blankets.

A line of deputies at the park's edge — armed with high-powered rifles, billy clubs and tear gas launchers — swaggered toward the crowd. They mowed down anybody in their path. A group of people held arms to stop the rioting police from getting to the families. I turned toward the throng of officers. One guy told me to go back: "We'll fight tomorrow."

But there were no more tomorrows for me. I had had enough at the hands of alien authority.

Come on, then, you helmeted, wall of state power. Come and try to blacken this grass, this shirt of colors, this festive park filled with infants and mothers and old men, surging forth in pride. Come and try to blacken it with your blazing batons, shotguns and tear gas canisters. I'm ready.

A deputy in a feverish tone shouted for me to move.

"*Chale*, this is my park."

Before I knew it, officers drove my face into the dirt; there was a throbbing in my head where a black jack had been swung. On the ground, drops of red slid over blades of green. The battle of Laguna Park had started.

Bodies scurried in all directions. Through the tear gas mist, I saw shadows of children crying, women yelling, and people lying on the grass, kicking and gouging as officers thrust black jacks into ribs and spines. Deputies pursued several people into the yards and living rooms of nearby homes. In a murderous frenzy, they pulled people out of back yards and porches, beating and arresting them.

A deputy pushed me into the back of a squad car. Somebody lay next to me, his hair oiled in blood. I didn't want to look in case his brains were coming out. I gave him a piece of my favorite shirt, soon to be soaked.

The first round of arrestees were crowded into a holding tank for hours in the East L.A. jail — the same jail where in a year's time, seven prisoners reportedly "committed suicide."

Later that night, we were piled into black, caged buses and taken to the Los Angeles County Jail, the largest in the country, then to juvenile hall and again to the county jail. At one point, officers sprayed mace into the windows of the bus while we sat chained to one another. Our eyes and skin burned as we yelled, but no one could hear us.

There were three other young dudes with me: another 16 year old, a 15 year old and his 13-year-old brother. In the county jail, deputies placed us in with adults — with murder, drug and rape suspects. We weren't old enough to be incarcerated there, but they didn't care about this. There was an uprising in East L.A. and we were part of it. One black guy recalled the Watts rebellion and shook our hands. I watched deputies come into the cells and beat up prisoners — breaking the arm of one guy.

At one point, the four of us juveniles were hauled to the Hall of Justice jail, known as the Glasshouse. The deputies threw us into "murderers row," where hardcore offenders were awaiting trial or serving time. I had a cell next to Charles Manson.

They threw me in with a dude who had killed a teacher and another who had shot somebody in the Aliso Village housing projects. One of the dudes pressed a stashed blade to my neck. But I knew, no matter what, never show fear. I stood up to him, staring without blinking. Then he backed off. Soon we played cards, told jokes and stories.

That night, we heard the "East L.A. riot" — this is what the media was calling it! — had escalated throughout much of Whittier Boulevard. Stores were burned down and looted. Police had killed people. Fires flared in other Chicano communities such as Wilmington and Venice.

Then a radio reporter announced that sheriff's deputies had killed Chicano journalist Rubén Salazar. Salazar had been a lone voice in the existing media for the Mexican people in the United States (he was a former Los Angeles Times reporter and KMEX-TV news director). At word of his death, the tier exploded into an uproar. Inmates gave out gritos and cell bars rattled; mattresses were set on fire.

The next day, Manson, who stayed in an enclosed cell with only a small glass-and-bar opening to see him through, had to attend a hearing. Early that morning, guards woke up everybody and made us face the walls of our cells. Some protested. The dude next to me said it was at Manson's request.

"Fuck this," I said, but we were forced to comply.

At midday, they allowed us to roam the tier. I talked to inmates from the other cells, most of whom were black or Chicano. For the most part, the four of us young dudes from the unrest were treated with respect. When it was time for Manson to walk the tier, however, the guards made everyone else go back into their cells. Manson emerged from his enclosed box. He ranted and raved about "niggers and spics," about how whites should kill us all. The other inmates yelled back, threatened his life, but Manson knew the guards wouldn't let anyone get to him.

I disappeared in the criminal justice system. I was being held without a hearing. Whenever one was scheduled, my parents would show up and then the courts canceled it. Dad and Mom searched for me everywhere. They checked for my name in court records and arrest sheets. They fell into a maze of paperwork and bureaucrats. At least once, I was being pulled away in chains while my mom and dad sat confused in a hearing room. Days built up on days while they waited word about my release.

Finally in the middle of the night, a guard awakened me, pulled me out of the cell and led me down brightly-lit corridors. Through a thick-glassed window, I saw my mother's weary face.

They brought me out in my old clothes, caked with dirt and blood. Mama forced a smile.

"I ain't no criminal, ma," I reassured her.

"I know, *m'ijo*," she replied. "I know."

☩ ☩ ☩

The Watts Rebellion of 1965 changed forever the civil rights struggle in this country. The fires that swept through my old neighborhood that summer swept through me, cutting deep lines, as it swept through America, turning it toward its greatest fears and hardest questions; demarcating the long-glossed-over class and national differences which have historically divided the country.

A trajectory from Watts converged with the more-than-century-old fight of the Mexican people for their own freedoms to ripen into the Chicano Movement as manifested in East L.A.

And what a time it was to be in East L.A.!

In 1968 several thousand junior and high school students walked out of the Mexican east side schools to demand quality and accountable education. Students in schools throughout Los Angeles followed suit — in South Central, the Harbor, the West Side and San Fernando Valley.

A handful of us at Garvey School joined with the East L.A. school "Blowouts," as they were called, when we walked out of the school yard. Led by a girl named Norma and myself, our walkout turned out as a solidarity gesture. The students didn't have enough cognizance of the issues to carry it to the heights taken by those to the west of us. Still it became my first conscious political act — I was 13 years old — for which I received a day's suspension from school.

Around this time, Chicanos formed various defense organizations. The Brown Berets followed the example of the community-based Black Panthers. MEChA, the Chicano student association, had chapters in all the major campuses. La Raza Unida Party, founded in South Texas, became the arm of the movement's burgeoning political campaigns.

In prisons, where a disproportionate number of Chicano males ended up, *pinto* organizations and publications flowered into existence.

East L.A. also birthed artists, musicians and writers out of the wombs of conflict. Art centers sprouted up such as Mechicano, Goez Studios, Self-Help Graphics and Plaza de La Raza. East L.A. boasted more murals per square mile than any other place in the world. Residents of federally-subsidized housing projects — once designated as havens of crime, drugs and gang warfare — covered up the bland pastel walls with bold-colored, message-laden works of art.

Over the years, bands like El Chicano, Tierra, Los Lobos, Con Safos, Los Illegals and Califas carried forth the people's message through Latinized jazz-rock compositions, and later in punk and traditional *corrido* forms.

Publications arose such as *La Raza* which chronicled through photos and prose the ongoing developments in the movement. Also *Con Safos*, a *caló*-tinged street-oriented magazine (and a forerunner of later magazines such as *Lowrider*, *Q-Vo*, and *Firme*); *Regeneración*, the rebirth of a publication founded during the Mexican Revolution by the Flores-Magón brothers; and *ChismeArte*, a literary and art publication.

A result and impetus of all this activity became the Chicano Moratorium Against the War. It was one of nine major disturbances in the barrio between 1970-72.

And for a time, for a most productive and wonderful time, gang violence stood at a standstill. For a time it appeared the internal warfare had given way to the struggle for land, language and liberty — when we had something more important to fight for.

☩ ☩ ☩

St. Anthony's Church sponsored a teen dance soon after my ordeal in the Los Angeles County jail system. I came, not knowing what to expect. The place swarmed with perfumed-and-preened young women, and dudes with plastered down hair and oven-heated shined shoes. The women danced with so much verve, so much music. Sometimes, I preferred standing on the sides to observe the stream and tide of their motion, their gyrations, the fusion of feet and fingers with the fever from some dark, tribal, ancestral homeland.

I noticed one woman with long, luxurious black hair, embracing cinnamon-colored skin, who danced as if she were outside by herself, in the rain or beneath a starry sky, just for me. She closed her eyes and let the band's beat press through her, fingering her flesh and sprouting in violent plumage across the dance floor.

Entranced, it took a while before I realized she was Viviana from Sangra.

Even though we had not seen each other for two years since we met during the Mission's Fiesta Days carnival, I felt compelled to confront her. Viviana turned slightly in my direction when I tapped her shoulder. Then after a few seconds' glance, she did a full body turn and looked straight into my face. She remembered. We both remembered — and it was as if no time at all had passed between us.

"You look and sound so different," Viviana later said, as we held each other following a couple of slow dances and some kissing.

"I've been through some hard times lately — I was just in jail."

"Somehow, I could tell. Something about being in jail changes a dude's expression, his voice; how he feels to touch."

"You're still nice to talk to," I said.

We spent the rest of the evening catching up. Viviana had kept herself pretty much out of trouble. But her brothers were getting crazier and deadly. The three oldest were hardcore members of Los Diablos; one of them, called Coyote, became Chava's right-hand dude. As she talked, a sparkle from her eye reflected a light on the dance floor and it appeared to be a warning: I would fall for this woman; I would fall hard.

I rode a ten-speed bike late at night to visit Viviana. I tried to look nondescript, with an oil-stained coat over unpressed denim pants. I had to enter Sangra territory to see her. But I wouldn't let that stop me; Viviana was worth the risk.

Beneath the porch light of her house, Viviana and I talked, caressed and endured. One time Coyote came up the walkway.

"What's up, sis?" Coyote said as he shot me a look that could have cut glass, like a diamond.

"Nothing," she replied.

Coyote stopped at the steps. I didn't look away from his gaze. With weight and boxing training, I looked like I could hold my own. And I had the look from *la torcida*. He figured I had to be from somewhere.

"¿*Dónde eres, ése?*" he finally asked.

"Oh Freddie, let him be," Viviana intervened. "He's here with me — and I don't want no hassles from either of you, understand?"

"¡*Aquí para Sangra — y qué!*" Coyote/Freddie said before he entered the house. I was safe, for the time being.

"I hate this shit," Viviana said. "You're not the first dude who has to go through my brothers just so I can have a friend. But I'm sick and tired of it."

"Thanks for backing me," I said. "But this can't go on forever. Someday they're going to find out I'm from Lomas."

"I know," she said looking away, distressed.

Viviana taught me poetry. Not the words or forms of it. The feel of it: The soul-touch she gave me, the way her words clutched at some dark and secret place inside of me. She had a way of saying almost nothing but when she did speak, her words radiated with truth and power. I looked forward to the visits. I didn't even mind the dudes I had to go around or ride past in silence to get there. Or her brothers. For Viviana, I would have done anything.

One night we kissed and kissed, then found ourselves unable to stop. Until then, we did nothing more than fondle and linger in easy talk, but something snapped between us; this unseen barrier which often kept us at a distance, despite being so close there, appeared to break. Our inhibitions were freed and my hands groped her supple body as her tongue freshened the inside of my ear.

I gently pushed her down on the porch and she followed willingly, eagerly. Her rising rate of breathing gave way to moans and sighs and woman-sounds that culled forth a measure of something sweet and taut within me. My hand moved to the top of her pants, where a button had been loosened, and I pushed my hand through and found I could go all the way to the stem of her pleasure, to the silkiness of her vagina, while she squirmed and tightened and squeezed as I felt myself swimming, drowning, in the ocean of our lovemaking.

The moments dripped, then Viviana exploded in a rush of orgasms; I rocked next to her like a baby in a cradle. Suddenly the porch, the trees, the walkway and row of houses became intruders. An uncomfortableness crept around us. Viviana sat up, buttoned her blouse and pants, then placed her hands to her face and sobbed.

"What's the matter, baby?" I whispered.

"You have to leave," she said between her fingers.

"Why?"

"I can't explain, just leave — please."

"I don't see why. Let's just sit here and..."

"Louie, you don't understand nothing, do you?" she said, her attitude a sharp contrast to the moments before, almost as if those moments were just dust from dreams, which often appeared real, but only dust.

"All right, baby, all right, I'll go."

I stood up and pulled the bike up from the grass. I felt so dumb, unable to find words, some sentences which could ease the pain. Anything.

"I'll be back, Viviana," I mustered while on my way out. "Don't ever forget what happened here tonight."

She laid her head on her arms, which were on top of her knees, as she sat on the porch steps.

"Go, please — just go," were her last words.

Viviana failed to return my calls. Deep, hoarse voices answered the phone and said: "She's not here."

I wrote Viviana letters, but doubted the wisdom of sending them. At night, I woke up suddenly, after dreaming of her coming to me, embracing me and dancing, and when I sat up I struck the walls, grasped the pillow and cried out her name.

Some nights, I rode my bike to her house and stared from across the street. Windows darkened. Porch light out. I felt like running up the steps and banging at the screen door and yelling for her to come out, but I could never do this. I hoped she would slide open the curtain, feel me near her. That she would let me in.

Viviana never looked out that window; she never opened the door.

A month or so passed and I went to another dance at the El Monte Legion Stadium with my sisters, Shorty and Ana. As usual, the place was jam-packed with *vatos* and *rucas* from barrios all over the San Gabriel Valley. Lowriders graced the rows of cars in the parking lot. Different gang members exchanged hand signs and spray-painted the names of all their homeboys on the walls.

This was a huge hall. I rambled around looking at the people, feeling like shit, but still open to make the most of the evening. Then my heart jumped. Viviana was there, at a seat, by herself. I walked fast to get to her, but before I did some dude came out of nowhere and offered her his hand to dance. She accepted. *Chingao*: I just missed her. My palms were wet. My tongue dry. I felt like there was an oven in my chest.

Then Viviana returned and this time I sat down next to her.

"Baby, how are you doing?" I said.

She turned her head, looked at me and smiled. God, it felt good. She acted coy, diffident, but alluring. There wasn't much to say. I leaned over and kissed her and she then placed her hand to the back of my neck and I felt her moan and squirm in her seat, taking me back to that night on her porch. We kissed a long time before she gently pulled me away.

"*Prieto*, I need to do something, will you wait here?" Viviana requested with her hands on my chest.

"Sure, I ain't going nowhere."

She got up from the seat, her hands brushed her dress over the curve of her hips, and then walked out. I felt so much relief. Love leapt out of my ears. Viviana, Viviana — how I prayed to every god known to man for this moment!

I sat there for an hour. Viviana didn't show. Others were being coupled already. Slow dance after slow dance caused me great anxiety. *Where was Viviana?* I looked around, but wouldn't leave the seat. It took me longer than most, but it finally hit me: She wasn't coming back.

I stepped away from that spot, walked through the sweat and cologne, through the stale smoke and wine breath. I made it to the exit. Then Viviana appeared, in a darkened corner, making out with another guy.

By the time I caught up with Shorty and Ana, I was wound up, bumping strangers, talking loud. Challenging everyone. A dude would give me any kind of look and I pushed myself up on him.

"What you looking at, *puto!*"

"Louie, come on, let's go," Shorty said, pulling me away. "Forget it, man."

I told my sisters what happened with Viviana. I wanted to kill someone. To help lessen my anger, Shorty and Ana plotted to wait outside of the El Monte Legion for Viviana and jump her.

"We'll do it for you, bro', okay?" Shorty said.

At first I liked the idea. I stood outside by my sisters as the place closed up and crowds of teenagers streamed to the parking lot. But the sadness and anger which first overwhelmed me soon started to choke me. All I wanted to do was get the hell out of there.

"Forget it, man," I told my sisters. "I don't want anything to happen to Viviana. Let's go home."

It was over. Finally, over.

☩ ☩ ☩

Mr. Madison looked tense, sitting there in short-sleeved shirt and casual slacks. In front of him were about 20 teenagers from Lomas, lying around in a circle on the front yard of my homeboy Alex's house. Mr. Madison had been persuaded to meet with us about how to improve the conditions at Mark Keppel High School.

"As principal of your school, I plan to make this the best learning experience of your lives," he said. "But no one man or administrator can do anything unless you decide to put everything behind it."

He seemed to be open, willing to consider our ideas. Chente told me to give him the benefit of the doubt, but not to let him off the hook either. Chente didn't want us to be given the runaround or appeased without real educational advances. But he said the students had to play the leading role in insuring those advances were realized.

"I can't make any guarantees," Mr. Madison said to finish the meeting. "The wheels of progress turn slowly. But I will promise to do all I can. If you work with me, I'll work with you."

He got up and shook everybody's hand. The next school year, I was allowed to come back.

Chicanos made up almost 40 percent of the student body at Keppel, although it seemed like it was 80 percent. The dark faces under the tree on the lawn, the daily brawls among us, and police coming through the hallways made it seem like nobody but Chicanos attended the school.

The Anglo students plugged along among their own, isolated in the upper-floor classrooms. They were in the journalism club that put out the school newspaper, ironically called "The Aztec." They were in school government sessions making decisions about pep rallies, the annual Christmas party and the Prom. They made up the school teams, the cheerleading squads and most ironically, they were the school mascots: Joe and Josephine Aztec.

The mascots were always Anglo, cloaked in deerskin, Indian-like garb. They usually acted like clowns, tripping over each other during football games, while "rallying" the team to victory. Sometimes they did tumbling acts — nothing whatsoever to do with being Aztec.

The Chicanos started their own student club called To.H.M.A.S. — To Help Mexican American Students. The other high schools in the district also did the same: San Gabriel High School had M.A.S.O. — Mexican American Student Organization; and Alhambra High School had HUNTOS — which means "together."

My first few days back in school, I felt like an outsider again. There seemed to be more activity though. I saw some Chicanas dressed in pep squad gear and a few Chicanas were members of the journalism club. The strict demarcation between the whites and Mexicans in some areas appeared to be breaking down.

I spent a lot of time in between classes at the Chicano Student Center, which was an office and lounge space in a bungalow in the middle of the school, next to the lunch benches. Mrs. Baez was the Home-School Coordinator, a woman who lived in Rosemead's South Side, a mother of teenagers, and active in Chicano affairs; she was also on the board of the Bienvenidos Community Center. Mr. Pérez, the print shop teacher, was the club's adviser. Two college students were hired as part-time assistants: Blanca Glendon, a Chicana married to a black, and Carmela San Juan, who was part Mexicana and part Filipina.

ToHMAS meetings were held once a week. At the first meeting dues were paid, officers elected, issues of concern raised, and activities planned. The most significant of our activities then were the Cinco De Mayo festivities, including our own float in the annual observances, and efforts to raise funds, like holding dances.

At first the club concerned itself only with benign aspects of school life. But the barrio realities, and the long-standing issues of inequality and neglect, kept rearing their heads. During the meetings, I kept quiet in the corner, not volunteering for anything, until something, I didn't know what, would snag my attention.

"Mrs. Baez, come outside," a student shouted through the door of the Chicano Student Center. "There's a fight."

Mrs. Baez left the paperwork she was working on and quickly followed the student outside. Bam Bam and another student, Alfredo, were going at it in the courtyard. Before this, the school administration would have automatically suspended or expelled the students. Mrs. Baez now could intervene and try to work out the problems among the Chicanos before the school staff got involved. This meant a lot of gray hairs for Baez and her assistants.

I sat in the lounge area, my hair long and slicked back, with a couple of other students. Blanca opened the door and asked us to step out for a time so a student session could be held. Mrs. Baez brought in Bam Bam and Alfredo and had them sit. I walked out and looked back through the window as an intense argument ensued between Bam Bam and Alfredo, with Blanca and Mrs. Baez trying to work out some solution. This is what they had to deal with every day.

The leading members of ToHMAS were mostly women, among them Esme, Cha Cha, Amelia, Yvonne, and Flora. A few dudes helped, such as Ysidro, Alex, Chuy and myself. But the women ran everything. It was through ToHMAS, and through the example of Mrs. Baez, Blanca and Carmela, that the women from Lomas found a place to address some long-standing grievances. Their leadership found shape and form through ToHMAS, as they took to heart the battle for their respect, and that of their people.

We dealt with two dominant aspects. One was something called Project Student, with Carmela as our sponsor, which targeted the physical deterioration of the school: Walls were cracked, stairwells in disrepair, and the freeway behind the school drowned out lessons from second-floor classrooms. In the summer, the air conditioning system rarely worked, making for long, sweltering days. In the winter, rain accumulated in buckets from roof leaks. Project Student, in fact, involved more than just Chicanos; whites and others also had to endure these conditions.

The other aspect involved the issue of dignity for the Chicano students.

"You don't mind if I don't call you Chin do you?" Mrs. Baez asked.

"*Chale*, what's up?"

"We'd like to propose you and Esme try out for Joe and Josephine Aztec."

I looked over at Esme and then back to Mrs. Baez.

"You're joking, right?"

"We're very serious," Esme said. "We're tired of them paddies — excuse me — but them Anglos putting down our culture. They make the mascots look like Pocahontas with tommy hawks and then prance around like fools."

"That's true, but what are our chances — I mean, how are we going to win when the Anglos do all the judging?"

"We plan to do an authentic Aztec dance, in authentic Aztec dress," Esme said. "If they deny us, then everyone will know how racist this school is."

"But I don't know any Aztec dances."

"We have somebody willing to teach you," Mrs. Baez said. "He's an instructor for a *folklórico* dance troupe at one of the colleges. You look Indian enough with your long hair. And I think it would help involve some of the hard-core Lomas students in what we're doing if you tried out."

"What do you say, Louie?" Esme asked.

They knew they had me. I accepted as a formality.

Esme and I went to East L.A. College and met with a Señor Franco, the *folklórico* dance instructor. He taught us some basic steps and helped us find the material and designs for our dancewear. To get it right, we dedicated hours of our evenings to rehearsal.

Esme choreographed the dance routine, based on Señor Franco's instruction. Our mothers created the costumes, and they were so strikingly beautiful, even Señor Franco was impressed. We added some non-Aztec touches too.

The rehearsals were secret. When the time neared for the tryouts, we walked into the activities office and signed up. A couple of the white students there gave us funny looks. Esme and I signed our names and then left.

The day of the tryouts, all contestants were to meet in the gym. Parents, teachers and students took up some of the bleachers. A row of judges, including some teachers and students, stayed near the performance area.

I entered the gym area in Aztec dress; I had on a leather top, arm bands and loin cloth, with a jaguar-imaged headgear propped on my head and bells strapped around my ankles. And I must have been a sight with tattoos on my arms and an earring. I saw a couple of rows of bleachers filled up with Chicanos; Mrs. Baez had organized the students to attend. As I entered, they cheered and hollered. I considered getting out of there but Esme came up behind me and held my hand. We were both nervous.

Esme and I were the last ones to perform. We suffered through a number of tumbling acts and screwball routines. Then an announcer came on the speaker:

"Now we have the team of Esmeralda Falcón and Luis Rodríguez."

Silence saturated the gym area. I walked up solemn and straight, a wooden chair in one hand and a conga drum in the other, and sat down in the middle of the basketball court. I paused for 10 seconds, then began the beat. Esme came in slow, purposeful, with a turquoise sequined-and-feathered garment and multicolored headgear that arced around her head like a rainbow; she also had bells.

Esme could have been a priestess from Tenochtitlan, her face pure and brown, with slight make up that accented her already slanted, indigenous eyes. She danced around me, as if calling forth a spirit; the bells on her ankles swirling around the beat, in time with the rhythm of the drum. At one point, I arose and danced with her, in unison, round and round through various steps, leading up to the climax.

We had to be serious — no laughing, no smiling, in keeping with the integrity of the dance.

A murmur swept through the bleachers when Esme and I crossed our feet together and swung around and around, hooked by our ankles, going faster and faster, the force of our swirling keeping us locked, letting the motion pull and embrace us at the same time, like in a battle. When we finished, one of my knees fell to the floor as Esme stood above me, the victor.

A few seconds passed, then an uproar of applause and cheers burst out of the bleachers. None of the other contestants received the response we did. I even saw white students and some judges clapping. They had never seen anything like it.

Esme and I waited by Mrs. Baez as the judges mulled over their decision. Finally:

"The winners are — and the new Joe and Josephine Aztec mascots of Mark Keppel High School — Esmeralda Falcón and Luis Rod...."

The yells drowned out my last name. Esme shrieked, threw her arms around my neck and hugged me. Other ToHMAS supporters came over with smiles and handshakes. In other people's eyes, this may have been a small victory. But for the Chicanos at Mark Keppel High School, this meant another barrier had been torn down and an important aspect of our culture recognized. I surprised myself and felt warm inside. I tried to shake it off, but couldn't. A flush of pride soon covered my face. *We won!*

More Chicanos became involved in ToHMAS. We started our own *folklórico* group in which Carmen San Juan taught the students some basic Mexican and Flamenco dances. Esme and I started a *teatro* group, based on what the Teatro Campesino of Cesar Chávez's farm workers union were doing in rural California. Our *teatro* group, however, had an urban slant.

I wrote the three plays we performed. One involved a dramatic verse monologue of a Chicana about to be arrested by the cops. Another involved a one-act about being proud of our culture. But the most controversial one dealt with getting Lomas and Sangra to stop fighting each other.

This play began with someone from Sangra crossing out Lomas on a huge, piece of white paper pasted on a wall. Then the action moved toward a point when the dudes from both neighborhoods go at each other. The upshot is as the two barrios fight, local government officials are on the side determining the site of a new mall or where the next freeway will go while making plans to uproot the very land the dudes were killing each other for.

"Who wants to play the dude crossing out Lomas?" I asked. Nobody raised their hands.

"What's the matter, it's only a play."

"Hey, Louie, we ain't about to cross out the Hills," Chuy said. "I know what you're trying to say, but somebody might get hurt."

I decided to play this part; I had to stand by my play.

We presented the productions at a joint cultural event sponsored by ToHMAS, MASO and HUNTOS. That day, a large grouping of dudes from Lomas came by and sat in the back. They acknowledged me, but I had to go through with the play.

When we finished, a few dudes stormed out yelling "Lomas Rifa."

But for those who stayed, we discussed ending the warfare between the barrios. Then Esme's portrayal of the Chicana getting beaten by the cops, in rhymed verse, helped keep the spirits high.

The wheels of progress turned too slowly. While we kept up with ToHMAS activities, the school could not keep up with all the students' needs. Red tape and outright opposition stalled Project Student. Then one night a group of white kids broke into the school and spray-painted the walls surrounding the Chicano Student Center with stuff such as: *Mexicans Go Home! Greasers Stink! Remember The Alamo!*

Esme called a meeting to determine what should be done.

"We should draw up some demands," Amelia suggested.

"That's right. People are still prejudiced here," said Flora.

"Well, what do we ask for? They've given us a lot so far — what can we get that we don't have already?" Esme asked.

"I got an idea," I said. "Chente over at Bienvenidos took me to the East L.A. schools. After the 'Blowouts' they got more Chicano teachers and even Chicano studies. This is what we need. We should demand a Chicano studies class and a Chicano teacher."

"Maybe Mr. Pérez will teach it," Amelia said.

"Or even Mrs. Baez — it's a great idea. How many are for it?" Esme said. It was unanimous.

The next day we presented our plans to Mrs. Baez. I wrote up a statement with the heading: *We Demand Justice!* The statement called for the school to find the culprits who defaced the Chicano Student Center, for more Chicano teachers, and for a Chicano Studies class. But Mrs. Baez didn't like it.

"Why? If we don't do something the *gabachos* will try to roll back the little we've got," I said.

"I think it's too rash," Mrs. Baez implored. "You don't know the kind of trouble you can get into. I know Chente has introduced you to a lot of the East L.A. student leaders — but this is not Garfield High School! We are a minority in this school. We have to do things differently. We can't just act like anybody should give us anything."

"But the Chicanos in this school have been pushed around for too long," Esme said. "We're tired. Every time we try to better ourselves, we're told to wait, to hold on, that things will get better. But it never does! We have to do something — we have to do it now."

"I can't support this," Mrs. Baez said. "But you do what you feel you must."

"We can't do it without you," Flora said. "And you know it."

Then Flora walked out. Disappointment crossed over everyone's faces. Defeat seemed to set in. But Flora's actions gave me another idea: Why not have a school walkout like they did in East L.A.? Our demands would be for Chicano Studies, more Chicano teachers and the new classrooms, air conditioners and repairs needed as part of Project Student. It would be a walkout for our self-respect.

The word spread. Esme and the others made sure everyone talked to everyone else. Only the Chicanos were involved. I discussed with Chente what we planned to do. He wasn't sure a walkout was a good idea, but he was willing to help us out. He ran off mimeographed copies of our demands.

The next day, everyone went to school like normal. At 10 a.m., the students were to walk out of their classrooms and assemble in front of the school.

"Do you think they'll do it, Louie?" Esme asked, while on our way to classes that morning.

"I don't know. But we'll soon find out."

In my history class, I kept an eye on the clock. As soon as the hands struck the magical hour, I grabbed my books and then proceeded out the door.

"Rodríguez, where do you think you're going?" Mrs. Tuttle said, the one we called Mrs. Turtle and who treated us like we were in kindergarten. "Young man, come back here this instant!"

But I kept on walking. In the hallways, a number of students emerged out of their classes. Not a lot, but more than I had imagined. Books were dropped in the hallways. When I made it to the front steps of the school there were already 80 to 100 students converging there. Esme and the other ToHMAS members had made crudely-painted signs and gave them to the students. I grabbed a handful of the demands from a bag and passed them out. Some of the students came up and grabbed stacks of the leaflets to help get them to other students.

In a matter of minutes, we had some 300 people on the front lawn. Teachers, and those students still in classes, stuck their heads out of classroom windows. Mrs. Baez received a phone call from Mr. Madison.

"Did you know this was going to happen?" Mr. Madison said.

"No, I didn't know about a walkout. I discouraged them, however, from presenting their demands," Mrs. Baez explained.

"And you refused to inform me about this?" Mr. Madison yelled. "You're supposed to tell me what's going on — that's why we have you here."

"Oh, I wasn't aware of this," Mrs. Baez said, her voice also rising in anger. "I thought I was to be here for the students, so they can have someone to talk to and represent their interests. I didn't know I was supposed to be your eyes and ears."

"Mrs. Baez, come into my office right now — we're going to have to put a stop to this," Mr. Madison said and hung up.

When Mrs. Baez showed, Mr. Madison stood up, getting ready to do some more yelling. But Mrs. Baez interrupted him.

"Mr. Madison, you can stop right there. I am a grown woman and a mother. I am not one of your high school students. I refuse to have you talk to me in this disrespectful and condescending tone."

"Oh you too?" Mr. Madison said. "Everybody wants respect around here. What about respect for me and this institution! We have a school to run. I can't have the school board find out about this — I can't let some disgruntled students ruin it for everyone."

"I would suggest that you pay attention to these disgruntled students and stop worrying about what the school board will do," Mrs. Baez said. "You've promised these children some action. So far, all they've received is a lot of fine talk and smiling faces. I don't support their tactics. But I believe the worst thing to do now is to sweep this under the rug. I won't be a part of that."

Mr. Madison looked stunned. His Home-School Coordinator had turned the tables on him. But he knew whatever he thought of her, she was still his link to the students.

"Okay, we'll let them have their say."

Mr. Madison sat down and made a phone call to the Dean of Students, Mr. Walsh.

"We're calling an assembly," Mr. Madison said. "I want those students back into the school. And then we'll hear what they have to say. But we won't begin to talk unless they're inside the school building."

Mr. Walsh came out to the lawn. The students had been chanting: We Want Chicano Studies! We Want Justice! ¡Ya Basta!

It took some doing, but Mr. Walsh convinced us to convene in the auditorium and discuss the issues.

"Bring in the whole school," I yelled. "You can't separate us. We want to speak to the whole school."

At first they refused. But finally, when it looked like the students weren't going to budge, Mr. Walsh agreed to let all the classes gather in the auditorium.

It was a session the likes of which Mark Keppel had never seen. Esme walked up to the stage and read out the demands. White students also stood up, some in tears, crying about why we were so angry.

"What have we done to you?" one blond-haired girl demanded to know.

Some Chicano students yelled back, about being neglected, treated like second-class citizens, about being denied access to school resources.

"This is not against whites," I said. "It's against a system that keeps us all under its thumb. By screwing us, the school is screwing you."

"It's your fault," said Stan, the student body president. "You Mexicans just don't want to get involved; you don't want to get ahead."

More yelling. More heated responses. It was difficult, but this had to happen. Everything had stayed bottled up for too long. Each group doing their own thing; complaining about the other group, but not reaching out. The tears, the yelling, the talk served as good medicine for all the students.

Even some hard-nosed dudes got up to say something; some of them had never spoken out in public before. Near the end, I stepped on the stage and made a speech.

"Chicanos only want what you want," I said. "We walk these halls together and yet we don't know anything about each other. We're scared of each other, we're ignorant of each other, and then we're surprised when people get up like this with so much hatred. It's for a reason. There's nothing wrong with *us*! We're not just making this up. Something drastic has to change, or there's going to be even more anger. More than you can imagine."

The result: Mr. Madison approved a new course, a class on Chicano history and culture, and he offered to provide a Chicano teacher for the class. Finally, he said the school would put some meat behind Project Student; it became a school-backed initiative to present to the school board.

Esme and I hugged again. We had only just begun.

♥ ♥ ♥

Shorty's eyes fell; her voice cracked and tears blurred her vision.

"He's dead, mama," she said.

"¿Quién?" Mama asked. "¿Quién se murió?"

"Fernando — he killed himself last night!"

14-year-old Fernando Luna had been one of Shorty's best friends. He was a member of the Lomas Dukes, the younger set the United Sisters usually partied with. He called himself Gallo, which means rooster. His older brother was Lencho, who was more involved in the affairs of the Hills than Fernando would ever be. Fernando was one of those guys who tried hard to belong, to be as crazy and committed as anyone. But none of us were aware how lonely he was in midst of the crowd.

His mother, Toncha, was active in the Bienvenidos Food Co-op. But as a single mother, on welfare, with five boys to raise, Toncha's hands were full — and I'm sure through no fault of her own, Fernando's needs weren't always met.

Shorty had been seeing a few of Fernando's homeys, like Bosco and Conejo. And although she confided with Fernando many of her problems, they never became intimate. She saw him as a good friend; somebody she could talk to. Now it comes out: Fernando liked my sister very much.

The night before, Fernando had phoned late to talk with Shorty. Usually she was full of stories, jokes and concerns. But Shorty was in bed and tired; she gently suggested he call her back the next day.

"Or let's talk in school," she said. "We can get together at lunch."

"Sure, okay," Fernando responded; there was nothing unusual in his tone.

The next day, Toncha discovered Fernando's body swinging from a pole in the closet.

✝ ✝ ✝

"It's not enough to accuse, to wail and spit on the face of all oppression — this can be ignored," Skin said. "It takes a scientific approach to uncover the source of exploitation, to unravel society's delicate and intricate tapestry, stitched with the skin of our mothers, the bones of our ancestors, the blood of all who toil."

"This is why we can demand — with full moral authority — what has been stolen from us," Ofelia said.

"And this they cannot ignore," Skin added.

Another session with the collective, most of it held in an eloquent and educated Spanish I could not speak myself, yet I grasped everything being said.

The group aimed to train a corps of leaders. Unlike others in the Chicano Movement who strove to *enter* the American capitalist system, it prepared for a fundamental reorganization of society.

"It's also time you understood whites aren't the enemy," Chente said. "Take that 'tradition,' all that energy expended against each other — what a waste!"

Others with their own answers also converged on the barrio. Born-again Christians, many of whom were ex-cons and ex-junkies, preached salvation; I attended some of their testimonials. Democrats, Republicans, libertarians and nationalists also plied their wares. Some wanted our minds, some wanted our souls — some wanted warm bodies for polling booths.

But the collective didn't depend on powers of belief or stale promises. They were social scientists, all the time probing and summarizing.

"You don't have to be a genius to figure out what's in front of you," Chente said. "Yet this is the hardest thing to do precisely because what we see is not always expressing what's beneath it."

"But all we know is *this* life," I questioned. "You can't change that!"

"Luis, change is what we're all about," Chente offered. "Change is constant, stagnation is relative. But change follows laws of development, a process that, if appreciated, sets the conditions by which people make their own history."

"What we're here to do is transform the way people have been accustomed to living," Sergio said. "The first step is removing the shackles on our minds."

The collective explained how workers of all colors and nationalities, linked by hunger and the same system of exploitation, have no country; their interests as a class respect no borders. To me, this was an unconquerable idea.

I also learned there was no shame in being a janitor or a garment worker; I never looked at Mama and Dad with disdain again.

So fundamental. So Christian. So American at times. Yet this conflict would be the most intense and prolonged of our lives.

✝ ✝ ✝

A party below the Hills swung with music, *ruquitas de aquellas* and anything to get high with. Suddenly, this dude Rudy rushed into the living room, breathing hard and sweating.

"Where's Santos and Toots?" he demanded.

"What the fuck you want?" Santos yelled from the kitchen.

"The *gabachos* on Marshall Street tried to jump me, man."

"Slow down — what happened?"

"I was walking my girl home when the bikers from the old gray house — you know the one before you get to the Church — anyway they come out of the house with chains and bats, call us fuckin' greasers and chase us down the street."

"I know who they are — they're in a bikers' club, the Sinisters," Toots said.

"Fuck 'em," Santos responded. "Let's get them white boys."

A caravan of three cars pulled out of the party toward Marshall Street on the other side of the freeway. I piled into a vehicle so packed — two dudes were stuffed into the trunk — I could hardly breathe the whole way up there.

The gray house had been known as a bikers' hangout for years. The grassless yard filled with automobile and motorcycle parts. Real poverty row.

When we arrived, dudes piled out of the cars and began to attack the white picket fence, tearing off sections of it and yelling out "Here Stand Las Lomas!" A rock smashed a window.

A long-haired, leather-and-denim clad dude stepped onto the porch, cradling a shotgun; he fired and Pokie received some of the pellets in his face, and he dropped to the street. Dudes began to run in all directions. Many jumped back into their cars. I ran off too, and came across Santos with a knife. He started poking me and a couple of others with it.

"You don't fuckin' run!" he yelled. "Lomas never runs!"

But in the confusion, there was nothing else to do. Toots and Cuervo picked up Pokie to take him to the hospital. I got into somebody's else car and we boogied back to the party.

Later at the party, Santos gathered all the dudes together and again shouted about the cowards we were. Puppet had heard what happened and called the house. But Puppet was pissed off we went after the bikers. He said nobody, but nobody, was to go back there.

Santos wasn't having it.

"Toots, Cuervo and I will go in one car," he said, displaying a handgun through his pant's belt.

"Chin, you get a couple of other dudes and come by five minutes after we do. Can you get a *cuete?*"

"*Simón*, I think so."

"*Orale*, then do it — and follow us over there."

I knocked on Roger Nelson's window. He opened it. Roger was a half-Mexican, half-white guy who I knew had weapons.

"What ya want Chin? It's 2:30 in the morning."

"I need a rifle, man, any one you got."

"What's going on?"

I explained the situation to him. Roger knew the Sinisters. In fact, they were long-time enemies. The Sinisters hated Mexicans. They also hated Roger because, although he looked white, he decided to cleave closer to his Mexican side and spent a lot of time with dudes from the Hills.

Roger handed me a Ruger Long .22 semi-automatic rifle with scope.

"Bring it back in the morning — I'll take care of it for you," he said.

I took a dude from the Imperials Car Club named Darío, who had a sharp, cherried-out Riviera. This was my first mistake. My second mistake was taking Conejo from the Dukes. He was my sister's ex, a 13 year old who was eager to go with me, so I figured it wouldn't hurt.

We were supposed to follow the old, beat-up car that Santos and the others were in. But by the time I got everything together, they were long gone. I told Darío to drive slowly down Marshall Street. As we approached the gray house, it looked like a tornado hit the place. The bikers were scrambling about outside; a couple of bodies were on the ground. Darío pulled up and I stuck the rifle out the side window.

"They're back!" a woman yelled.

The bikers rushed around, some jumped over trash cans and others tripped into the dwelling. I didn't know what to do. A massive biker dude stood nearby on the yard and looked at me while he tried to figure out his next move. But instead of running, he turned around, wound his arms over his head and bent over. Without thinking, I shot him — right in the ass!

"Take off, man, take off!" I yelled at Darío.

We sped off toward Del Mar Avenue, not far from my house. But we didn't get too far. Police cars came out of nowhere, from every direction. Darío stopped the car in the driveway of an apartment complex.

"Come out with your hands up!" a cop yelled.

We did as they ordered. I emerged from the car and perhaps ten .38 revolvers were pointed at my head. They told us to lie on the ground with our hands on our heads. I saw a cop reach into the back seat of the car and carefully remove the .22 rifle with his fingertips.

"I got it," he declared.

Conejo cried the whole time we were hauled to the San Gabriel jail house. I told Darío and Conejo not to say anything. After the booking rituals, we found out what happened.

The first car had come to the house on Marshall Street and opened fire on the bikers who were hanging around. Three bikers went down. Then a few minutes later, we came by in Darío's ride while the bikers were still figuring out who had gotten injured. Another biker down. The first car escaped.

The second car with three teenage male suspects was apprehended and a fired weapon confiscated.

Darío, Conejo and I were booked for assault with intent to commit murder.

CHAPTER EIGHT

"They say of the poet and the madman we all have
a little." — Sandra Cisneros

The cells babbled with the poignant tongues of despair licking the walls. Every now and then the air reverberated with *gritos*, the Mexican yell of a man who's drunk and angry, reaching as deep as he can to shout all his pain and glory to the world. Jail in the barrio is only a prelude; for many homeboys the walls would soon taste of San Quentin, Folsom and Soledad, the pathway through The Crazy Life.

From the age of 13 on, I ended up in cells like those of the San Gabriel jail house — places like Pomona, Temple City, East L.A., Monterey Park, East Lake's juvenile detention hall and the L.A. county jail system following the Moratorium. Sometimes the police just held me over three nights and then let me go at the start of the week to keep me off the street. But this time, at 17 years old, I faced a serious charge of attempted murder. This time Mama didn't come for me.

"*Ese malvado — deje que se pudra*," Mama told the Spanish-speaking youth officer after hearing of my arrest.

The cell walls were filled with the warrior's art. Most of it declaring Sangra in the beautiful, swirling style of theirs. Smoked outlines of women's faces were burned onto the painted brick. There were love messages: *El Loco Con La Bárbara, P/V* (por vida) — and poetry:

Aquí estoy
En la calle sin jando.
Nadie sabe mi placa
Y a nadie le importa

Voy al chante de mi ruca
Pero se queda mirando

Le hablo con mi alma
Pero la puerta se está cerrando. *

and:

En el bote del county
Con toda mi loca pasión
Puse tu placa en la celda
Y con ese pensamiento
Estoy sufriendo mi desgracia. **

Pachuco blues. Somebody in another cell let out a soulified *grito* with the funk of burnt burritos, debris-strewn alleys and fervent love-making thrown into the mix. The holding blocks were made up of two cells and an area for inmates from the shared block to sit around. I gathered up toilet paper, soaked it in water, and rolled it to the size of handballs. When it hardened, I passed the time by throwing it against the wall.

A Sangra soldier named Night Owl sat in a cell next to me and threw challenges.

"Lomas ain't shit," Night Owl said. "I heard your homeboy crying — what are you, babies?"

"Fuck you," I answered. "You can say that behind thick walls, but I'll be out and I'll see you in the street."

Hours of this opened up into other discussions: about family life, about songs we liked — we even shared a few verses — and about women.

"You know Viviana?" I asked. "Her brothers are Coyote, Negro and Shark."

---

*Here I stand / in the street without money. / Nobody knows my name / and nobody cares.

I go to my woman's house / but she stands there just staring. / I speak to her with my soul / but the door is closing.

**In the county jail / with all my crazy passion, / I place your name on a cell wall / and with this thought / I suffer my disgrace.

"What you mean, do I know her?" Night Owl said. "Everybody knows her. They say she fucked around with some dude on her porch while her brothers were inside watching."

¡Qué jodida! It's me they were talking about! Then it struck me as very funny and I laughed.

"What are you laughing about?"

"Nothing, man — whatever happened to her?"

"She got knocked up — she's living with my homeboy Cyclone."

A pang of hurt, I shook my head, then changed the subject.

Darío, Conejo and I were scheduled to go to juvenile hall. Our parents refused to get us. It sounded like a conspiracy. Then I received a visitor.

"You messed up, Luis," Chente said.

"I know — Mama doesn't want anything to do with me."

"Can you blame her?"

"Not really. Did anyone die yet?"

"There was a dude in serious condition, but he's doing better. One woman lost a couple of fingers. I know why it happened, but why did you have to get involved?"

"I don't know. Something snapped inside of me. I have nothing against bikers. But these were older dudes, man. About 40 years old. They had no business fucking with us. I just couldn't let them get away with it."

"The center is trying to get you guys released. We talked to your parents and they're willing to work with us. We're doing all we can to help you. But you've got to stay cool. Don't rattle these bars, okay?"

Chente left. A day later an officer came and opened my cell.

"You're getting out. There's people waiting for you."

I could see my mom and dad with a couple of Bienvenidos staff members in the front desk area. I looked over where Night Owl was still holed up.

"Hey dude, here's for Sangra," and I stuck out my hand.

Night Owl looked at me for a second, then smirked, and shook my hand through the bars.

"You ain't so bad after all," he said. "*Suerte, ése.*"

The next weeks were stacked with uncertainty about the case. Meanwhile, the people at ToHMAS welcomed me back at school.

"I don't know what to say, Louie," Esme said. "I'm just glad you're okay."

Mrs. Baez saw me in the Chicano Student Center lounge talking to Blanca and Carmela as I related to them the incident. A clipping with the headline, "Five Injured In San Gabriel Shootout," had been tacked onto a bulletin board.

"Luis — our Joe Aztec — a fine example you turned out to be," she said.

"I'm sorry Mrs. Baez, I let you down."

"If you wanted notoriety you got it. Unfortunately, the younger guys around here think you're God."

"I didn't mean for this to happen."

"Nobody ever does," she responded.

"I have something for you though."

I dropped a folder with papers on her desk. In it were vignettes, poems and stories. I left as Mrs. Baez picked up the folder and began to peruse it.

The bikers refused to identify Darío, Conejo or me. Instead they pointed to Roger Nelson. He was there, they said. It was his gun. They saw his stringy long hair as he stuck his head out of a car window. For some reason, they wanted Roger.

The police picked up Roger and charged him. Of course, I knew he was in bed the night of the incident. Then another strange thing happened. The authorities let me and the others go. They never did find the first car. They contended only one car was involved and Roger had escaped before the police caught us.

"What's going on Chente?" I said while at the youth center. "As much as I don't want to get sent up for this, it's all lies."

"I don't know, but I can tell you this," Chente said. "The law isn't always about truth."

Instead of being the one facing a hearing, I became the key witness for Roger, who was 18 and had to appear in adult court.

A number of the bikers showed up for the trial, including a woman in a cast and the dude I shot in the butt — the bullet had lodged in mounds of flesh so no serious damage had been done.

Roger wore a suit and now sported a close-cropped haircut. His fiancé, Margarita, sat next to him.

"This goes way back, Louie," Roger explained. "My family had a beef with the Sinisters. Somebody got killed. They always thought my dad did it. He's in the joint now, but they've been after me for years. Since it was my gun, they say I set them up. They want to see me put away — like my dad."

"I think it's going to backfire on them."

"I hope so," Roger said.

Defense attorneys called me to the witness stand, and I related how I obtained the gun, how I got Darío to drive to the gray house — how there were already people shot when we got there. The bikers got on the stand and flubbed their testimony: There was one car — there were two cars; Mexicans were involved — there were no Mexicans. Most of the arguments made the shootings appear as something only between bikers. I couldn't figure out why. Maybe Puppet had a reason for not wanting us to go back to the gray house the night of the party.

A jury found Roger not guilty. Soon after, Roger and Margarita drove to Las Vegas and were married; I went along as their best man.

✝ ✝ ✝

Staff members and volunteers from the area's community centers met to discuss how to end the barrio violence. They stepped into dangerous, shifting ground. Police, city officials, even businesses had a stake in this endeavor.

"We should organize a meeting in which the various groups could agree to a truce," proposed Sal Basuto from La Casa.

"I don't know if we should condone their existence by doing this," a woman from the Zapopan Community Center countered. "We need more police protection — we need to stand up to these hoodlums and put them behind bars."

"That sounds like cops talking," Chente said. "These aren't criminals without faces. They are our children! What you propose only pits the community against itself — and the police would like nothing better than that."

"I think we should treat these youth as adults would treat warring nations," Sal continued. "They have to negotiate. They have to draw up treaties. They have to sign them and abide by them. These young people might as well be prepared for the world they're entering."

"This sounds fine — I don't oppose it offhand," Chente said. "But we also must consider how to provide something real and sustainable. Role-playing and game-playing won't make it. These young people need a strong economic foundation, a viable future — if you're not addressing this, then you're not serious about solving anything."

I'd been asked to sit in on the meeting, but I didn't say anything at first. I listened. It became important for me to find a way for the barrios to unite.

"What do you think, young man?" one of the staff members asked me during a low point in the talks.

"I don't know about stopping violence. But it wouldn't hurt if we had jobs."

The group decided to have a barrio unity meeting at La Casa. I had to convince my homeboys to show up. Not an easy task. Chicharrón agreed to attend. I even tried inviting him to a study session, but he refused, although in jest he began calling me the "Chinmunist," a combination of Chin and communist.

I walked up and down the Hills talking to dudes about the meeting. The younger guys seemed interested. I got most of the Dukes to say they'd come. But I needed some of the *locos*. My break came with Cuervo.

"I'm sick of this shit," he confided one day. "I've seen too many people killed."

"Great, I need you to help get others."

"*Orale*, Chin — count me in."

One evening, a homeless man tripped over a bundle laid out among bushes at Smith Park in Sangra. He looked closer; a woman's soiled foot stuck out of one end. It was Cokie's body, wrapped in bloody blankets.

The coroner's office reported she had been pumped full of pills and brutally raped. They had no suspects. But as always there was talk; somehow people knew who did what even when the authorities didn't.

The street talk said dudes from Lomas did the job. Cokie had long been a thorn in the side of the Hills. But it was a crime which scared a lot of us. What were people willing to do? It's true Cokie was behind a lot of hurting, but who knows if she deserved the kind of hurting she went through before she died.

Chava, just released from Camp Gonzales, a youth detention facility, declared that anybody in Sangra who participated in the barrio unity meeting would answer to him. Sal said he needed time to work everything out. He canceled the meeting.

✝ ✝ ✝

ToHMAS membership leapt off the rolls. I recruited students by going to the lawn and telling them about our activities. A large number of them were there passing the time, scoping each other out, not going to classes. ToHMAS provided some of them the incentive to break out, to do something, even to stay in school.

We had "Brotherhood" dances to unite the Chicanos throughout the area. We also sponsored a Queen contest to raise funds. Beauty was not a criterion; the winner was the person who could raise more money in a designated period of time. The first year's queen was Amelia, who was short, chubby, not-good-looking but full of spirit and drive. What mattered to us were actions, contributions — essential things. The Anglos still selected their queens on looks and status (most Homecoming Queens came from money).

When the football season came, Esme and I attended every game as the school's mascots. I remembered a couple years back when "the tradition" exploded during a football game and I pulled dudes off bleachers to beat on them. This time, I stood on the sidelines in Aztec apparel, performing solemn rituals. Change is a mother!

Even the varsity team opened up. Ricardo Reyes from the Hills became the school's best running back. Soccer became a school-sponsored sport and the newly-arrived Mexican immigrants were competing in L.A.-area and state-wide leagues. The Spanish-speaking students had their own club called ALAS (Association of Latin American Students), which in Spanish means "wings."

Mrs. Baez was instrumental in creating the soccer team. Although they had no uniforms, no pep rallies or any school support, the first year they competed, they took the regional championships!

One day pretty Delfina Cortez, the boxer Hector's old girlfriend, came to a ToHMAS meeting. She looked fine — 14 years old but shaped like a full-grown woman. She wore skirts and dresses which seemed to come off the pages of fashion magazines.

"You're popular around here," she told me.

"I don't know about that. You're the one who's popular."

"I mean, ToHMAS is big right now; people say you had a lot to do with it."

"Not any more than Esme, Flora and the others. Will you join us?"

"Sure, as long as you're in it."

She smiled and walked away. There must be something to being popular — where somebody like Delfina would have anything to do with a big-jawed, awkward and long-haired dude like me.

The Brotherhood Dance involved students from the three local high schools. We brought in a popular East L.A. band. Weapons weren't allowed in the gym where the dance was held. We wanted to have a dance in which no one had to fear for their safety. Esme, as president of the club, introduced the members and winners of our contests. Then it was party time.

Delfina arrived alone. She stood around with the rest of the ToHMAS members. I went back and forth between the dance floor and back stage making sure everything went smoothly. I stopped for a minute and Delfina was still there, still smiling.

I asked Darío, who became a friend after our arrests, for a favor.

"Let me borrow your Riviera, man. I'd like to take Delfina to the Boulevard tonight — with class."

"No way, dude," Darío said. "But I'll tell you what. Let me drive you guys over there. And, if you'd like, I'll leave you alone while I go to a late show or something."

"¡De aquellas! I go for that."

I asked Delfina if she'd hang out with me after the dance. I didn't notice Esme was within earshot of our conversation.

"I'd love to," Delfina said.

Esme came by and bumped into me. She gave me a hurt-crossed-with-anger look, then walked away. She didn't talk to me the rest of the evening.

Darío drove Delfina and me through the Boulevard a few times. Fancy "shorts" danced on the asphalt with only the eyes and beany caps of the drivers visible through the windshield. Music blared out of a multitude of speakers as a river of headlights streamed toward the silhouette of downtown skyscrapers and back.

Darío parked his thin-striped, white Riviera with chrome rims and chain steering wheel behind the Boulevard Theater. A gold plaque with "Imperials" faced out the back window.

"I'll be back about an hour and a half. Don't go anywhere, all right?" Darío said.

Delfina and I lay in the back seat, talking, then smooching, then talking.

"If you don't mind, I'm taking this off," Delfina said as she removed her bra from beneath her silk blouse. Her nipples made impressions through the blouse as she put the bra in her purse.

Before long my hand traveled through her skirt toward her crotch. I felt something. She quickly reached under the skirt and pulled her legs through the underwear, which had a sanitary napkin stuck on the inside. I could see a tinge of blood.

"This is not a good idea — maybe we should walk around," I said.

"Why? It's only blood — my blood — there's nothing wrong with it!" Delfina shouted.

"Hey, Delfina, I didn't mean anything by it. I just never went all the way with a girl on her period before."

"You're just like everybody else!" she yelled. She grabbed my hand and slipped my fingers through her vaginal lips. Then she showed me the soft red liquid which leisurely smeared the fingers.

"See, it's nothing terrible!" Then she cried and I didn't know what to do. I hugged her, trying to keep my fingers from touching the silk blouse.

"I'm sorry. Believe me, I'm so sorry."

"Oh, Louie, I think I love you."

☩ ☩ ☩

Love is a word which so easily skims across our lips. Girls cut their wrists for it. Dudes try to kill for it. Notes professing devotion are passed in the hallways, dropped on desktops or placed discreetly inside school folders. It doesn't take much: a woman brushing her hair, the sniff of a dude's cologne, an after-school walk — and we're in love.

Babies are easy too. Many homegirls become mothers, although they are unfinished children. Whatever comfort and warmth they lack at home is also withheld from their babies. Girls drop out of school. Homeboys become fathers even in their early teens. But there's nothing at stake for them; at the most, having a baby is a source of power, for rep, like trophies on a mantel.

Daddio, before he died at 16 years old, had children from girls in Lomas, El Hoyo Maravilla and La Puente.

Some babies end up without fathers. Like Daddio's offspring. Like John Fabela's daughter. Some cry for milk as a mama presses a needle through a withered vein on her arm. The babies wail for feeding, for touch and the internal knowledge of being special, wanted. If it doesn't come, as soon as they commence the bleeding, they ache for what they never had, with an emptiness which is never filled.

Sheila told me I was somebody she could relate to, who wouldn't turn away. She told me she was pregnant. I took her to the teen clinic. A few days later, it was confirmed.

"It's Eight Ball's baby," Sheila said. "But he doesn't want anything to do with it. What should I do?"

"Why don't you tell your parents?" I suggested.

"I can't — they'll kill me."

"They won't kill you. Maybe they'll get mad," I said. "They might even help you. Try it. If it don't work, we'll see if Mrs. Baez can do something."

The next day, I asked around for Sheila. Nobody knew where she was at. I entered the Chicano Student Center.

"Hey Blanca, have you heard from Sheila?"

"You mean you don't know?" Blanca said.

"What?"

"She told her father she's having a baby," Blanca replied. "He got so mad, he broke all her fingers."

✝ ✝ ✝

Chente's face twisted and snarled as he examined the murals inside my garage room. It looked like he hated them. I never took art lessons; I drew, Chicano-style, freehand, mostly barrio images. I didn't realize that Chente could see the spirit behind my work was more promising than any actual technical ability.

"I have a job for you," he finally said. "This summer, we're doing a mural project. The City of Rosemead is footing the bill. We'll cover the costs of a coordinator and some Youth Corps slots. The city will pay for the paints, brushes and equipment. How does this sound to you?"

"Listen, Chente, I really don't know what I'm doing."

"If you can do what you did here, you'll do fine," he said. "Besides, I'll hook you up with some muralists in East L.A. who can help you."

Then Chente reached into a bag he brought and passed me a box.

"This is for you."

I opened the box. Within it was the most beautiful book I had ever seen: a hard-bound, almost three-inch-thick coffee-table edition about the murals of Mexico with several hundred color and black & white photos. The book included the works of Siqueiros, Orozco and Rivera, Mexico's renowned masters.

"Look this over," Chente said. "It'll show you what public art's all about."

I became the mural project supervisor. The center provided me with 13 young gang members, about half of them girls. We drove around looking for walls to paint. The good ones already had tons of graffiti. We approached the building owners and provided them sketches of what we intended to do. Most owners declined to participate, even though they weren't paying out of their pockets. Finally a few consented, especially if it meant an improvement over the anarchy of scrawl.

I took the mural team to the Goez Art Studio on First Street in East L.A. The leading artists behind the Estrada Courts Housing Projects mural program were based there, and they showed us how to prepare the walls, whether masonry, stucco or wood. They taught us to do miniatures of the mural on paper to the proportion of the area we were working on, then how to square every section of the miniatures which we would replicate on the wall with a chalk line. We learned about the kind of acryllic, all-weather type paints to use, where to get them at discount and how to choose brushes. The Goez Studio also assisted us with human figures, perspective and color schemes.

The first wall I worked on was at the John Fabela Youth Center with a local muralist, Alicia Venegas. After this, the mural team obtained permission to do a large mural at a bar down the street. We were ready.

My sketches dealt with pre-Columbian structures and street images such as hypodermic needles, *cholos* and coffins. On one wall of a hardware store, I ventured into surrealism with floating objects and distorted faces. The team also painted an Aztec warrior at the concession stand in Garvey Park — one of the places I broke into when I was younger.

I soon met a few of L.A.'s best known muralists such as Willie Herrón, Judith Baca and Gronk.

And another world opened up to me.

† † †

One night, a couple of Temple City sheriff's deputies stopped a group of young men drinking in front of the Southside home of Miguel Robles, my old buddy from the days of Thee Impersonations, and later, the Animal Tribe.

Over the years, Miguel completely removed himself from violent activities. He devoted himself to sports — becoming a prize-winning track runner and baseball player. His leadership qualities stayed with him as he participated in San Gabriel High School's MASO club at the same time I was embroiled in ToHMAS. In fact, he had the respect from both barrios as someone who could transcend the obstacles and amount to something. He even talked about being a police officer.

This particular night, the deputies ordered Miguel and his friends to line up and be searched. Miguel's older brother Mooney emerged from the house to investigate. One of the deputies recognized Mooney from an outstanding warrant. Mooney ran back into the house. As a deputy held a gun on the guys spread-eagled against the squad car, the other one pursued Mooney.

The pursuing deputy tackled Mooney in the living room. Miguel's mother and sister, both in the kitchen cooking, rushed out when they heard the noise. His father was resting in the bedroom with his legs in casts from a work injury.

Miguel broke away from the others and ran to the house to help Mooney. By then the deputy had pulled his gun and fired at Mooney's head, clipping his ear. Their mother screamed. The father fell out of the bed and crawled into the living room. Miguel then jumped on the officer, who pulled Miguel off his back and threw him toward the sofa. Without warning, the officer fired another shot, this time striking Miguel. His mother fainted. His sister froze in terror. Miguel's father crept in just as his son fell back onto the sofa, blood oozing through fingers stretched across the abdomen.

Sheriff's deputies arrested everyone — Miguel's father, despite his casts, his mother and his friends — and hauled them to the station.

Mooney survived, but was then re-jailed on the warrant. Miguel remained in critical condition. Meetings were held in which the witnesses testified about what happened. The community demanded that Deputy Fred J. Coates, a 14-year veteran, be brought to justice. The sheriff's office transferred Coates to another subdivision of the county while they investigated.

Meanwhile, the Brown Berets organized a march which went through various San Gabriel Valley barrios to protest the shootings.

Sal Basuto reset a date for the barrio unity meeting at La Casa. Bienvenidos people held mini-conferences around the police shooting in anticipation of the meeting. We now had a rationale and a cause: Justice for Miguel Robles!

La Casa's meeting hall overflowed with people. Sal had volunteers pass out brown arm bands to remind everyone of Miguel's condition. Sangra Diablos had their representatives sitting on one side of a round table in the middle of the hall; community members sat behind the table in a circle. Lomas representatives included Santos, Cuervo, Toots, Pokie, Chicharrón and me.

At the table were Viviana's brothers Negro and Shark, also Turtleman, Boy, Hapo and Night Owl. I gave Night Owl a wink as I sat down and he smirked like he did when we were in jail together. Chava did not attend, but this time he didn't oppose anyone else being there; Sal said he did this to save face.

Sal had drawn up an agreement which declared a truce between Lomas and Sangra. Violators would be reprimanded by the barrios involved. Joint events were planned to keep the peace. At the bottom of the agreement it said: End Barrio Warfare! Justice for the Robles Brothers! We all signed and then the hall broke out in hand claps, slowly at first, then progressing into a thunderous roar in the style of the Chicano movement.

Afterwards, we celebrated under the ramada. Everybody acted tentative. A truce between our barrios had never happened before. Later, Chava arrived with a few other Diablos like Coyote, Danilo and Gato. He kept cool at first. But Santos felt uneasy, coming up to me, trying to stay cool but feeling his blood boil. I tried to calm him down.

Sure enough, Chava walked up to Santos and stared him down. Santos stared back, his arms out in a ready-to-fight stance. Suddenly, Chava came at him, bare-fisted. Santos and Chava threw blows, back and forth. Others tried to get involved but people from La Casa and Bienvenidos called for calm, pulling others away from the fighting.

The two ended up in the middle of the street; Chava had Santos by the throat, Santos grabbed Chava's gut and squeezed. Neither would let go. Sal tried to break them up, but couldn't disengage them.

"Párenle — we don't want to give the police an excuse to shut us down," Sal implored.

At that point, somebody pushed through the crowd.

"Miguel is dead!...Miguel is dead!"

Everybody stood still and listened.

"We just got a call. Miguel died earlier tonight."

Santos and Chava let go of each other. Chava then turned around and walked away, a few of his homeboys at his heels. I felt the heat within me again, and I wanted to cry but no tears would come: Miguel, oh, Miguel, you were the best of us!

Deputy Coates now faced a murder charge. It was an opportunity to put away, for the first time ever, a "peace" officer for killing an unarmed citizen in Los Angeles County.

Soon the Brown Berets organized openly in the area. I became acquainted with a couple of their San Gabriel Valley representatives. They had goatees, long hair, looking like Che Guevara, with berets covered in buttons and slogans. A branch of the Movimiento Bookstore opened in South San Gabriel, an offshoot from the original one on Brooklyn Avenue in Maravilla. A former prison activist, Al "Pache" Alvarez, ran the store, and I often came in to glance at his books, posters and magazines about Chicanos and other groups waging the struggle, such as the American Indian Movement, the Black Panthers and the Puerto Rican resistance group, The Young Lords.

✢ ✢ ✢

A deputy squad car drove through the unilluminated roads in the Hills. Unseen voices cried out "Lomas" from the bushes; the trees and darkened homes followed the squad car's journey up the winding streets as the voices echoed against the shadows of collapsed fences, shacks and branches.

From somewhere in the foliage, gunfire riddled the side of the vehicle.

"Code 999!...Code 999!" a deputy radioed in. "Officer under fire....Bailey and Marsh Avenues."

The deputy sped out of there as fast as possible; he made it without injury. Later for weeks, sheriff's deputies blocked off entrances and exits to the barrio, checking license plates and marking down numbers and names.

Then on a moonless evening, the sheriff's helicopter criss-crossed the neighborhood as usual, forcing everyone to stay inside their homes. It hovered across the path of an empty shed on the highest hill in the barrio while covering a patch of ground with its spotlight. A loud crack resounded nearby as a powerful projectile struck the side of the helicopter, causing it to sputter and twirl as it descended toward earth.

The pilot kept the helicopter in the air while he maneuvered it out of the path of trees and homes, finally striking soil and landing in an empty field.

The media declared the greater South San Gabriel/San Gabriel area a hotbed of unrest. The helicopter incident had been duplicated in other neighborhoods as well, the most famous being in the Casa Blanca barrio of Riverside, some 60 miles east of us. In East L.A., a group calling itself the Chicano Liberation Front had allegedly planted bombs in power stations and government buildings. Whole sections of the city and county were placed on alert.

One warm, summer afternoon, Santos casually walked up Graves Avenue to see Indio, a homeboy who lived with his wife and two children in the flat area below the Hills. Indio sat on the front steps with his three-year-old boy by his feet. Santos crossed the yellowed yard as Indio stood up to greet him. At that moment, an unmarked car speeding down Graves Avenue slowed in front of Indio's house. Two bullets burst out from inside the vehicle before it sped off, never stopping. No barrio was claimed. The bodies of Santos and Indio lay across the lawn, killed instantly, as a small boy wailed for his mother. Another drive-by?

The funerals for Indio and Santos were massive. Hundreds of cars lined up on Portrero Grande Drive for miles from the church, where the bodies had lain in state, to the Resurrection Cemetery where most of the barrio dead were buried. In school, everybody wore black arm bands again, reminiscent of Miguel's death, John Fabela's and others'.

Rumor had it Sangra shot Santos and Indio. Those trying to maintain peace knew this violated the truce and could mean warfare again. Leaflets issued by Bienvenidos and La Casa tried to cool the rising tempers. But there were those on both sides who didn't want peace.

✝ ✝ ✝

As many of the *locos* as possible were to assemble in the basement of an old Victorian brick house — one of the few remaining in the barrio — where Puppet lived.

Groups first gathered in the various vacant lots: the one on Toll Drive, the Bailey Street fields and the ravine where Berne Street dead-ended. I went up Toll Drive towards a battalion of dudes with Pendleton shirts, buttoned from the top only, *vato*-style, and starched khaki or juvenile hall-issued pants we called "counties." They had an assortment of bandannas, hats and gloves: battle gear, even on a hot day.

When I reached the others, somebody passed me a bottle of muscatel wine. Others talked about the women they had been with, the rampaging they had done: smart, slick talk — our *totacho*.

"*Caiga, ése,* how's the *ruca* I saw you with last night?

"*Más firmota, ése,* but she talk too much."

"*Orale,* what you do — talk back?"

They were about *locura,* the spirit of existence which meant the difference between living life to the fullest or wandering aimlessly upon the earth, taking up space, getting in the way. The *vatos* hated those without daring, those who failed to meet the challenge, the fear and exhilaration of this presence.

We moved toward Puppet's *cantón* and trickled down into the basement, out of view from the street. Outside, Puppet's sister Rachel walked Eight Ball around, who had overdosed on smack, so he wouldn't pass out.

I climbed into the basement. *Yesca* smoke infiltrated my eyes and nose. I barely saw the flicker of gazes through the haze. Whispers and the sleepy drawl of some hyped-up dude surrounded me. Fluorescent posters, crosses and the spray-painted names of homeboys covered the basement's walls and ceiling.

My eyes scanned around and then stopped. There before me lay the largest collection of weapons I had ever seen: shotguns, in different gauges; handguns from .22s to 9 millimeters; semi-automatic rifles with scopes, thirty-thirty and thirty-ought-sixes; and the automatics — 16s and all sort of subs. In a corner were several wood boxes piled up with hand grenades. Here was an inventory of the barrio arsenal, most of it stolen from military armories.

Dizzy from the scene — the laughter, the weaponry and blurred faces — I squeezed in between Enano and Bone.

Soon Puppet came down the steps with Fuzzy, confidence in their stride. Puppet and Fuzzy were the self-appointed lieutenants in the coming battles. They were accepted by an unspoken respect. Even Peaches, Ragman, Natividad or the maniac Valdez brothers accepted this.

Puppet looked around and spotted Chepo, a younger dude from the Dukes.

"No Dukes," Puppet declared.

"Hey, man, I just came to..."

"I said no Dukes," Puppet repeated.

Nobody disagreed. Chepo got up and left.

Puppet, dark and broad-shouldered in a short-sleeve knit shirt, squatted in the middle of the room. On his forearm was a tattoo of a peacock. On the inside of his other arm, a spider poised near a Mexican girl in a *sombrero*, caught in a web.

Next to him stood Fuzzy, a light-skinned dude with a rugged face, goatee, and short, almost nappy, hair on his head. He had his shirt off and "Las Lomas" tattooed in large old-English lettering across the wide of his back.

"*Orale*, homeboys, what are we going to do about Sangra?" Fuzzy asked the *vatos*. They responded with yelps and *gritos*.

"Fine, let's work out some tactics," Puppet said.

Everything became quiet; I could hear my heartbeat.

"We know the *chota* is expecting us to move. So we have to do it quick. Sangra won't know what hit 'em."

"They'll know it was the Hills, *ése*," Bone interjected.

"They'll know it's us. But they won't know exactly who," Puppet said. "The *chota* will come down hard, but we're going to make sure nobody gets popped. This means we got to take care of each other. And we have to be *trucha* for *dedos*."

Dedos meant fingers and is used to describe snitches. They were also called *ratas* — rats.

"*Guacha*, Toots and Ragman will carry the *cuetes*," Puppet explained. "I want Fuzzy and Nat to..."

"I have something to say," I called out.

Everybody turned to my direction.

"Have you thought about what Sangra is doing right now?" I said. "They're probably getting ready to hit us too. And we hit them and they hit us — when does it stop?"

Puppet gave me a look which signaled something unpleasant.v

"Nobody says you have to do anything. Go on out there with Chepo then."

"We can't pretend a war with Sangra won't mean others won't die," I responded, knowing I couldn't back off. "That our brothers and sisters, or even our moms, won't get hurt."

"We're doing it for Santos and Indio," Fuzzy said. "Besides, you the dude painting murals over our *placas*. That's dead! We were talking about *dedos*. Where do you stand, *ése*?"

"You all know I'll take on anybody," I countered as I stood up. "They were my homeboys too. But think about it: They were killed by a speeding car, both of them shot right through the heart. Nobody yelled out nothing. Who's trained to do this? Not Sangra. I say the cops did this. I say they want us to go after Sangra when we were so close to coming together."

"We have to use our brains," I continued, talking to everyone. "We have to think about who's our real enemy. The dudes in Sangra are just like us, man."

Treacherous talk.

Then Puppet stood up.

"Only *pinche putos* would tell us to back off on Sangra, talking bullshit about uniting barrios."

"Listen, don't misunderstand..."

Just then a fist slammed against my mouth; a warm wet trickle slowly wound its way down my chin.

Puppet appeared ready to swing again but he looked surprised; he gave me one of his best blows, yet I didn't fall.

My measured reasoning turned to anger. I felt like throwing a blow of my own. But I looked around at the faces of my homeboys — at Chicharrón — and realized I was alone. Fuzzy gave me a large grin.

"Look, *puto*, you messin' with the Hills," Fuzzy said. "And nobody messes with us. Understand?"

No direct threats. All threats had to be carried out. This served as a warning. The uneasiness in the place could be cut with a blunt knife.

"All right! We got better things to do then waste our time with this *pedo*," Puppet declared. "So if it's all right with Chin over here, we move on Sangra tonight."

Puppet looked at everybody and there was approval. He looked at me and there was silence.

Chapter Nine

"You don't have solo rights to anything anymore, not even your crazy life."
— Letter to me from a Jewish teenager
after a youth conference in 1972

A low, primered 1968 Impala idled in front of a beige-white, Spanish-style stucco house in a cleanly-lit section of San Gabriel. Music spilled out of open windows along with laughter and the talk of young people. A party! The car pulled into a spot near the house. Yo Yo and Hapo jumped out the front seat while Coyote clambered out of the back and looked around. The swirl of Santa Ana winds cooled the summer heat, clearing away the eye-burning smog which has smothered the valley for days. Chava stepped out from behind Coyote.

"Let's check out the *borlote*," he declared, and the four marched toward the pulsing beat.

They entered the front door without invitation and surveyed the scene. A row of girls sat around with beer cans and cigarettes in their hands. The intruders could not make out the handful of guys scattered among them; they looked cool, but not *barrio*.

Coyote eyed a pretty *ruca* by a coffee table topped with bowls of chips, salsa and onion dip. Yo Yo indicated he had to go to the head. Chava and Hapo shuffled through the kitchen and out the back door; outside, a few people danced near a carport lined with trash cans brimming with ice and beer.

"¡*Sangra Rifa!*" Hapo yelled, by impulse really, perhaps thinking it will keep the dudes at a distance. Chava looked annoyed at him, but it was too late.

Eight dudes stepped out of the darkness beneath the carport. Chava immediately recognized them: Eight Ball, Fuzzy, Enano, Topo, Lencho, Toots, Bone and Puppet — from the Hills!

Hapo backed into the house. Coyote and Yo Yo sensed something was wrong. Hapo looked at them, terrified.

"*Trucha* — run!"

"What?"

"I said run — it's Lomas!"

Coyote, Yo Yo and Hapo flew out the door toward the Impala. But Chava did not run, could not run; he stood alone in the back yard as the legion of shadows approached, yelling back, shadows which surrounded their prey and pounced in a deadly pantomime, steel blades penetrating flesh. Chava did not cry out.

He toppled to the ground, touched the wet sweet-smelling blades of grass, and it was these simple, slight odors, sensations and sounds which gripped his attention: the peal of chimes near the back door, moths colliding into a light bulb — a treble pressing out of woofers and tweeters from dual stereo speakers. Eight dudes, eight punctures into sides, the abdomen, the ribs. *No more, no more!*

But there was more.

Somebody picked up a rusted tire rim from the cluttered driveway, raised it high, and thrust it down on Chava's head.

"No more, please, no more!"

But this was not Chava's voice. Somehow his voice sounded only as an echo in a canyon inside his body. This was a woman's voice, Rita's voice, as she jumped over Chava's prone figure and pleaded with the shadows standing over him to stop.

The shadows backed off. Rita turned Chava's barely-breathing body onto its side and somebody nearby screamed, like the wailing inside a black dream, into all the screams ever screamed, as the grass blended into crimson from wounds in his body and his head, a soaked mass of hair, eyes and jawbone.

✝ ✝ ✝

Chicharrón pulled up in front of Mark Keppel High School.

"Hey, Chin — want to hear a joke?" he asked.

"Only if it's a good one."

"Knock, knock..."

"I said a good one."

With him was a year-old baby. Chicharrón and Shoshi weren't together anymore, but he held the legacy of their brief relationship in his arms. They named him Junior. Having a baby didn't seem to fit Chicharrón, but he looked proud as Junior took in the surroundings, full of unknowing.

I stood in front of the gnarled tree among students sitting in the grass, talking and relaxing in the sun. Chicharrón, as usual, started in on me.

"I see you still got them potato shoes."

Chicharrón poked fun at my brown shoes which I wore until the leather withered, looking like a spud. He also made fun of the fact I peed a lot, especially when I drank. He once handed me a picture he drew of me with a tiny piss sac and potato shoes — underneath he wrote: The Chinmunist.

In my senior year, I became ToHMAS president. The club had succeeded in obtaining a Chicano Studies class with a powerful and engaging teacher, Mr. Sosa. I also became the student council's Speaker of the House and a columnist for the school's newspaper, which the journalism teacher offered after he liked my response to an anti-Chicano editorial. I called the column "Pensamientos."

In one column I wrote: "It's important that Chicanos feel this is their school too. It's about time we became part of America." And once I did an article about how Lomas Dukes held a car wash to benefit an elementary school where the children had no money to buy milk or lunch. Somebody on the newspaper staff asked why the Dukes didn't use the money to clean the graffiti off the school walls. I told him: "It's a lot better to feed some hungry kids than to clean up your fuckin' walls, that's why!"

As we sat around, making the baby laugh, Cha Cha, a leading member of ToHMAS, came up behind me, a tremor in her voice.

"Louie, I need to talk with you."

"What's going on Cha Cha?"

"You know Mr. Humes, the history teacher, he just threw me out of his class for being late — but not before he called me a chola whore!"

"What?"

"It's true. I told him I had to take my little brother to the babysitter's because my moms is sick. But he got real mad and cursed me out — in front of the whole class!"

"Who does he think he is? Let's see about this."

I went into the school. A few of the students on the lawn, including Chicharrón and the baby, walked in behind me. I ran up the stairs to the second floor. Cha Cha pointed across the hallway to a classroom in session.

When I entered, Mr. Humes, with graying hair, short-sleeve striped shirt and tie, stood in front of the blackboard, addressing a scattered row of students.

"Young man, you have no business barging into my class like this, you better leave..."

"No, I won't leave. What's this about calling Cha Cha a chola whore."

"I don't have to answer to you!" Mr. Humes yelled. "I'm tired of this dictatorship of students we have here."

"Oh, I see — you want to be able to call somebody a whore and get away with it. That's over with, man. We refuse to take any more abuse."

"And I won't take this abuse," he countered. "I want you out of my class — now! If not, we'll see Mr. Madison about this."

"Well, you're just going to have to see Mr. Madison."

Mr. Humes stalked out the class. As he slammed the door, the students in the room and in the hallway broke into cheers. It was far from over.

Mr. Madison called Cha Cha and me into his office.

"You can't go around disrupting classes," he said. "This conduct has got to stop."

"Nobody should get away with what Mr. Humes called Cha Cha," I said.

"But there are other ways to resolve this. There are channels. There's me — why didn't you come to me first?"

"We're taking this into our own hands. We have no way to control the outcome if we don't. We just don't trust how anything gets resolved around here."

"But I have the authority, not you," said Mr. Madison. "I can't have students interrupting classes whenever they feel like it."

Then Cha Cha spoke: "Listen Mr. Madison, you've forgotten that Mr. Humes called me a whore. Who cares about us 'disrupting' a class. What are you going to do about Mr. Humes? It's my life here. It's the lives of others like me. What are you going to do?"

It was far from over. Other students found out what happened. Again the anger held inside boiled over. Somebody slashed Mr. Humes' car tires.

Later a group of Mexicans beat up some Anglos in the gym. This escalated to fights in the cafeteria and parking lot. Cha Cha's encounter served as the catalyst for that year's Tradition.

The student council called a special session. Daryl, the student president, proposed a "Communicators" group which would consist of leaders from among the Mexican and Anglo students. Mr. Madison approved the suggestion and provided a meeting place for the group. A list of 60 names were drawn up; I was on the list.

The Communicators were to stifle any rumors. Stop any fights. Resolve any differences. The Communicators wore red armbands. We were excused from classes and allowed to roam the hallways and talk with students. The fights ceased after two days as the Communicators walked up and down the school espousing calm.

On the third day, the 60-member group met in the auditorium to determine how to deal with disruptions. I proposed they take affirmative steps for people to talk out their problems, to address the inequities, and allow more power to fall into the hands of students. This led to a wild debate. As we argued the finer points, a teacher ran into the auditorium.

"They're at it again!" she yelled out, her hair disheveled. "They're fighting in the halls!"

"Okay, everyone," Daryl said. "We've got to go out there and stop this."

The Communicators poured out of the auditorium to where a knot of students gathered near a stairway. Screams and shouts greeted us. I saw one dude jump in crazy anger from the top of the stairs onto the crowd of students below.

I rushed up to the melee and tried to pull apart a couple of students on the ground. But as I got a hold of one guy, I looked up and a crumpled soda can filled with sand smashed against my mouth. The jagged edge and weight of the sand burst open my bottom lip; blood streamed out as if it were a waterfall. Others stopped fighting as I stood there in a daze. A student and a teacher grabbed my arm and escorted me to the nurse's office.

When we got there, a number of students were already sitting around with various injuries. The nurse looked at my mouth. The crumpled can had sliced the lip and chipped off a piece of tooth. She suggested I be taken to the medical clinic.

"You're from Keppel, right?" the doctor said as she came into the operating room where I lay holding soaked towels to my face.

"We've been getting a lot of you guys this past week," the doctor said. "Let's take a look."

I removed the towels. The doctor looked stern, but not alarmed.

"Ain't no big thing," she said. "We'll get you some stitches, and you'll be good as new."

I liked her already. She prepared the cat-gut while I lay back.

"I'm not using any anesthesia," she declared. "You seem like a tough dude. I'm sure you can take it."

I hated her guts. Yet I didn't say anything. I let her sew up the lip without any painkiller; I felt the needle enter in and out of skin, stitch after stitch. I didn't wince or complain. I just tightened my grip on the bedsides so the doctor wouldn't see.

After the doctor finished, she looked at me with a devious glint in her eye.

"I guess you could take it," she said. "Not even a whimper. Okay, tough guy — you can go home now."

But I didn't go home. I went back to the school with an immense gauze bandage on the lower lip. By then hundreds of students were gathered outside. It was an impromptu walkout following my injury. I walked up to the crowd which roared at the sight of me. Esme addressed them from the top of the front steps. I came up next to her, the gauze and the pain keeping me from smiling.

"Louie, can you say a few words?" Esme asked.

I took my time, but I managed.

"We've come a long way in this school. But something keeps coming up to show us we've got a long way to go. All I can say is, we can't stop fighting until the battle's won."

The students exploded in a frenzy of clapping. Inside the school doorways, I could see Mrs. Baez was pleased to see me asserting myself. But Mr. Madison, trying so hard to contain the controversy, looked tired.

Not long after this, the school fired Mr. Pérez. Mr. Pérez ran the print shop. It was the most popular class for Chicanos; many meetings were held there. He not only sponsored the ToHMAS club, he was also the school's best teacher. Mr. Pérez arranged field trips to downtown, the beach, even to Beverly Hills; he wanted us to see the world, see how others lived and know why we didn't live the same way. But teachers who helped students think were considered radical.

One day Mr. Pérez received a notice. The school claimed he was insubordinate and unresponsiveness to the students' needs — the exact opposite of the truth.

I walked into the Chicano Student Center. Esme's face covered with pain; Amelia, crying. Mrs. Baez held a phone in her hand, although not talking into it.

"This is it, man," I said. "I've had it with these people. Another walkout, man, we're going out until they bring Pérez back."

"No, Luis, not this time," Mrs. Baez said, waving the phone at me. "You can't walk out every time something isn't to your liking. The school and Mr. Pérez need to work this out."

"That's just an excuse," Esme said. "They've wanted to get rid of Mr. Pérez for a long time. He's the only teacher willing to take chances, to challenge the way things are."

"Yeah, Mrs. Baez, I don't buy it," I said. "We're going out."

"Luis, don't forget you're a Communicator," Mrs. Baez said. "You're supposed to keep the peace."

"Not any more — I quit!"

This time, I worked the halls hard, telling as many students as I could about the pending walkout. This time, the school was prepared. For a year or so, Alex, who lived in the Hills, worked with Mr. Madison to diffuse any tension. The day of the proposed walkout, Mr. Madison had a talk with Alex, who then went around the school telling everyone the walkout was off.

Some students came up to me, confused. I began to see the plan: Mr. Madison wanted a tug-of-war between Alex and me — and he was betting on his stooge Alex. In fact, the walkout's strength had waned because of Alex's misinformation tactic. But still, Mr. Madison implemented Plan B.

I had designated 1 p.m., following the lunch period, for everyone to meet on the lawn. But just before the lunch break, the loudspeakers made an announcement: At 1 p.m. there was to be a special school-wide assembly at Aztec Stadium.

"They're doing this to stop the walkout," Esme said.

"I know, there's nothing we can do now," I said. "Let's see what Mr. Madison has in mind."

Hundreds of students assembled in the bleacher stands. I found a seat at the very top and sat down, my face a mask of indifference.

Mr. Madison made a long-winded speech about cooperation, about harmony and understanding; how certain elements were out to undermine all Mark Keppel High School stood for.

I sat there, feeling the flux and flow of power within me. I had called off the walkout, that much I had to do. But I also knew all this — the school assembly, the address to the student body, Alex's role — all of this was because of me!

I recalled when I first entered school in Watts, how I had been virtually written off, pushed into a corner with building blocks and treated like a pariah; how in Garvey I had been heaved out of classes and, later in high school, forced to drop out and labeled a failure!

Now I was somebody they couldn't dismiss — somebody who had to be heard.

✟ ✟ ✟

"I finished reading all the work you gave me a while back — remember, your poems and stories," Mrs. Baez said.

"Yeah, sure — they're no good, right?"

"Luis, how can you say that! They're wonderful. We should get them published."

"Great — but how?"

"Well, I picked up a newspaper the other day where they announced a Chicano Literary Contest in Berkeley. It's from Quinto Sol Publications. Let's send them the work. But it has to be retyped — your typing is terrible."

"I know, I know...but who's going to retype it?"

"I'll find some help. I'm sure there are people willing to do something. What do you say?"

"I guess okay — I mean, it's worth a try."

About the same time, the California State College at Los Angeles offered me an Economic Opportunity Program Grant — despite my past school record, lack of credits and other mishaps. Chente, Mr. Pérez and Mrs. Baez teamed up to help me get accepted.

And a Loyola-Marymount University art professor asked me to paint a mural for the school; he offered some pay and student artists to work with.

My head spun with all the prospects.

But the kicker was when Mrs. Baez returned the newly-typed versions of my writing; I couldn't believe I had anything to do with it. The shape of the words, the forms and fragments of sentences and syllables, seemed alien, as if done by another's hand.

The fact was I didn't know anything about literature. I had fallen through the chasm between two languages. The Spanish had been beaten out of me in the early years of school — and I didn't learn English very well either.

This was the predicament of many Chicanos.

We could almost be called incommunicable, except we remained lucid; we got over what we felt, sensed and understood. Sometimes we rearranged words, created new meanings and structures — even a new vocabulary. Often our everyday talk blazed with poetry.

Our expressive powers were strong and vibrant. If this could be nurtured, if the language skills could be developed on top of this, we could learn to break through any communication barrier. We needed to obtain victories in language, built on an infrastructure of self-worth.

But we were often defeated from the start.

In my case, though I didn't know how to write or paint, I had a great need to conceive and imagine, so compelling, so encompassing, I had to do it even when I knew my works would be subject to ridicule, would be called stupid and naive. I just couldn't stop.

I had to learn how, though; I had to believe I could.

One day, I received a phone call. It was from Dr. Octavio Romano of Quinto Sol. I had been chosen as one of two honorary winners in their $1,000 literary contest. My award was $250, a paid plane trip — my first ever — to Berkeley, and a publishing contract.

At the news, I felt so alive, so intensely aware of my surroundings. After I hung up the phone, I raced out of the house in the rain and danced: an Aztec two-step, boogie-woogie, a *norteño* — it didn't matter, I danced.

Mama looked out at me and said I had gone crazy for sure. And I was crazy — like my Tía Chucha, who continued to create without recognition, despite being outcast from the family; crazy like the moon which jitterbugged in the night, crazy like the heartbeat which kept pumping its precious liquid when so much tried to stop it.

I won $250 — the most legitimate money I'd ever obtained in one chunk. I danced for the 'hood, I danced for the end of degradation, I danced for all the little people who ever tried to make it and were crushed.

Berkeley...my own book contract...250 bucks!

I finally graduated from high school. Quite an achievement. I didn't attend the official ceremony and prom because I felt it had nothing to do with me.

ToHMAS had its own celebration where I received a certificate in appreciation of my activities of the previous two years. Mrs. Baez and Chente were among those present, both smiling with perhaps a sense of some accomplishment. They helped make me.

I gave Esme, Flora, Amelia, Chuy, Cha Cha and the others my sincerest hopes for the future. A few of them were continuing as Keppel students and planned to carry on the fight we had begun. Delfina was there and I walked up to her. She was to be next year's Josephine Aztec.

"Louie, I wouldn't be here if it weren't for you," she said.

"I'm glad — I'm just sorry it didn't work out between us."

We hugged, and then I made the rounds embracing and shaking hands with the other students. When it came time for me to say a few words, I told the group: "I believe anything I've done, anybody can do — and do better. I'm no exception. Everyone here is a potential leader."

I managed to go to Mr. Madison's office and pick up my diploma. Mr. Madison handed it to me without a word and shook my hand, looking ambivalent. I felt he didn't hate me, but he had never known anyone like me — and I suspected he figured it would be a long time before he'd meet another.

As I left the school, I carried with me numerous scars, but there were also victories: Mr. Pérez got his job back, the school hired another Chicano Studies teacher — and Mr. Humes received an early retirement.

In my last year, ToHMAS members attended Mexican American Leadership Conferences with students from all over Los Angeles County. The Belmont High School teacher Sal Castro, a leader of the 1968 East L.A. "Blowouts," and other Chicano leaders were key speakers.

We also participated in L.A.-wide conferences with youth of other communities: Jewish students from the Westside, Anglos from the San Fernando Valley, Blacks from South Central L.A. and Compton, sons and daughters of the longshore, refinery and canning industries in the Harbor — many of whom were undergoing similar predicaments. We told our story to enraptured groups and struck a chord.

Most importantly, Anglo students at Keppel began to grasp the significance of struggle and pressed for their own demands.

One of them, Maureen Murphy, ran a controversial campaign for school office on a program of unity and justice. She wrote me a letter following her victory: "You are one of the three persons in this world I term a 'real person.' You showed me many times where I was wrong and where I was right, and even where I have to fight and what to give up. I'll be frank...I'm scared. I need someone to help me. I'm not really that happy I won for if the color of my skin was different, like you, I would have lost."

Some like Maureen understood that the foundation for the sinking levels of instruction for all students, for their own diminished rights, lay in the two-tiered educational system. As long as some students were deprived of a quality education, they all were.

✝ ✝ ✝

I began Cal State-L.A. in the fall of 1972, majoring in Broadcast Journalism and Chicano Studies. I even bought my first car, a blue bug with chrome rims and tires which stuck out several inches from the side. A lowrider Volkswagen.

While going to college I had to continue working since the grant I received would only cover part of the cost. I worked part-time gigs as a school bus driver, a warehouse employee and a truck driver for a lamp manufacturer.

I signed a contract with Quinto Sol and worked on the publication of the book, tentatively titled "Barrio Expressions."

Chicharrón continued to visit, sometimes letting Junior play in the back yard. I stayed in the garage room to save money. Besides, the place carried so many memories; I didn't want to leave, even when Mama offered to let me stay in the house again.

I became active in MEChA, eventually becoming vice-president and editor of the club's newspaper. We set up a MEChA Central which trained and organized Chicano students from high schools all over the Eastside: Roosevelt, Garfield, Lincoln, Belmont, Franklin and Wilson. I traveled to these schools talking with youth and serving as liaison to the college.

On one of those excursions, I met Camila Martínez. She was a student at Garfield High School, an almost 100 percent Chicano school with one of the highest dropout rates in the city. I attended a MEChA meeting there and was asked to speak. I addressed issues of organizing, drawing a lot upon my Keppel experiences. But I became terribly distracted by a cute, Filipina-looking, curly-haired, dark-eyed student in front of me. She had on a short skirt out of which emerged some killer legs. I didn't know it then, but this girl knew what she wanted, and she wanted me.

Camila showed up at all the meetings, gently interrupting my talks with questions and comments, constantly keeping herself in my view. I invited her to study sessions we were starting in various East L.A. homes. She came, participated, picked up readily the concepts and fell in well with the discourse. Before I knew it, I invited her to a dance MEChA was having at Cal State. During a slow dance, she said she liked me. I felt something kindle in my chest. I was falling for Camila.

But I was already seeing two girls who lived next door behind my brother Joe's house. By then Joe had married a woman he met when he was a truck driver for a company where she worked on the assembly line. Her name was Elvie. They moved in next door and soon had a son they named after me, Louie, and later a daughter, Tricia.

The girls, Rosie and Terry, were runaways who ended up staying with Joe and Elvie. Before long, they moved in on me. Terry used to throw dirt clods at my garage room door in the middle of the night. I'd open the door and she'd jump over the fence and spend the night. My mother asked me about the splattering of dirt on the outside of the room, which I pretended I didn't know anything about, but I sensed she knew what was happening.

Rosie got involved with me soon after, I believed to get back at Terry. One day Rosie came to my room and knocked.

"Who is it?"

"It's Rosie, I need to talk with you."

I let her in. Rosie stood in the doorway, the sunlight behind her, and then she took off her blouse. She had nothing underneath.

"I know this is very forward — but I want to make love to you."

I also dated girls Elvie hooked me up with, including her Puerto Rican friend Evelyn. There was also a *mechista* who I liked from Cal State.

And there I was, falling for Camila!

One day, a bombshell was laid at my doorstep. A letter. In it, Terry said she was pregnant — and claimed it was my child!

I was stunned. Here I was on the verge of changing my life, in college, with a book about to happen, working in my spare time and possibly getting more mural-painting jobs. I didn't want this child. But I didn't know how to respond. Unfortunately, I didn't talk to anyone before I confronted Terry.

"Listen, Terry, I like you very much. But I'm not ready to have a baby."

"What are you saying, Louie?"

"I mean, there's many things happening for me right now. A year ago, I would've been game. But I don't want to stop what I've started. I think you should have an abortion."

Terry looked horrified, then ran off. Soon after everything caved in. Elvie said Terry threatened suicide. Rosie all of a sudden took my side of the issue, causing greater conflict. When word got to my family, I faced divergent pressures: I should be responsible and have this child. I should be responsible and make sure Terry gets an abortion. I didn't know what to do. I wanted to get out of there. I called Chicharrón one night and got dead drunk.

The next day, Rosie came to the room in a harried state.

"Terry's gone!"

"She's gone? But why, she's going to have a baby, no?"

"Louie, I don't know — it's hard to tell with Terry what's real and what ain't. But she left last night, took everything, and didn't say where she went."

"You mean, Terry may not be pregnant?"

"I mean, with her you don't know if she's just playing games to get to you, or if she left because she doesn't want to lose the baby."

"Shit, we have to find her...but I can't go now. I'm working and going to school."

I talked to my brother and his wife to figure out what to do. They offered to look for her. My sister Gloria went along. The next weekend, they went as far as the Mexican border, following on leads Rosie gave them. Terry's family stayed in San Diego and they tried there. But no Terry.

In two days, they returned.

"Sorry, Louie, we couldn't find her," Joe said. "Nobody knows where she's at. She could be having a baby. She could be living it up somewhere without one — or she could be dead."

Later, Rosie returned back to her family. I never did find out where Terry went. I never knew for sure if she had a child, and if so, if it was mine.

The peace between the barrios never got off the ground after Santos and Indio were killed; I still maintained the sheriffs were behind their murders. Regardless, the wars continued, worsening in some cases, extending in others. In one incident, a group of dudes were standing around in front of La Casa when a carload of *locos* cruised by. Tiburón walked out, a handgun in the small of his back.

"You and me, Coyote," he called out.

Coyote walked out to meet Tiburón. Tiburón then reached behind him, pulled out the gun and began shooting. Other dudes with him opened fire as well. The Sangra guys scattered. One of them walked off for a few steps, fell, got up and then fell again; he died there on the sidewalk.

In the wee hours of the morning, plainclothes detectives busted into several homes belonging to Lomas members. They were being arrested for the murder of 16-year-old David Alcón. One of those they picked up was Chicharrón.

The police issued a warrant for Tiburón's arrest. He was nowhere to be found. For weeks, the police combed the Hills, visited his family, even called on authorities in Mexico.

Then in the Hills, in the quiet of night, somebody thrust a shotgun through a bedroom window and opened fire, striking Tiburón's 13-year-old brother in the head. Pellet holes and blood scattered on the far wall. Sangra claimed the shooting. Soon after, Tiburón turned himself in.

A jury found Tiburón guilty of murder and he was sent up to San Quentin. Chicharrón, who was 17 then, was found guilty of accessory to murder and sentenced to YTS prison in Chino. A couple other dudes from the Hills received various lesser charges relating to Alcón's death.

Junior no longer came to play in the back yard. Shoshi took care of him following Chicharrón's verdict. Chicharrón then left to serve his time — I was the last of anyone who ever claimed *los cuatro*.

I started to see more of Camila. She moved in with an older sister after being thrown out from her mother's house. But once her mother found out I was seeing her, she started to spend more time at the house on Ferris Avenue where Camila and her sister, Irma, lived. The first time I took Camila to a movie, her mother forced Camila's younger brother to come along, armed with a kitchen knife in case I "got out of hand."

Once I drove a large bob-tail truck to the front of Garfield High School to pick up Camila after school. As I strolled the walkway leading up to the main building, dudes moved out of the way, some giving me nods, as Camila waited for me, smiling, on the school's steps. She looked so pretty with skin of soft brown, shapely legs and a shapely behind, and one of the cutest faces I'd ever seen. I felt proud to be her boyfriend.

Everything seemed to come my way — with a beautiful woman at my side.

✝ ✝ ✝

The woman screamed but nobody appeared to hear. I saw a couple of deputies push her against a car parked in the lot of an after-hours club in Norwalk. I looked to see if anybody else was around, but the few who were there turned away, ignoring the screams as a deputy punched the woman in the face.

"Hey, get off her!" I yelled.

I didn't know who she was or what she did; I just couldn't stand there and witness the beating.

"Get the fuck out of here — now!" shouted an officer as he pulled hard on the woman's arm so he could put handcuffs on her. Her face smashed against the asphalt, bleeding from the mouth.

"*¡Pinche cabrones!*" she managed to say.

"Leave her alone — can't you see you're hurting her?"

At this, a couple of deputies pounced on me. I fell to the ground. Officers pulled on my arms, picked me up and threw me against a squad car. I felt the blows of a blackjack against my side and back. I tried to pull them off me, when suddenly eight other deputies showed up. As they pounded on me, my foot inadvertently came up and brushed one of them in the chest.

The deputies threw me inside a squad car, the woman in another. By then a crowd had gathered, but they appeared helpless as more deputies swarmed the club's parking lot.

For about a half-hour the squad car drove around. A deputy hit me in the stomach. Another struck me in the face:

"You got something to say...it looks like you got something to say to us," an officer implored.

I didn't say anything. Not even fuck you. I felt my cheek swell. Another fist smashed into an eye, the end of a blackjack into a rib. I clenched my teeth, holding back a cry so that they couldn't use anything I said or did to intensify their attack.

The deputies drove me to the prison ward of the L.A. County Hospital to have my injuries checked. Within hours, I was declared fit and taken to the County Jail. Familiar territory. This time, I was an adult and belonged here. This time I faced a hard-time prison sentence for assaulting a police officer.

On the bus to the County Jail, a woman sat chained with her head down in a caged area near the driver. She looked up and saw me.

"Hey you...yeah you, *ése* — what's your name?"

"No talking!" shouted a deputy sitting nearby with a shotgun in his hand.

In a few minutes, somebody passed me a gum wrapper. I grabbed it, although my arms and legs were also in chains. On it was a phone number and a woman's name: Licha.

Licha Rubalcava and I appeared together for our preliminary hearing. She faced charges of drunk, disorderly conduct and resisting arrest. I had disorderly conduct, resisting arrest and assaulting an officer — presumably when my foot struck one of the deputies. Licha was 27 years old, a mother of three children, whose husband was serving time in Tracy prison in Northern California. She lived in Riverside and worked as a barmaid. She was in Norwalk with friends that night just to party.

We were assigned a public defender, since neither one of us could afford our own counsel. The judge and the PD worked to determine whether we would be released on our own recognizance or forced to make bail. Both Licha and I were denied release. Licha ended up at the Sybil Brand Institute for Women. I went back to county jail. Before we split up we made a pact:

"Whoever gets out first, has to go see the other one, all right?" Licha said.

"That's fine with me."

Despite some bruises, a swollen and cut lip, Licha looked real nice.

Trying to get somebody to post bail became an arduous task. My parents didn't have any money. Neither did my brother. I called Chente and also tried the people at Cal State. Eventually I came up with enough for a bail bondsman, which was 10 percent of the required amount.

As soon as I could, I went to Sybil Brand, which was over the freeway from Cal State in City Terrace. I was taken to a room where a scattered number of people visited with prisoners who were behind thick plates of glass. A guard brought Licha to where I was standing. She had on a blue smock, her hair in disarray and bags beneath her eyes. She seemed embarrassed and didn't look at me at first. But she smiled prettily.

"Man, I'm so happy to see you," she said.

"Me too, how you been?"

"What do you expect! These god-damn bitches treat you like shit here. All day they fuck with me!"

"Hey, don't get mad at me, *mujer!*"

"I'm sorry...you've been so sweet."

She looked down, embarrassed again. I looked at her wrists and saw a red tag.

"Why do you have red on your wrists? What's that mean?

"Oh it's nothing," Licha said. "Naw, why lie...it means I'm suicidal. I tried to cut my wrist here the other night."

"No, Licha, don't do that — we'll help each other. You'll see, you'll be out in no time."

"I'm so glad you're here, Louie. I really need you."

We didn't know each other, but our experience brought us real close, real quick. We talked about so many things. I told her I'd help her make bail so we could work on our case together.

I hustled money everywhere, even getting advances from work and using some of my college money. In the next weeks, I didn't attend any classes. I failed to follow up on the Loyola-Marymount mural project and lost the account. But none of this mattered. What lay before me was a possible future in prison — for something I didn't do! I had to do all I could to avoid this; I wasn't sure it would work.

Licha was finally out on bail. We had a court hearing together and I began to get help in trying to win the case.

I approached a judge in San Gabriel who helped me out once when I was a juvenile offender. He remembered me and, although it was a shot in the dark, wrote a letter to the court on my behalf. I then obtained letters from Mrs. Baez, from Chicano Studies professors at Cal State and from EOP coordinators.

I read all the letters. So many nice things were said about me, sincere efforts to keep me out of *la pinta*. I realized how much support I had — and I felt bad about failing all these people again, although I knew this time, it wasn't entirely my fault.

I called my public defender about the letters. He didn't know if they were going to do any good, but he would work with them. Unfortunately, Licha couldn't get anybody to write letters for her.

We called each other almost daily. We made plans for me to visit her in Riverside. She gave me an address, and I figured out the best way to get there.

On a Saturday afternoon, I jumped on a bus from downtown Los Angeles to the desert. With all the stops, it was about a two-and-half-hour ride. I pulled into the Riverside bus station in the early evening, and stepped off, a small bag in my hand. There were a lot of people hanging around, some looking as if they had no other place to go — drifters, the homeless and tired, men and women, unbathed and hungry.

I continued past them, looking for Licha's street. I got lost a few times, asked directions, started out again, then lost more time because of wrong directions, but finally pulled myself back on track by the time it had gotten dark.

I located Licha's street and kept going. It was a curbless road, small but well-kept homes to the sides of me. This was the Casa Blanca barrio, one of the bigger Mexican enclaves in Southern California. I also knew it was tough territory, so I had to avoid bumping into any *vatos*.

Licha's address finally popped up. But the house was dark. My heart seemed to drop in that instance. I took a deep breath, then walked up the weed-filled grass to the door and knocked. No answer. I found a doorbell, but it didn't work. So I knocked again. Still no answer. I stood there for 45 minutes, not believing Licha wouldn't be there. She never showed.

I kept on walking. By then it was late and awfully cold. It was too late to take a bus, so I couldn't get back home. But I knew something about surviving in the streets.

I found a church with a set of double, hardwood doors. I pushed in one door — it was open; many churches stayed open all night for prayer. I walked up an aisle. Rows of pews radiated to the sides; an immense statue of Jesus Christ on the cross in front of me. Nobody else around. My footsteps rung out as I neared a pew at the front. I sat myself down on the hardness. The cold increased in intensity. I looked around. At the statue. The lit candles. The stations of the cross. It had been a long time since I'd been inside a church. Although at my mother's heeding I had gone through all the required Sacraments, some years back I stopped religious instruction, making confession or attending Mass. A priest once called me a bonehead heathen, and I never returned.

I lay back on the wood, closed my eyes, and descended into sleep.

More bad news: Quinto Sol Publications was embroiled in an internal squabble. One of its editors split from it and started his own press. This editor took along with him a number of Quinto Sol's authors, splitting up the contracted books. My book, unfortunately, was too far off in production and had to be put on hold. Eventually it got dropped in the jostling, and Quinto Sol reorganized into Tonatiuh Press without me.

I also got word the deputies who filed the assault charges on me were going to attend the hearing. The public defender said this looked bad. If I pled not guilty, I would have a trial. But if a jury were to convict, I would obtain a prison term. The public defender made an offer:

"I think you should cop a plea."

"No, man, I didn't do anything wrong. I didn't assault no cops — they assaulted me! And I got the scars to prove it."

"It's their word against yours. You got nothing to stand on. Nobody is going to testify for you, they're all scared. This happens all the time. Your only hope is to plea bargain."

"I just can't. It's the principle..."

"Fuck principle — it's your ass here! You got some good letters. They're good enough for the judge to consider another plea. But you have to cooperate. You have to say guilty to something else, okay? Come on, Luis, this is the only chance you got."

"Louie, do it," Licha interjected. "Take the lesser charge."

Although Licha had stood me up — she said she forgot I was coming — she didn't give any excuses and apologized. I felt she didn't owe me anything, so I let the incident drop.

"I don't know," I said. "It's not right — they'll do it to somebody else."

I turned away; I also felt scared. I knew the chances of a judge giving me a break if I pled not guilty were practically nil. But I recalled the beating, the way the fists came at me, the taunting, the thrust of blackjacks. I just couldn't let these deputies get away with it. I called Chente to hear what he had to say.

Chente understood the dilemma. But he also felt I needed to get out of this as fast and as cleanly as possible.

"You're fighting something more powerful than your puny plea for justice," Chente said. "Your day will come — our day will come! But, right now you can't make up for the Chicano Moratorium, for Miguel Robles and all the others who've suffered because of this society. It's more important you are around — to do the hard work required to help change this."

Licha and I showed up together for the next hearing. She looked sharp in a tight-fitting, gray-and-black dress-suit. She had her hair streaked, her face healed; so much beauty shone through again.

"You look pretty today."

"Oh, *querido*, you look pretty too."

Then the public defender arrived.

"The judge is prepared to offer a plea, Luis. The judge has the letters. But you got to tell me now. This is it; there's no backing off. What do you say?"

"Are the arresting deputies in there?"

"Yes, they're there and looking for a kill. Don't mess with this. Take the plea."

"Okay, okay...I'll do it."

Licha swung her arms around my neck. She smiled and kissed me on the cheek. The PD went away to work out the deal. Inside, my nerves jumped up and down. At the same time, I felt somewhat relieved. I wanted out of this mess. I had no choice, but I would never forget what the deputies did to me — the humiliation, the pain, the indignities — I would never forget.

We were called into the courtroom. On the side were the officers in uniform. The public defender addressed the court, saying I would accept guilt for the lesser charge of drunk and disorderly. I looked over at the deputies, who exhibited a tinge of disappointment.

The judge didn't take much time. He had the letters on his desk. He remarked to me about the break he was giving me in consideration of my support and new-found objectives. Although Licha didn't have the same support, he gave us both a break. My sentence involved a fine and few months incarceration in county jail.

The PD shook my hand. Licha hugged me, real tight, as tears streamed down her face. She had to do her time at Sybil Brand.

"As soon as we're out, let's get together, all right?"

"Licha, I'm sorry it worked out this way — but with everything bad, something good usually comes along with it."

The day I left county jail, Licha came for me. Again, she looked radiant, although she was almost 10 years older than me and a single mother of three.

"Come with me to Riverside and stay a few days?"

"It's not going to be like the last time, is it?"

"No Louie, I told you that wasn't my fault — man, you don't forget nothing do you?"

"Okay, let's start over, that's what I want to do — just start over."

By then, I was so far out of it that I forgot about Camila, my art, and the book — I was back to the way of the 'hood.

We drove the long stretch of Interstate 60 to Riverside. When we arrived in town, she took me to the bar where she worked to pick up an old check they held for her.

I entered the bar, although I was 18 years old and this was a 21-and-over joint. But nobody questioned me. Besides, for years I looked older than my actual age. Licha directed me to the back room; I lingered next to a time clock as she rummaged through a drawer to get her check.

"Stay here, I'm going to get it cashed."

When she returned, Licha stood by the time clock and filled out a time card.

"I got my job back — man, I'm so happy."

As she turned toward me, I pulled her near me and our lips touched, a light contact, but driven by sensuous quest. We kissed again, this time long, deep and smothering, something we both desired for a long time, neither of us wanting to stop.

"Louie," Licha finally took a breath. "Let's go home."

I left Riverside with images of the weekend etched in my mind: Milk dripped from Licha's breasts as the nipples puckered with excitement; tremors rumbled throughout our bodies; me crumbling beneath her fingers. Before I left, Licha went into the house and gave me a record, "Daddy's Home," by Shep and the Limelighters.

But a month later as I tried to negotiate a time to see her again, she said I was too young for her — the relationship would never work. I tried to argue against this. One day in the mail, Licha sent me another record: "You're Still A Young Man," by Tower of Power. There were no more arguments from me.

CHAPTER TEN

"I glimpse in the distance certain roads, clearings
silent in the morning after the night's demons have
fled: the future, the ageless future, where there is
always time to create." — Maurice Sachs

Alone at a bus stop in the first hours of a day, I wrapped
myself in a long, black trench coat — no longer used for *jambas*
or *jales*. "*¡Qué jodida!* — it's cold," I stammered out loud, to no
one in particular. Trucks rumbled by and an occasional
lowrider, sweet salsa sounds radiating from outside speakers; I
jumped to the beat inside the trench coat as a breeze played
havoc with my insides.

I reflected on writing and art, on class struggle, on family
and a woman's touch — what mattered to me then.

I stopped attending Cal State after my release from jail;
I'd been set back too far. Besides, I ran out of money. I now
worked full-time on the graveyard shift of a paper factory. I
also realized sitting in a classroom didn't work for me; it
revived images of what I endured as a child and something
within me blocked against it. I preferred my own inquiries,
reading everything I could when I needed to.

The incidents of violence continued. A week before, a dude
from Sangra strutted down Mission Boulevard when a carload
approached and someone opened fire; the dude dropped to the
ground and rolled over beside a mail box. But the car turned
around and somebody stepped out with a shotgun and blasted
him again; it was at such close range, the wadding from the shell
embedded in his stomach.

I now looked on these matters with different eyes. I
recalled when this first happened. Chente and I had been at his
house, talking about the Hills and how I had to defend it,
whatever the cost.

"That's exactly what the rulers of this country want you to do," Chente said. "Instead of directing your fury at the real source of the problem."

"But this is my 'hood — there's so much to be done here."

"There's much to be done everywhere. You need to broaden your experiences — find out what the rest of the world is all about."

"I understand, but I can't leave now; Lomas is everything, it's my family — it's my world."

Chente then placed a small globe in my hand and twirled it once.

"Okay, Luis, tell me: Where is Las Lomas on this globe?"

I gazed at the revolving sphere: the colors, the place names, the lines of mountain ridges and contours of islands and nations. I stopped the globe from its spin and found the United States. I turned it slightly to California, then cast down to a dot which claimed "Los Angeles." But there was no Lomas. No South San Gabriel.

"You see — Lomas is so tiny, nameless, it doesn't even warrant a dot," Chente explained. "The *vatos* defend a land which doesn't even belong to them. All the death — for what?"

I thought about the globe. Chente was right. A bigger world awaited me. But I also knew: Once you're in Las Lomas, you never get out — unless you're dead.

"Chente, I thank you for all you've done, but I can't leave," I said. "I have to try and reason with the homeboys, to stop the killings in my own way."

I spent a few nights pacing up and down the Hills, talking to the *vatos*; they listened and appeared as if maybe, just maybe, I made sense. When this happened, I wanted to stick it out. They would understand, I thought, if they were willing to learn, if they had the proper leadership.

One night in the fields, I stood among a line of dudes against a wall. Somebody passed around a Super Kool, a cigarette laced with "angel dust." Every one before me inhaled it; but when it came to me, I refused.

"Come on, *ése*, just a toke," said the guy in front of me.

"*Chale*, I don't go that way no more."

"Fuck it — you take it then," the guy said to someone next to me. But to our surprise he also refused. Then the next guy. And the next. Nobody wanted the Super Kool after me! As soon as somebody took a stand and turned it down, the others did the same.

I arrived at a point which alarmed even me, where I had no desire for the internal night, the buoyancy of letting go, the bliss of the void. I required more, a discipline as bulwark within which to hold all I valued, a shield against the onslaught.

I figured I could help the homeboys become warriors of a war worth fighting, convinced they would let go of the intoxications — even heroin — if they had something more meaningful in their lives; if only...

Just then, a 1955 Bel-Air came toward me. I recognized the car. It belonged to Enano. I looked closer at the occupants inside: Peaches, Topo, Enano and Fuzzy. Three of them had blue bandannas above fierce, dark faces. I smiled, gave them the Lomas hand sign. The bomb stopped in front of me.

Topo, the first one to initiate me into the 'hood, sat on the passenger side with a small-brim hat on his head. He looked straight at me, returned the smile, then picked up his hand to reveal a handgun.

My face flushed. For seconds, time stood still. For seconds, my mind raced, trying to figure out what was going on. Thoughts promenaded back and forth, telling me to drop down, to protect myself, at the same time denying everything in front of me.

Topo pulled the trigger and a familiar blast burst forth, sharp and furious. I fell in that instance, popping noises blasting about my ears.

I heard the car screech away while I crawled as fast as I could behind a brick wall. They would come back, I thought; if they knew I was alive, they would come back!

I leaned heavily against the wall, breathing hard and sweating *la gota gorda*. Through a window, I could see an illuminated painting of La Virgen de Guadalupe. Around me were an array of trash cans. An alley cat emerged from the garbage — scared, as I was scared.

For a long time nothing transpired. Nobody came. The bomb did not return. There was just me, a mangy cat, a bench full of bullet holes and Mother Mary, perpetually smiling.

I slowly rose to my feet. None of the bullets had struck me. My eyes burned with fury, with sorrow. I wanted to yell, I wanted to cry — I didn't know what I wanted.

In thinking back, I realize if they'd wanted to kill me, they would have. These were warning shots, as if to say: "Next time you're dead."

The homeboys tried to kill me, *vatos* whom I had known as brothers, with whom I scurried down muddy streets and slept next to in jail, with whom I partied and hung out in front of courthouses and the fields; they were dudes I fought for and with whom I shared a taste of *la carga*.

I would have died for them.

☩ ☩ ☩

There comes a moment when one faces the fresh features of an inner face; a time of conscious rebirth, when the accounting's done, the weave in its final flourish, a time when a man stands before the world — vulnerable, nothing-owed — and considers his place in it. I had reached such a moment.

"I'm ready to leave, Chente. There's nothing for me here anymore."

Chente arranged for me to hide out in a federally-subsidized housing project in San Pedro. I spent two months there trying to clarify the issues before me. During spare moments, I played street football with others from across the country who were also there, some from kindred conditions.

Before I left for San Pedro, I closed the doors of my garage room for the last time; my books and papers packed in boxes, my few belongings stashed away until I could reclaim them. I said goodby to my mother and father, who looked old and drawn out.

"I never liked the walkouts, the revolutionary talk and the books you read," Mama said. "But you stuck by what you believe in — and I respect you for that."

This meant much to me, hearing it from my mother. I gave her a sustained and sad-filled embrace. My father didn't say a great deal. He gave me a brief, awkward hug and then shook my hand.

"If you need anything — money, a place to stay — you have it here."

"That's good to hear, Dad — thanks."

Although my father had been jailed and falsely accused like me before he left Mexico for the United States, we never related our experiences; he was a man of few words, and I stopped expecting more. As I drove away from the house, I swung by the Hills, everything eerily quiet. It felt strange to leave such a place and such a time in so much silence.

I visited the Resurrection Cemetery, passing through the large, ornate gates, and parked. I strolled across the sheen of wet grass and up easy slopes, sprinkled here and there with marble headstones; flowers everywhere. A small boy in a wrinkled suit raced past. Nearby, a family stood around a recently-covered burial spot.

There wasn't much to see that day compared to the times when cars stretched for miles, winding around the curves of cemetery roads as they led to a casket next to chairs, wreaths and a mound of red dirt.

I recalled the old people who came here, the men in brown suede hats and canes, and black-shawled women with rosaries clutched inside vein-streaked hands. I recalled the mothers who had to be restrained as they lay across the casket, beseeching to be buried with their son or daughter. I recalled the working men with their calloused palms and sun-beaten faces whose hardened eyes were forged from the heat of foundries or from under the sun's gaze — and I remembered the stream which emanated from those dense eyes, how it pulled something raw and smoldering from every one of us.

I recalled the young people: dudes in long-sleeve shirts and pressed pants, and girls with harsh makeup and, sometimes, infants against their shoulders. The deafening yells, the wet-stained cheeks, the touch of a trembling hand — I remembered it all.

I left before the teardrops fell — for fear they'd never stop.

☥ ☥ ☥

In South San Gabriel, as elsewhere, events crashed into each other. A jury found Fred Coates, the deputy responsible for Miguel Robles' death, innocent of all charges — as they had done for virtually every deputy ever accused of maiming or killing an unarmed person of color. The sheriff's office assigned Coates to another part of the county. Soon we heard reports he faced an investigation for beating up a black youth.

By then, a prison group known as *La Eme* — otherwise called the Mexican Mafia — had penetrated the Southern California gang structures, starting with the home of their birth: Maravilla. They pulled in *soldados* from the various barrios to carry out high-level organized crime operations, including drug deals and murder. The talk in the Hills was that Fuzzy, Topo and Cuervo had become soldiers for *La Eme*.

Even Puppet failed to escape the transitions. A couple of Mexican immigrants shot him when he chased them following a minor argument. He lived, but I later learned he accepted Jesus Christ as his personal savior.

The scourge of PCP — "angel dust" — had begun to grip almost every facet of barrio life. Whole neighborhoods became like ghost towns as increasing numbers of young people were hooked into this overpowering narcotic, easily manufactured in back-room laboratories and distributed widely and cheaply. Although PCP preceded the crack epidemic, it was enough to make blabbering idiots of once-vigorous boys and girls.

La Casa Community Center became a major casualty of PCP. I once visited Sal Basuto who showed me around so I could see the devastation: pieces of pool table on the floor of the youth center, torn mattresses where runaways hid to snort, shoot up or smoke "angel dust" — anything of value gone, as if everything around Sal, all he had fought for, caved under PCP.

In a matter of a year or two, the murals I painted through the Bienvenidos Community Center were whitewashed; the backlash against them proved swift and extensive. Only one mural survived, the one I finished on Chicano History for the inside of the Del Mar Children's Library. Once in a while, I'd wander in there and sit down to gaze at the panels, without saying a word; one of the few remaining "shrines" of that tumultuous period.

Mark Keppel High School continued in crisis — including undergoing a major confrontation the following year after I graduated. The police attacked a group of students on the lawn — at one point smearing the face of a pregnant girl into the ground and yanking students from the hallways. About 20 young people were taken to the police station and booked.

A meeting was immediately called in which the police responded to inquiries about the incident. I returned to attend and saw fathers and mothers — people who paid taxes, who obeyed laws, who came to this country to work and better their lives — approach the police representatives as if they were going to pluck out their eyeballs. The police got flustered and had to promise to return all the mug shots to the parents and remove any statements of wrongdoing from the students' records.

I also learned the Movimiento Bookstore shut down when the body of Al "Pache" Alvarez was found in Garvey Park with a bullet hole through his head. His murder was never solved.

But the most critical blow came with the closing of the Bienvenidos Community Center. According to some insiders, *La Eme* had taken over various community centers across the county. There also appeared to be a move to take over Bienvenidos.

Mrs. Baez, who chaired the board, figured the only way to keep the center out of *La Eme*'s hands was for the board to disband — a sort of "scorched earth" policy.

Although the Food Co-op continued on its own for a while, even opening up a separate storefront, the center's programs, the John Fabela Youth Center, the dropout school and day care, all closed their doors — leaving Las Lomas with what it had once before: Nothing.

Along with all this, the neighborhoods also changed. What I had unknowingly conjured up in my *teatro* productions came to fruition as land developers, along with county and city officials, tore up whole streets to build new townhouses, malls and expensive condos.

One year, I visited my mother and father who still lived in the house in San Gabriel. By then the house had been stuccoed over, another bathroom added and a second house filled the back yard. My old garage room had been repainted and now served as storage.

My mother explained how many more Asians had moved into the newly-constructed areas. One day, a new mall opened where the drive-in used to be; Mama and my sister Ana walked over there to check it out. But as soon as they got there, they slow-walked through the crowd, feeling out of place. There were hundreds of Chinese, newly arrived in this country, talking only in their language. None of the items in the stores were marked in English or Spanish. Mama didn't mind the Chinese people — in some ways their culture recalled her Mexican-Indian upbringing — but it was evident the mall had no place for the Mexicans remaining in the area. There were no efforts to reach out, no means of inclusion — something our family had long experienced.

This wasn't about being Asian. Money talked here. Big money. Similarly a good part of the Hills found itself swept away with the massive land deals and influx of investments during the 1970s and 1980s. Between the police, prison gangs, Pacific Rim money and developers, the Hills didn't have much of a chance.

✝ ✝ ✝

After San Pedro, I traveled to Chicago with Chente and a few others to attend a meeting with people from throughout the United States, Canada, Mexico and Puerto Rico.

The morning we arrived in the city, the skyline rose from the horizon, glittering in the sunlight, like an Emerald City, so magical and massive. Yet as we drove through it, Chicago struck me as dark and dirty, the brick buildings covered with black soot as the smoke and silt from steel mills, bucket shops and other industry slaughtered the sky and dusted the streets, alleys and gangways. Here was a city unlike any I had ever seen, another world, and it beckoned like books, like the passage to knowledge and the ripening spring of a new world; the city pulled me in, and although it would be another 12 years before I ended up there, it never let me go.

When I returned to Los Angeles, I moved to Boyle Heights and later to neighborhoods such as White Fence, Florence, South Pasa, La Colonia Watts and Gerahty Loma. I found work in foundries, refineries, steel mills and construction sites, which I would do for another seven years before pursuing the disciplines of journalism and literature.

I soon worked with community leaders who battled against police terror, labor issues, the rights of the undocumented, for tenant rights and decent education — they were welfare mothers, war veterans, trade union members, students and unemployed — a mixture of nationalities and colors, linked by an economic equality, a commonality of survival.

One day at the Aliso Village/Pico Gardens Housing Projects, where I organized among some of the most neglected youth in the city, I asked Camila Martínez to marry me.

In the summer of 1974, soon after I turned 20, Camila and I wed at the Guadalupe Church on Hazard Avenue: a traditional East L.A. wedding, complete with a lowrider caravan, fights and chair-throwing at the reception, and the bride and groom sneaking out in a beat-up bug for a honeymoon at a sleazy, crumbling motel where we ended up after running out of gas.

I began a new season of life. Intellect and body fused, I now yearned to contribute fully, embodied with conscious energy, to live a deliberate existence dedicated to a future humanity which might in complete freedom achieve the realization of its creative impulses, the totality of its potential faculties, without injustice, coercion, hunger and exploitation.

✝ ✝ ✝

I'm at a *quinceñera* dance at the American Legion hall in San Gabriel, my cousin's, one of Tío Kiko's daughters. I'm older, married with a child, and dressed in plain shirt and pants, hair shortened, not much to show for what I'd been through only a short time earlier.

I step outside to take in some air. I lean against a parked sedan, looking at the stars which seem extraordinarily large and bright this evening. Just then a short figure, wobbling, with a kind of limp, moves toward me. He has a blue beany cap over his head and a dark, hooded sweatshirt.

"You Chin....de Lomas," says the figure. I don't recognize him, not even the voice, which rasps as much as it slurs. No pangs of familiarity.

"I guess I am — but it's been a long time since anyone's called me that."

"You're going to die."

"What are you talking about?"

"You thought you killed me, but you didn't," the dude says, haltingly, measuring every word. "I took all your shanks...eight of them...right here."

The dude lifts up the sweatshirt. A ghastly number of scars traverse his torso. A plastic bag is strapped at his side, to hold his urine.

"You did this to me...look hard, you did this!"

"You got it wrong, Chava, it wasn't me."

"Sure — I've heard it all before. I know who did this...and you're going to pay."

From the sides emerge two other guys, healthy and strong, looking like street, although a lot younger than the both of us.

"Chava — listen," I say. "I heard about what happened that night. But I wasn't there. For some time now, I've been working my way out of that useless existence. Now I've found something to live for, bigger than you and me, bigger than Lomas and Sangra. You don't want me."

Chava gets closer, alcohol on his breath. I can see tears forming in his eyes.

"Lomas did this — somebody has to pay!" he yells while pulling off the beany cap, revealing a misshapen head with scattered slivers of hair. The scars on his body don't compare to those on his head and the side of his face; they're larger with indentations and purplish membranes.

"Look what you did to me. Somebody has to pay for this!" Chava repeats. He's so disturbed, I can see him pulling out a knife and stabbing me just to salve his pain. I look at the guys next to me, and they strike me as too young and inexperienced to act. I keep talking.

"There's some things to fight for, some things to die for — but not this. Chava, you're alive. I feel for you, man, but you're alive. Don't waste the rest of your days with this hate. What's revenge? What can you get by getting to me? I'm the least of your enemies. It's time to let it go, it's time to go on with your life."

Chava begins to shudder, to utter something, a guttural sound rising to his throat, a hideous moan. I think he's trying to cry, but it's hard to tell. I don't know what to do, so I pull him close to me. He twists away, the dudes to the side look lost, not knowing their next move, unprepared for what follows. I again pull at Chava, and hold him. He breaks down, a flood of fermented rage seeping out of every pore.

"If I thought my life could cleanse you of the hurt, of the memory, I would open up my shirt and let you take it from me. But it won't — we're too much the same now, Chava. Let it all out, man...let it out."

I hold Chava as if he were cornmeal in my arms, then pity overwhelms me, this complicated affection which cuts across the clear-cut states of being we'd rather seek: Here's friend, here's enemy; here's sadness, here's happiness; here's right, here's wrong. Pity draws from all these opposing elements and courses through me like an uncooked stew, mixing and confusing the paradoxes, because now this man I once admired, if not revered, I once feared, if not hated, stands here, a fragment of the race, drunk, agonized, crushed, and I can't hate him any more; I can't see him as the manifestation of craziness and power he once possessed; he's a caricature, an apparition, but also more like me, capable of so much ache beneath the exterior of so much strength. Pity links us in a perverted way, transcending our veneers, joining us in our vulnerability, and at the same time distancing us from one another. I want to escape from Chava's tired, perplexed and tattered face, to run away from how something so beautiful, in its own way, can become so odious.

After an eternal minute, Chava pushes me away, wipes his face with a soiled sleeve, and then turns. The dudes next to us don't seem to know what to do but follow. I see Chava hobble away, two confused teenagers at his side, and as he vanishes into a flicker of neon, I hear the final tempo of the crazy life leave my body, the last song before the dying, lapsing forever out of mind as Chava disappears, enveloped in flames breaking through the asphalt, wrested into the black heart of night.

EPILOGUE

"Go ahead and kill us, we're already dead..."
—Young Latino participant in
the 1992 Los Angeles Uprising, as
quoted in *USA Today*, May 1, 1992

This book is a gift to my son Ramiro, to all my children, who will traverse a more severe and uncertain path to maturity than I had to undertake. I look at him now, at his handsome face, at his almond-shaped eyes and cinnamon color, and it's hard to believe how many impacted layers of hurt and abuse these features conceal. He has a right to be angry. And he's not the only one.

From Chicago, we watched the fires that consumed miles of Los Angeles and some other American cities beginning on April 29, the day a jury in Simi Valley, California declared four police officers innocent of excessive force in the beating of Rodney King.

Fire for me has been a constant motif. I was 11 years old when the 1965 Watts Rebellion tore through my former neighborhood. At age 16, I participated in the Chicano Moratorium Against the Vietnam War — the so-called East L.A. riot. Later, mostly as a journalist, I witnessed uprisings in such far-flung places as Juchitan, Oaxaca; Overton in Miami; and "Da Bulls Revolution" (after the Chicago Bulls won their second N.B.A. Championship on June 14, 1992).

The heart of the L.A. uprising was in the African American community. But it soon involved large numbers of Latinos (who make up almost half of South Central's population) and whites — Latinos were the largest group among the 18,000 arrested; at least 700 of those detained were white. Some called it the country's first "multi-ethnic" revolt; the common link was the class composition of the combatants.

247

Los Angeles 1992 was the first social response to an economic revolution which began years before: The shift from mechanical productive energy to one based on electronics. In Los Angeles, this translated into tens of thousands of jobs lost as factories such as Goodyear, Firestone, General Motors, Bethlehem Steel and American Bridge closed down forever — many of which I worked for during the 1970s. Along with this came the cyclical crisis of glutted markets and a shrinking consumer base, where more was being produced by fewer people (as the new technology could only integrate a few). The mode of distribution began to break down. From cars to electronic items — including such necessities as food, clothing and homes — goods lay idle while an increasing number of people had to do without.

The resultant economic decay — L.A. has the second largest homeless population in the country — was the foundation for the kind of response that followed the Rodney King verdicts. Add to this one of the most brutal police forces in America, and you have a riot in the making; it was only a matter of time.

Government officials at local, state and federal levels proved they would not allow any serious challenge to the economic and political underpinnings of poverty in this country. They dispatched National Guard and Army troops, who turned their guns against Americans — barely more than a year after the bloody (for the Iraqi people) Persian Gulf War.

The L.A. violence also uncovered a two-year effort to unite the two largest gangs in the city — the Bloods and Crips. A "Bloods/Crips Proposal For L.A.'s Face-Lift" was soon circulated; it proposed building parks and community centers, repaving streets and schools — not just reconstructing the taco stands, liquor stores and exploitative businesses which dotted the South Central landscape before the uprising (a radio broadcast stated that in a three-mile radius of South Central, there were some 640 liquor stores, although not one movie house or community center!).

A major decline of gang-related incidents was reported throughout the South Central community. Graffiti sprouted up with sentiments such as "Mexicans & Crips & Bloods Together," although police later removed most of the unity-related scrawl.

In the months after the uprising, police broke up as many gang "unity" rallies as they could, arresting truce leaders, and inflaming the ire of housing project residents in which many of the rallies were being held. The LAPD told the media they feared the gangs were going to turn on them, possibly ambush them. Yet no police officer has been killed or severely hurt since the King verdicts — even during the uprising, although instances have emerged of police shooting several people, some in the back, during and since the riots.

Then several hundred FBI agents were sent in to "break up the gangs" involved in the April/May violence — the largest investigation of its kind. Although there were some 600 Los Angeles youth killed in 1991 from gang and drug-related incidents, the federal government never before provided the commitment or resources that they have since the Crips and Bloods declared peace.

At the same time, the immigration authorities terrorized Mexican and Central American immigrants, placing the largely Salvadoran Pico-Union community under a virtual state of siege (this area was one of the hardest hit in the fires).

This is not the first time the federal government has intervened. It has derailed and, whenever possible, destroyed the unity which emerged out of the Watts Rebellion, out of the Chicano Moratorium, out of the Wounded Knee protests. In the 1960s and 1970s, the Black Panthers, the Brown Berets, the American Indian Movement, the Young Lords, the Weathermen, Puerto Rican liberation groups, the Chicano Liberation Front — and more recently MOVE, the Republic of New Africa, FALN, the Black Liberation Army — every major organized expression for justice and liberation was targeted, its leaders killed or jailed, its forces scattered.

To challenge how power is held in America meant facing a reign of terror, some of which I witnessed over the years, most of which failed to reach "mainstream" America — although this is changing. L.A. helped bring it home.

This is the legacy of the period covered in this book. This is what my son, Ramiro, and his generation have inherited.

What to do with those whom society cannot accommodate? Criminalize them. Outlaw their actions and creations. Declare them the enemy, then wage war. Emphasize the differences — the shade of skin, the accent in the speech or manner of clothes. Like the scapegoat of the Bible, place society's ills on them, then "stone them" in absolution. It's convenient. It's logical.

It doesn't work.

Gangs are not alien powers. They begin as unstructured groupings, our children, who desire the same as any young person. Respect. A sense of belonging. Protection. The same thing that the YMCA, Little League or the Boys Scouts want. It wasn't any more than what I wanted as a child.

Gangs flourish when there's a lack of social recreation, decent education or employment. Today, many young people will never know what it is to work. They can only satisfy their needs through collective strength — against the police, who hold the power of life and death, against poverty, against idleness, against their impotence in society.

Without definitive solutions, it's easy to throw blame. For instance, politicians have recently targeted the so-called lack of family values.

But "family" is a farce among the propertyless and disenfranchised. Too many families are wrenched apart, as even children are forced to supplement meager incomes. Family can only really exist among those who can afford one. In an increasing number of homeless, poor, and working poor families, the things that people must do to survive undermines most family structures. At a home for troubled youth on Chicago's South Side, for example, I met a 13-year-old boy who was removed from his parents after police found him selling chewing gum at bars and restaurants without a peddler's license.

I recall at the age of nine my mother walking me to the door, and, in effect, saying: Now go forth and work.

People can't just consume in this society; they have to sell something, including their ability to work. If decent work is unavailable, people will do the next best thing — such as sell sex or dope.

I've talked to enough gang members and low-level dope dealers to know they would quit today if they had a productive, livable-wage job. You'll find people who don't care about who they hurt, but nobody I know *wants* to sell death to their children, their neighbors and friends.

If there was a viable alternative, they would stop. If we all had a choice, I'm convinced nobody would choose *la vida loca*, the "insane nation" — to "gang bang." But it's going to take collective action and a plan.

Twenty years ago, at 18 years old, I felt like a war veteran, with a sort of post-traumatic stress syndrome. I wanted the pain to end, the self-consuming hate to wither in the sunlight. With the help of those who saw potential in me, I got out.

And what of my son? Recently, Ramiro went up to the stage at a Chicago poetry event and read a moving piece about being physically abused by a step-father when he was a child. It stopped everyone cold. He later read the poem to some 2,000 people at Chicago's Poetry Festival. Its title: "Running Away."

There's a small but intense fire burning in Ramiro. He turned 17 in 1992; he's made it so far, but every day is a challenge. Now I tell him: You have worth outside of a job, outside the "jacket" imposed on you since birth. Draw on your expressive powers.

Stop running.

July 1992

GLOSSARY

✝: Pachuco Cross

A la brava: To do something whether you like it or not.

Amá, mira a Rano!: Ma, look at Rano!

Aquí estoy: Here I am.

Aquí nomás: Just here, doing nothing.

Aquí para Sangra — ¿y qué?: Here stands Sangra — what are you going to do about it?

Así es, así será: This is how it is, this is how it's going to be.

Barrio: Neighborhood. Also the territory of Chicano gang groupings.

Bienvenidos: "Welcome," the community center which once served South San Gabriel.

Blancas: White amphetamine pills.

Bolero: A slow ballad/dance.

Borlote: A party; a rowdy scene.

Botánica: A barrio herb and tonic shop. Known for religious and medicinal items.

Bruja: Witch.

Cabrones: Bastards.

Caiga: Come here.

Caló: Chicano street slang. Not just "Spanglish" but urbanisms which are neither Spanish or English. Linked to the Gypsy patois of Spain and Mexico.

Cantón: One's house; "the crib."

Camaradas: Partners.

Carnal(es)/carnala(s): Brothers or sisters, literally "of the flesh." Also an affectionate way to greet fellow barrio members.

Carrucha: A beat-up car.

Chale: Slang for "no."

Charrangas: A popular Cuban-based rhythm.

Chavalas: Slang for girls. Derogatory if referring to males.

Chicanos: The Mexican people in the United States.

Chicharrónes: Mexican-style pork rinds.

Chicos: Young dudes.

Chingao: A term of exclamation; "what the fuck?"

Chingaso: A hard blow; being struck down.

Chisme Arte: "Gossip Art;" an East L.A.-based literary and art magazine published during the 1970s and early 1980s.

Chiva: Heroin.

Cholo(s)/chola(s); cholillos: A low life. Appropriated by Chicano barrio youth to describe the style and people linked to local gang structures.

Chota: The police.

Chúpame: Suck me.

Churros: Mexican flour bread fried in grease and then dipped in sugar and cinnamon.

Clica(s): Slang for clique(s) or club(s).

Ciudad Juárez, Chihuahua: Juárez City, in the Mexican state of Chihuahua; a border town across from El Paso, Texas.

Coloradas (colies): Red barbiturate pills.

Compa: Companion; short for *compañero* or *compadre.*

Con Safos: Chicano slang meaning "nobody can mess with this." Usually used in graffiti after a gang designation (often with just the letters c/s). Later an affectionate term among barrio youth for whatever is hip and cool. Also the name of a Chicano magazine from the late 1960s, and the name of an East L.A. rock-soul band during the 1980s.

Comadres: Godmothers.

Controla: To control.

Corridos: Mexican "running" ballads, usually telling a story of heroism and heartbreak.

Costurera(o): Garment worker.

Cuete: A gun; literally a firecracker.

Curandera(o): A Mexican healer, often linked with magic and Native-Catholic beliefs.

De aquellas: Of fine quality; "way out there."

Dedos: Fingers, refers to snitches.

¿De dónde eres?: Where you from? Used to challenge rival gang-bangers.

De verotas: The real truth.

De volada: To do something in a hurry; without thinking.

Diablos: Devils; the name of a set in the Sangra barrio.

El jefito: The boss; affectionate term for father. Mothers are called *la jefita.*

El Loco Con La Bárbara, P/V: Loco with Barbara, for life (P/V is short for *por vida*).

El mero chingón: The top dog (the biggest, meanest fucker).

El pie: The foot.

Engabachados: To be anglicized.

Escamao: Caló term for "losing it;" shaken up or panicky.

Ése: A greeting among *vatos*; "hey you." In L.A., African American street youth use this term to mean any Mexican gang-banger, pronounced as "essay."

Eso, así: Yes, like that...

Ese malvado, deje que se pudra: That no-good, let him rot.

Esqüintar: To leave, derived from "making our squints."

Está bien: It's okay.

Está derecho: He's straight; on the mark.

Feria: Money; Spanglish from "fare."

Fíjese: Check this out.

Firme: Caló term for hip, cool; the best. Also the name of a lowrider culture magazine in the 1970s and 1980s.

Flaquillo: A skinny little dude.

Folklórico: Traditional Mexican/Spanish dance and music.

Frajo: Cigarette.

Gabacho/Gaba: A white American; Anglo.

Grifa: A reefer of marijuana.

Gritos: Referring to the long, deep Mexican soul yells.

Güacha: Pay attention; watch out.

Güantes: Gloves; slang for throwing blows.

Güerita: A little blonde or light-skinned girl.

Hablen in español, ya saben que no entiendo inglés: Speak in Spanish, you know I don't understand English.

Hijo: A term of exclamation. Short for "the son of..."

Híjole: A term of exclamation.

Hipócrita: Hypocrite.

Huapango: A popular folk music of Mexico.

Huevos estrellados: A serving of eggs, sunny-side up.

Huevos rancheros: Ranch-style eggs, over a tortilla with rice and beans.

Hura: The police.

Jaina: A girlfriend.

Jale: A job, also refers to doing "work" for the barrio.

Jambas: Robberies; stealing.

Jaspia: Hunger.

La carga: Heroin.

La Casa: "The house;" the community center serving the Sangra barrio.

La Colonia: The colony. Also the name of the main Chicano barrio in Watts.

La Eme: The "M," stands for the Mexican Mafia, the oldest, and one of the largest, American prison gangs.

La Gerahty Loma: Major barrio in the hills of East L.A., situated on county territory.

La gota gorda: "The fat drop."

La Llorona: The weeping woman, a widespread legend among the Mexican people in the United States and Mexico.

La marqueta: Spanglish for "the market."

Lambe/Lambiche: A kiss-ass, literally "licker."

La pinta: Prison.

La Vida Loca/Mi Vida Loca: The Crazy Life/My Crazy Life, symbolizing the barrio/pinto gang experience.

La Torcida: Jail, prison time.

Las Lomas: The Hills; a barrio east of Los Angeles on county territory.

La Raza: The Mexican people. In the late 1960s and early 1970s, the name of a leading Chicano *movimiento* magazine.

La Santísima Madre de Dios: The Holy Mother of God.

Lo chingaré: I'll fuck him up.

Loco(s)/loca(s): The crazies. Another term for barrio youth.

Locura: Craziness; referring to a state of being, not so much a state of mind, among barrio gangs.

Los Cuatro del Barrio: The Barrio Four.

Maldad: Meanness.

Masa Harina: A popular brand of flour sold in heavy cloth sacks and used to make tortillas.

Más Firmota: A total fox.

Marrano: A pig. To be filthy.

Mechista: A member of MEChA (Movimiento Estudiantil Chicano de Aztlán), a Chicano student activist organization.

¿Me quieres?: Do you like me?

Mescal: Mexican spirits produced from the maguey cactus plant. Liquor known for the worm at the bottom of the bottle.

M'ija / m'ijo: Shortened and affectionate version of *mi hija(o)* — my daughter/my son.

Movimiento: The Movement; the Chicano Movement.

Mujer: Woman.

Nadie se mueve: Nobody move.

Nayarit: A northern state of Mexico. Many immigrants to Los Angeles originated in the north of Mexico.

Norteños(as): Music of northern Mexico, also known as *conjunto* music.

Orale: Hello. Hey. Okay.

Pachuco: Mexican youth of the 1930s and 1940s who developed their own style and language in the barrios of America; linked to the urban youth style of major Mexican cities.

Párenle: Stop.

Pedo: A fart; term used for anything that's a waste of time.

Pégale: Hit him.

Pendejo(a): A stupid person.

Pensamientos: Thoughts; ideas.

Pinche: Damned.

Pinto: An ex-con.

Placa: One's barrio name.

Plato: A fight.

Poblana: A traditional dress from Puebla, Mexico.

Pobreza: Poverty.

Por el amor de Dios: For the love of God.

Prendida(o): Slang for "lit up" or eager.

Prieto: Dark one.

Puto/puta: A male whore/ a prostitute.

Puta madre: Mother whore.

¡Qué cábula!: What a kick! *Cábula* also means to mock, jest or joke.

¡Qué desmadre!: What a holy mess!

¿Qué está pasando?: What's happening?

¿Qué hubo?: What's up? (sometimes written as Q-vo).

¡Qué jodida(o)!: What a fucked-up situation.

¡Qué Maravilla!: What a marvel!

¿Qué pasa, hombre?: What's happening, man?

¿Qué pasó aquí?: What happened here?

¿Qué pues?: What's up?

Querido(a): My dear one.

Qué Rifa: We rule.

¿Qué se yo?: What do I know?

¿Qué traes tú?: What's up with you?

¡Que viva La Raza!: Long live the Mexican people.

¡Que viva South San Gabriel!: Long live South San Gabriel!

¿Quién se murió?: Who died?

Quieres algo conmigo, pues aquí estoy: You want something with me, well here I am.

Quinceñera: A coming-out celebration for a 15-year-old girl.

Ranchera: The music and style of the "ranch," equivalent to country music in the United States.

Ranfla: A cherried-out lowrider car.

Refín: Food.

Regeneración: Rebirth. Name of an early 1900s magazine published by the Flores-Magon brothers, two leading Mexican revolutionaries. Later it was "regenerated" during the Chicano Movement by activists linked to the growing public arts movement in East L.A.

Rifa: The best of all.

Río Grande (Río Bravo): A river which partly serves as the borderline between the United States and Mexico.

Ruca(s): Barrio woman, literally means "old lady."

Ruquitas de aquellas: Fine, foxy women.

Salsa: Latino Caribbean-based rhythms popular in major American cities.

Sangra: The barrio surrounding the San Gabriel Mission church.

Señor(a): Mister, missis.

Sonora: A northern state of Mexico.

Sinaloa: A northern state of Mexico.

Simón: Caló term for "yes."

Soldados: Soldiers, those linked to *La Eme,* known as *soldados azules,* blue soldiers. Members of *La Familia* prison gang were linked to the color red.

Sombrero: Hat. Popularly used to describe the wide brim Mexican hats used by mariachi bands.

Suerte: Good luck.

Tarahumara: A native tribe of Mexico, whose ancestral home is the mountain range in Chihuahua. They are among several tribes known to have never succumbed to the Spanish. They continue in the old traditions and today are extremely impoverished in Mexico.

Teatro: Street theater in the tradition of the Teatro Campesino of the United Farm Workers Union movement.

Tecato: Heroin addict.

Telenovelas: Spanish soap operas.

Tijuanera(o): Somebody from the border city of Tijuana, Mexico. A derogatory term for newly-arrived immigrants.

Tina: A vessel to hold liquids.

Totacho: Our talk, slang.

Trago: A drink.

Trapo: A rag.

Trenzas: Braids.

Trucha: Caló term meaning to watch out, be alert.

Un camarada de aquellas: A real down dude.

Un chingo: A whole lot.

Vatito: Little dude.

Vato Loco: A crazy dude. This is what certain barrio members with intense street reputations were called.

Vatos: Dudes or guys.

Vecindad: A complex of linked homes around a common courtyard, widespread in parts of Mexico and the Southwest.

Veracruz: A state in Mexico on the Caribbean coast. Known for its African-based population and influence. Home of the standard rock song, "La Bamba."

Veteranos: Veterans of barrio street warfare. The African American gang equivalent is "Original Gangster." Among Mexicans, some of these veterans go back two or more generations.

¡Ya!: Now!

¡Ya basta!: That's enough! Popular slogan during the Chicano Movement.

Ya estuvo: That's it. It's finished, done with.

Yesca: Slang for marijuana.

¿Y qué?: What of it? Usually follows one's barrio designation; a challenge.

OTHER LATINO TITLES AVAILABLE FROM CURBSTONE PRESS

MIRRORS BENEATH THE EARTH
Short Fiction by Chicano Writers
edited by Ray González

"As I read the stories, ethnic boundaries collapsed, and I was in a universe without dividing lines, without borders. Read and see and hear for yourself how they open and describe worlds heretofore banned and ignored from American literature and how rich and substantial American literature becomes by their inclusion."— Jimmy Santiago Baca
$13.95 paper, 1-880684-02-0

THE CONCRETE RIVER
poetry by Luis J. Rodriguez

This collection of poetry by the Chicano poet, journalist and publisher, Luis J. Rodriguez, received the 1991 PEN Oakland/Joesphine Miles Award for excellence in poetry.

"Rodriguez writes from the inside out, with great knowledge, passion, and compassion....Highly recommended for contemporary poetry and multicultural collections."—*Library Journal*

"In the highly emotional and oracular register of Whitman and Ginsberg, Rodriguez speaks for a silent generation of Mexicans who came north for economic freedom....For Rodriguez, poetry is a sacred act that can rescue the poet's past in order to instruct his community about his relationship to it and the world."—*The American Book Review*
$9.95 paper, 0-915306-42-5

REBELLION IS THE CIRCLE OF A LOVER'S HANDS
a bilingual edition of poetry by Martín Espada
translated by the author and Camilo Pérez-Bustillo
foreword by Amiri Baraka

About this powerful collection of poems, which received the 1989 PEN/Revson Award for poetry, the judges (Carolyn Forché, Daniel Halpern & Charles Simic) said: "Whoever in the future wishes to find out the truth about our age will have
to read poets like Martín Espada....The greatness of Espada's art, like all great arts, is that it gives dignity to the insulted and the injured of the earth."
$9.95 paper, 0-915306-95-6

FOR A COMPLETE CATALOG, SEND YOUR REQUEST TO:
Curbstone Press, 321 Jackson Street, Willimantic, CT 06226